The Very Thing

The Very Thing

The Memoirs of Drummer Bentinck, Royal Welch Fusiliers, 1807–1823

Jonathan Crook

Foreword by
Donald E. Graves

Frontline Books
London

The Very Thing

This edition published in 2011 by Frontline Books,
an imprint of Pen & Sword Books Ltd,
47 Church Street, Barnsley, S. Yorkshire, S70 2AS
www.frontline-books.com

ISBN: 978-1-84832-598-2

CIP data records for this title are available
from the British Library

For more information on our books, please visit
www.frontline-books.com, email info@frontline-books.com
or write to us at the above address.

Printed in Great Britain by MPG Books Limited

Typeset in 11/14.5 point Arno Pro and Arno Pro Caption

Contents

———•———

Illustrations and Maps

Plates

Maps

Maps pages 22, 26, 35, 53 © C. Johnson, from D. E. Graves, *Fix Bayonets*.

Foreword

———◆———

I am very pleased to provide a foreword to *The Very Thing*, Jonathan Crook's editing of the Napoleonic memoirs of Drummer Richard Bentinck of the 23rd Foot, or Royal Welch Fusiliers. When I was working on *Dragon Rampant*, my history of that regiment from 1793 to 1815, Jonathan Crook very generously gave me access not only to the original memoirs of his relative Bentinck, but also his background research on the man, his unit and his times. This fine material proved very useful and permitted me to provide a fascinating glimpse into the life of the enlisted Welch Fusilier during the Great War with France because memoirs by enlisted men are much rarer things than those written by officers. This is largely due to the literacy barrier as most common soldiers could neither read nor write and therefore the discovery of a new memoir by an enlisted man is always a matter for celebration.

In the case of Drummer Richard Bentinck, he actually left two memoirs of his military service from 1807 to 1823. The first is a series of articles, which appeared in a small local newspaper, and the second is a personal recollection, which Crook believes Bentinck dictated to his son. The two sources can be differentiated by the use of the first or third person in the narrative sections below, the former being the dictated account and the latter the work of an anonymous journalist who interviewed Bentinck toward the end of the veteran's life. Having read both documents I can testify that Crook's edited version includes all the relevant passages from both sources and excludes reams of extraneous material. This is particularly true of the newspaper articles as the journalist who wrote them copied lengthy passages verbatim from Napier and other historians of the Peninsular War – sometimes giving the true authors credit but more often not. This was a common practice of the time and Crook has not only hewed out this copious dead wood but replaced it in *The Very Thing* with excellent background material that places Richard Bentinck and the 23rd Foot squarely in their place and time. The result is an extremely interesting book that can be read on many levels but which is centred, of course, on the rarely downhearted figure of Drummer Bentinck.

We march along beside this young man as he joins the 23rd Foot and we campaign with him in Denmark, Martinique, Portugal, Spain and France. We experience long marches, perilous sea voyages, short rations and wretched weather. We fight in bloody major battles and many smaller engagements, of necessity sew clothes out of blankets and cobble shoes out of cow hides, and suffer from the whims of martinet officers. But Bentinck also remembers the good times – many having to do with the sudden availability of large amounts of free or cheap drink – and we learn that it was not all hard times for the enlisted fusiliers but that there were days when the sun shone, the officers were kind and the women were friendly.

For a man discussing events that occurred a half-century in the past, Bentinck had a remarkably good memory. He does have occasional lapses – mostly concerning the chronology of an event – but Crook's own research has permitted him to correct any major errors. There are many fascinating episodes in Bentinck's story but my personal favourite is his description of the return to Britain of the 1st Battalion of the 23rd Foot in the early summer of 1814, following six years of foreign service. After more than two decades of nearly incessant warfare, peace has finally returned and Britain is in a mood to celebrate. After landing at Plymouth, Bentinck and the Royal Welch Fusiliers march along the southern coast of England to Gosport and their progress is one continuous triumphal procession. As Bentinck describes it, he and his comrades were 'cheered, fed and regaled as though each man [of the battalion] were some illustrious hero' and in 'almost every town they passed through they were treated to as much meat and drink as they could use by their fellow countrymen'.

The Very Thing is a fascinating and colourful memoir of a private soldier of Wellington's Peninsular army. It is a book that can be read with profit and enjoyment by the specialist and the general reader alike. Jonathan Crook deserves much credit for the adept way in which he has edited and supplemented the original text for a modern audience.

Donald E. Graves
Valley of the Mississippi,
Upper Canada

Introduction

———•———

D rummer Richard Bentinck of the 23rd Foot, Royal Welch Fusiliers, was the great-grandfather of my uncle, Bryan Boardman. In 1982 Bryan commenced research on his ancestor, gathering a large and diverse range of sources, but unfortunately suffered an untimely death in 1994 before he could complete his work. Bryan's family and my father's family came from Heywood, a small town north of Manchester. During his research Bryan became aware of a series of articles written in 1873 by a journalist on the *Heywood Advertiser*, based on interviews with Richard Bentinck in his later years.

These interviews are distinguished by revealing anecdotes told by Bentinck, mixed with references drawn from historical sources and the journalist's own perception of events. In addition, in his old age Bentinck had produced a narrative of his military experiences, which I believe was dictated to his eldest son, also Richard Bentinck, who had in time become a prosperous auctioneer.[1] Bentinck's account to his son is in the first person, whilst the journalist's version refers to Bentinck in the third person. Quotations from both sources are offset in the main text.

I joined the British Army in 1994 and in 2001 was posted to Colchester, physically close to Bryan's widow, Pat Boardman, who lives near Ipswich. Pat, well aware of my interest in military history, gave me the results of all of the research undertaken and material gathered by Bryan and I began my journey, learning about the life of Richard Bentinck and the 23rd of Foot in the Napoleonic era.

As a serving officer I was in a fortunate position to receive considerable help from the Museum of the Royal Welch Fusiliers at Caernarfon Castle and direct assistance from the then staff, particularly Colonel (Retd) Peter Crocker and Anne Pedley. However, 2001 also marked a change in the tempo of the British Army's life following the terrorist attacks of that September and for a number of years I found myself frequently deployed on operations and struggling to find the time and energy to conduct the required research on Bentinck. Over the years I have gradually chipped away at the task and have discovered a fascinating story of remarkable military exploits by Richard Bentinck and the 1st Battalion of the 23rd of Foot in the Napoleonic era.

Their noteworthy experiences and the numerous individual tales woven with the collective adventures prompted an ambition to expand the work in order to write a book about the battalion over the period in which Bentinck served with it, which included the military expeditions to Copenhagen and Martinique, the Peninsular War and the epic battle of Waterloo. These ambitions unravelled when I learnt that Donald E. Graves, an eminent Canadian military historian, had commenced work on a near-identical project. I recognized that, given my military responsibilities and inexperience in writing history books, there was no way I could compete with Donald. I thus sent him all my research and work in the hope that he would be able to weave the story of Bentinck into his study, which indeed has taken place with the publication in mid-2010 of his tremendous work *Dragon Rampant: The Royal Welch Fusiliers at War, 1789–1815*.

Donald examined my work and suggested that I should go back to the original idea of writing about Bentinck's life. Energized by his advice and considerable assistance, I took to the task. Bentinck's military life had fortuitous timing: within a few months of joining the Army and the 1st Battalion of the 23rd, he was participating in the brutal but measured expedition to seize the Danish fleet at Copenhagen. Shortly after the successful conclusion of this expedition, his battalion deployed to garrison duties in Nova Scotia, where the pace of peace did not appeal to many, although some did make the most of non-military opportunities. The discovery that the island of Martinique was poorly defended by the French led to the 23rd participating in a British expedition from Nova Scotia to capture that island, which was a considerable achievement. A following period spent back in Nova Scotia, recovering from the trials and tribulations of both the expedition and the climate of the Caribbean, was very timely before the battalion was committed to the Peninsular campaign.

A huge amount has been written about the Peninsular War and from my research I perceived two common themes: ultimate victory was testament to Wellington's skill as a commander and to the dogged fortitude of British troops. Bentinck's account, and indeed the experiences of the 23rd of Foot, reinforce this perception. At the start of their involvement, the men of the battalion were sarcastically referred to by more experienced troops as 'Johnny Newcomes'. However, the reputation of the 1/23rd grew and grew as the battalion consistently demonstrated its resolve and professionalism in the most testing and often most bloody of circumstances. Throughout the campaign, the quality and character of the battalion shone through, from charismatic officers to stoical soldiers. The general endurance and resilience to injury and illness illustrated by

Bentinck help explain the British reputation of military success, whatever the circumstances.

The title of my book, *The Very Thing*, is reflective of this substantial reputation and Bentinck's pride at being part of the Royal Welch Fusiliers. At the engagement of Aldea da Ponte in September 1811, Wellington identified a worrying tactical vulnerability and called for an infantry battalion to conduct an immediate manoeuvre. On being informed that the 1/23rd was best disposed, he is said to have smiled and commented, 'Ah, the very thing,' demonstrative of how the battalion had won the greatest of confidence of the most fabled commander in British history.

To some, Bentinck's experiences of Waterloo will be of considerable interest. He paints a very vivid picture of the frequent French cavalry charges and the battalion's dogged defence in square, and although he has the benefit of hindsight, the importance of the battle is quite apparent. The loss of Colonel Ellis, the 23rd's commanding officer, was a particular tragedy, after his many years of hard service. Bentinck's account and others from the regiment illustrate the tremendously high regard that Ellis was held in and perhaps more importantly his substantial influence in shaping the character of the 1/23rd.

Wherever possible, I have tried to use the notes at the conclusion of every chapter as a means to add context and detail to events, circumstances and people. The opportunity to see and understand the differing perspectives of events across the ranks has been fascinating. Thomas Jeremiah in his account of life in the 23rd of Foot adroitly commented that, 'So great is the ignorance of the poor soldier that he knows nothing of the debates between the greatest and most able statesmen until he finds himself plunged in smoke and fire.' Yet just prior to Waterloo, Wellington is supposed to have commented when looking upon a common British soldier, 'There, it all depends upon that article whether we do the business or not. Give me enough of it, and I am sure.'

From my own experiences of military operations around the world, these two shrewd comments could have been spoken but months ago. I hope that by telling the remarkable story of the military adventures of Richard Bentinck it will make a small addition to our understanding of the British Army in the Napoleonic era and how the building block of strategic success was, and continues to be, the military aptitude of the ordinary British soldier, men just like Richard Bentinck.

---

1. The author holds a copy of this narrative and it is also available via Suffolk Libraries.

Chapter One

Early Life and Joining the Army

———•—•———

The stormy period between 1790 and 1820 provided the opportunity for the Royal Navy and the British Army to achieve a formidable professional reputation, hewn from the experience of conflicts and combat around the world in pursuit of national interests and the necessity of defeating Napoleon's empire. Many of these conflicts happened at the same time so that Britain warred with several nations at once, on battlefields from India in the east to the Indies in the west. The foundation of a national psyche of military excellence can be attributed to these times of ceaseless arbitration of the sword, often all too necessary when Britain stood alone against Napoleonic Europe.

The martial character of the nation has a long ancestry, from those who resisted the landing of the first Roman legions, or strove to stay the Norman onslaught at the Battle of Hastings, to more recent times and a dwindling number who can still recount tales of fighting duels in the blue skies above the cliffs of Dover, or leaping under a silken canopy into the cauldron of Arnhem. Despite the generational differences there were always common factors; often the men who fought the battles were really but mere boys, while some were not always volunteers, but all rapidly became accustomed to the harshness of military discipline, the privations of campaigning and the terror of battle. All soldiers expect the scythe of death to skip over their young heads in its busy sweep but no matter the intensity of the battle or the length of the campaign, there will always be veterans – those who are left to fade away amidst enthusiastic tales of what they had participated in and witnessed.

In the Napoleonic era, the hardship and trials of life meant that there were few veterans who lived to a ripe old age to tell of the enthusiasm they felt and witnessed on Nelson's great victories being made known or on Wellington's brilliant feats being proclaimed. Yet each town in the United Kingdom generally had a couple of these veterans in the second half of the nineteenth century. One such place was Heywood, nine miles to the north of Manchester, which in 1873 was a large and thriving cotton mill town with a population of some 18,000. At this time there were known to be four ancient townsmen[1] who had fought in the Napoleonic wars of seventy years previously. They came to be regarded with a curious veneration by the rest of the town's population:

> Their war-worn frames made a feeble and melancholy muster requiring a wondrous imagination to connect them with the invincible warriors who bore everything before them in times when battles were not won by miles off by length of shot, but by strength of limb with the bayonet through the enemy's breast.

The purpose of this book is to provide a sketch of the military career of one of these veterans of Heywood, Richard Bentinck, who served variously as a drummer, a private and a bandsman. He had a number of eventful experiences, endured substantial hardship, desperate engagements and pitched battles during his service of 1807–23 with the 1st Battalion of the Royal Welch Fusiliers (23rd of Foot). This battalion became renowned for participating in nearly all the significant campaigns and battles of this era, with Bentinck starting his career with the ambitious expedition to capture the Danish fleet at Copenhagen and effectively concluding his war service with the epic struggle of Waterloo. The intention of this account is simply to provide a true outline of the share borne by a humble, ordinary soldier in that sanguinary epoch of the country's history.

> Richard Bentinck, the old veteran in question, is 84 years of age, and can yet thread a needle without the aid of glasses.[2] He was born in the parish of Bacton,[3] in Suffolk, in 1789, the year after the outbreak of the French revolution.[4] He came of a martial stock, his father, an agricultural labourer enlisting soon after the lad's birth into the Army Reserve and being drafted off to Gibraltar; and his Father's two brothers also taking to soldiering.[5] Perhaps one allurement thereto was the frequent marching of troops about there, to and from the barracks at the neighbouring towns of Stowmarket, Bury-St-Edmonds, and other Garrison places. The poor Mother, being left there with three boys and girls, was hard put to it for subsistence. After striving for herself and them for some time, however, her friends took and apportioned her children amongst them, and she got a situation as dairy servant.
>
> Kind as the friends were, it could not be supposed that they would keep the children idle a year longer than was necessary, so at the tender age of eight, Richard found himself shoved out upon the broad world to find his own porridge. This he did in the capacity of scout to a cattle jobber;[6] a sort of two-legged dog, whose duty was, like that of his four-

footed helpmates, to circumvent and bring back any rambling cow, calf or bullock to his master's drove. Many a hard chase did he have over those flat Suffolk fields, and many tears did he shed in scrambling through the big thorn hedges. Tiring of these discomforts, he next obtained employment with a miller, but finding that too confining for his fancy after a time, he engaged himself to a farmer. This master proved a very bad one, possessing implicit faith in the horsewhip, with which instrument he operated so frequently on the person of his little servant that the latter at length made up his mind to run away. He did so, one wild December morning. Having neither friends able to shelter him nor a situation in view, and thinking of the employment his father and uncles had chosen, he not unnaturally availed himself of that common expedient of the needy, enlisting into the army. This in spite of this youth, being then but 15 years old.[7]

At this period in time there was a near insatiable demand for troops, with a requirement for battle-casualty replacements, men to make up for the continual death toll from diseases endured in far-off places like the West Indies and India, and very simply because the Army kept increasing in size. On most occasions recruiting parties sent out by battalions and regiments were responsible for luring civilians into the Army.[8] However, Bentinck was not seduced by such a party but rather was the master of his own destiny as he made use of his local knowledge actively to seek the Army out.

Tramping afoot to Bury-St-Edmonds, where there were always detachments lying, he met coming out of the town 300 or 400 men of the Second Battalion of the 23rd Regiment, the Royal Welch Fusiliers, who had come up from Chester and were on their way to Colchester.

It was fortuitous that Bentinck came upon elements of the 2nd Battalion of the Royal Welch Fusiliers (2/23rd Foot) which was moving to reinforce the 1st Battalion (1/23rd Foot) which was at Colchester.[9] The demands of the campaigning of the Napoleonic era meant that most infantry regiments had 2nd battalions which were used by regiments as the location of a depot, where recruiting parties could find a base and subsequent recruits undertake training. It generally also became common practice for fatigued, wounded or sick soldiers from the 1st battalion to be given a respite from conflict.[10] The 2nd Battalion of the 23rd Foot was only granted establishment in December 1804 with headquarters in Wrexham. Years of campaigning and expeditions had taken its toll on the regiment and in the spring of 1805 the 1st Battalion was at quarter strength, whilst the 2nd Battalion numbered only 74 men. Over the next two years intensive recruiting efforts greatly improved the situation but the general circumstances demanded a constant stream of recruits.

> Recruits were eagerly caught up in those days, when soldiers were so numerously made into food for powder. So, young Bentinck, lad as he was, was pounced upon by the passing Officers and asked if he would enlist, to which he readily responded that he would. So without more ado he turned back and marched beside the big billy-goat which had led the old regiment since its formation, with gilded horns, and the same allowance of pay as any private for its maintenance.[11] This was in December 1806, and he was sworn in at Colchester on January 2nd, 1807.[12] At this time Colonel Jones was then commanding the First Battalion.[13] The Battalion was in full strength, with close to a thousand all ranks.[14]

Chance had been kind to Bentinck. The 1st Battalion, 23rd Foot, had an auspicious recent history, with service in North America 1773–84 which included a number of major battles. The declaration of war by France on Britain in 1793 provided additional testing experiences, with the battalion participating in the British campaign against French possessions in the West Indies over the period 1794–6. This was followed by garrison service in Britain for a couple of years before a raid on Ostend in 1798 and an unsuccessful attempt to liberate Holland from the French in 1799. In 1801 the battalion was part of the successful Egyptian expedition before undertaking garrison duties in Gibraltar. A miserable campaign in Germany followed in 1805, which achieved very little, and in 1806 the battalion moved to become part of the garrison in Colchester, where Bentinck joined.

> In consequence of the small size and tender age of their new recruit, the Officers were somewhat at a loss what to do with him, but ultimately they deposed a tall Drummer, and gave Bentinck his drum, and a bounty of £16. A sum significant of the havoc made with soldiers in those times. Much of this, however, had to be paid back to the Quartermaster for the outfit or 'kit' of the recruit. In the case of the Drummer, this included a coat so covered with lace that the red could hardly be seen.

Bentinck's memory of his bounty is most likely incorrect. At the time, soldiers signing on for life exchanged for a bounty of £23 17s 6d, most of which was absorbed by the cost of outfitting necessaries, personal kit such as shirts, shoes, pack, leggings, stockings, brushes, black ball, combs, straps for greatcoats, stock and a clasp. It was common for the recruiting party to encourage the recruit to part with any remaining bounty money by spending it on beer, which they could indulge in. Although he had evaded the recruiting party, the experienced soldiers in his company would no doubt have encouraged Bentinck to part with his bounty money to celebrate his enlistment. If he was lucky, Bentinck may have ended up with slightly more than the £1 he would at best have received roughly every six weeks as a farm labourer. Soldiers were paid a shilling (5p) a day but half of this was deducted for food. In addition the soldiers had to pay the equivalent of 2p a week for washing and 1p a week for cleaning materials. One day's pay a year was also given to the Chelsea Pensioners, leaving little to end up in the pocket of the soldier. However, Bentinck was fed, clothed, housed and had employment, which all in all could be seen to be an improvement on his previous circumstances.

The excesses of military dress provided the greatest challenge to garrison life for the young recruit:

'Ah,' says the subject of our story, 'the cleaning and titivating soldiers had to do in my time! Twarnt just a whisk and a whiff as it is now. Many a time have I cried, at first, over putting up my hair!'

This was not indeed a task to be laughed at, under the absurd military fashion then prevalent. In the first place every man had to use at least half a pound of flour a week to powder his hair with, making it look like an unbaked cake clapped upon his head and pressed carefully down upon his face.[15] But this was not all. The curling irons had to be used with great exactitude to make two or three little curls, like those on a drake's tail, on each temple, and woe betide the unlucky fellow who appeared on parade with one of these a shade out of twist. Then a tail of horse hair had to be fitted to the back of the head, bound up with a bit of leather shining like a mirror with 'heel ball'[16] and tied, every hair in its place with string or wire.[17] Those who could not manage this intricate business and who came in for the punishment drill rigorously imposed for any real or imaginary defect in his work (and there were many) paid sixpence a week to any dexterous comrade who would do it for them. Which was thus not over paid considering that a shake of the customer's head would subject the artist to penalties. Then every scrap of leather had to be heel-balled, every inch of piping pipe-clayed, and even the gun barrels were kept bright, for the great suffering of the unhappy warriors.[18]

However, Bentinck was fortunate in not having to endure garrison soldiering for more than a few months. Napoleon's policy of continental blockade, designed to starve Britain and place the country under unremitting pressure to sue for peace, had been met by determined opposition. Where possible, the Royal Navy would fight back and demonstrate the will of the British government to intervene wherever it deemed necessary to thwart the ambitions of Napoleon. In July 1807, the French and Russian governments signed secret articles in the Treaty of Tilsit whereby both countries were to force Denmark and Sweden to join their alliance against Britain. Napoleon, flushed by his recent victories on the battlefield and the securing of peace in Europe under his terms, was planning a further expansion of his rising powers. He particularly coveted the Danish fleet, then the sixth largest in the world. Secret articles in the Treaty and Napoleon's plans to capture the neutral fleet of Denmark were soon discovered by the British government. To assist the Danish royal court in making a decision in favour of Napoleon, French troops were deployed into the Danish province of Holstein. The fear that the French might eventually make use of Danish and Swedish sea power to mount an invasion of Britain prompted the government to take quick and audacious action.

It was decided to mount an expedition to Copenhagen in order to persuade the Danes to allow the 'temporary deposit of the Danish Ships of the Line in one of His Majesty's Ports', to be held there until a time when the situation with Napoleon was settled. At a very unwelcome 3.00 in the morning of 25 July 1807, the piquet of the 1/23rd of Foot woke all the men up and the battalion was mustered for departure to Harwich but an hour later. In company groups the battalion marched the distance of twenty-one miles from Colchester, completing the journey by 1.00 in the afternoon. However, the orders received were deliberately limited and the exact destination was kept a secret, which created much conjecture and debate amongst both the officers and the men.

---

1. The other veterans were Joe Mills, Tom Whitworth and James Smithies. Smithies's recollections were published in the *Middleton Albion* in 1868 and possibly influenced Bentinck to do the same.

2. Bentinck's date of birth is subject to debate. His discharge certificate lists his age as 18 on enlistment on 10 January 1807, implying a birth date in 1788–9, which would tally with him being 84 when the *Heywood Advertiser* published its articles in 1873. His

gravestone lists his date of birth as 1787. However, records show that he was baptized on 12 February 1792 at Bacton, Suffolk; if this is accurate and, as was customary, this was an infant baptism, his date of birth would likely be at most a few weeks before.

3. A small village some seven miles north of Stowmarket, Suffolk.

4. A historical error, the storming of the Bastille occurred on 15 June 1789.

5. It is very questionable that Bentinck's father enlisted in the Army Reserve and was posted to Gibraltar. At this time there was no Army Reserve. An Army of Reserve was formed in June 1803 with the June 1803 Additional Force Act, raised by ballot, with the same system of substitution permitted as for the Militia. However, troops could not be sent abroad.

6. A person engaged in the buying and selling of cattle.

7. If the date of 12 February 1792 for Bentinck's baptism is correct he might well have been 15 on enlistment.

8. 'The three greatest inducements when recruiting men were alcohol, cash bounties and unemployment. The sergeant of a recruiting party, resplendent in his best uniform, complete with sash, sword and ribbons would buy a drink for all males in a pub of his choice (usually chosen with a prior transfer of coin to the publican), spin a tale of "Gentlemen soldiers, merry life, muskets rattling, cannons roaring, drums beating, colours flying, regiments charging and shouts of victory!" and try to hook a fish.' Graves, *Dragon Rampant*, p. 54.

9. The 23rd Regiment of Foot had been raised in 1689 as Lord Herbert's Regiment, its first Colonel being Baron Herbert of Cherbury. In 1702, when issued with the new flintlock musket (*fusil* in French), it was re-titled the Welch Regiment of Fuzileers. At a time when most infantry were armed with the matchlock musket, a dangerous weapon around the quantities of black powder generally found in artillery positions, special units of 'fusiliers' equipped with the safer flintlocks, were created to protect the artillery. When all British infantry regiments were eventually armed with flintlocks, the three regiments of fusiliers (also known as fusileers, fuziliers or fuzileers according to the vagaries of eighteenth-century spelling) in the British Army – the 7th, 21st and 23rd Foot – lost their original function but retained their status as elite infantry. In 1747, the regiment's title was changed to the 23rd Regiment of Foot (Royal Welsh Fuzileers) but it obstinately refused to give up the archaic spelling 'Welch'. Although early in its history the 23rd Foot was linked with the Principality, it did not specifically recruit in Wales but from across the British Isles. The regiment had seen considerable action in its early years, fighting at Blenheim in 1704, Ramilles in 1706, Oudenarde in 1708, Malplaquet in 1709, Dettingen in 1743, Fontenoy in 1745, Minorca in 1756, and Minden in 1759. From Graves, *Dragon Rampant*, and Glover & Riley, *That Astonishing Infantry*.

10. In some circumstances, it was a military necessity to deploy the 2nd battalion. In the case of the 23rd Foot, this did indeed occur with the 2nd Battalion distinguishing itself at Corunna in 1809 and in the same year serving on the ill-fated Walcheren expedition.

11. The origin of the custom of the Royal Welch Fusiliers marching with a goat with gilded horns at the head of the regiment on parade has never been verified. However, it was apparently well established in 1777, when Major Robert Donkin wrote in his *Military Collections and Remarks* that, 'The royal regiment of welch Fuzileers has a privilegeous honor of passing in review preceded by a Goat with gilded horns, and adorned with ringlets of flowers', and that 'the corps values itself much on the ancientness of the custom'. Quoted in Glover & Riley, *That Astonishing Infantry*, p. 278.

12. This differs from the date of his discharge certificate which shows his enlistment as being 10 January 1807. The same date is also quoted in Holme & Kirby, *Medal Rolls*, p. 81. 'For a man to be legally enlisted he had to sign the proper forms, pass a medical examination and be "attested" before a magistrate who would verify that he was sober and then read him those sections of the Articles of War that dealt with mutiny and desertion. As both doctor and magistrate were paid by the Crown for these services, recruiting could be a profitable activity for them and many medical examinations were not that diligent, while magistrates attested men reeking of alcohol when legally they were supposed to be sober. Boys under sixteen years of age could be attested if they were above five feet four inches and their physical appearance suggested that they would be able to mature to cope with the rigours of army life.' Graves, *Dragon Rampant*, p. 54.

13. Lieutenant Colonel Evan Jones was a Welshman from Gelliwig in Caernarvonshire. He had joined the 23rd Foot in 1791 and had fought with it in the West Indies, the Helder and Egypt. He commanded the 1st Battalion in 1807 and participated in the Copenhagen expedition, subsequently retiring on return to run his property in Caernarvonshire. However, Bentinck is inaccurate to suggest that he was the commanding officer when he joined the battalion. The commanding officer was Lieutenant Colonel James Losack who resigned in February 1807 to be replaced by Jones, who moved over from the recently established 2nd Battalion.

14. On 26 March 1807, the battalion was inspected by Major General Thomas Grosvenor at Colchester. The total strength, all ranks, was 991. Two sergeants, two corporals and 192 privates were Welsh. Broughton-Mainwaring, *Historical Record of the Royal Welsh Fusiliers*, p. 217. It is recorded that the battalion was at full war strength for the Danish expedition, mustering a total of 925 men. The organization of a battalion was standard, but strength was not regulated as in many continental armies to a fixed 'establishment' in terms of numbers of men of each rank. A battalion comprised ten companies, each of around 100 men. Eight of these companies most frequently took a position in the centre mass of the battalion when established in line so were often called 'centre companies'. The other two companies were known as 'flank companies' – one company of grenadiers, who would stand on the right flank, and the light infantry company. The grenadiers were supposedly comprised of the largest and strongest men, the light infantry of men fleet of foot best suited to skirmishing and scouting. During campaigns and expeditions, it was usual to form brigades by grouping two to three battalions together. Two to three brigades would then form divisions.

15. This practice was abandoned in 1795 and Bentinck undoubtedly was educated by experienced soldiers in the historical trials and tribulations of soldiering prior to his enlistment.

16. 'Heel balling': the process of waxing and polishing the leather by hand.

17. The hair on the top was cropped short and the queue or clubbed pigtail, some seven inches long, doubled over upon itself with the end hidden and bound with a ribbon. It was then held together by candle tallow or hog's lard, kept off the collar by a piece of cloth worn under it.

18. On 20 July 1808, it was announced that the use of queues was to be dispensed with. Hair was to be cut close to the necks and frequently washed. Despite Bentinck's comments on the challenges of keeping hair in queues, the officers and men were not in favour of this change. The adjutant reported to the commanding officer, then Lieutenant Colonel Ellis, that the men were in a state of 'ferment'. Ellis acted rapidly and decisively. He called out a company, had them sit on benches on the square and then sent half a dozen men as hair cutters to remove the hair up to the neck. It is assumed that the officers marked the loss of their hair by replacing the grease protector that sat on the back of the neck with a 'flash'. For the next twenty-six years this was worn as an unauthorized decoration until royal assent was given. It was not until 1900 that the wearing of the flash was extended to all members of the regiment.

Chapter Two

The Copenhagen Expedition

For the expedition to Copenhagen, the battalion was at full war strength, with the total complement of the expedition being about 25,000 troops, under the command of the respected Lord Cathcart,[1] with the naval contingent, led by Lord Gambier, being 24 ships of the line and 22 smaller warships, as well as troop transports. Three divisions were deployed from England for the expedition: the 'Right Division' from the Downs, the 'Left Division' from Harwich and the 'Reserve Division' from Hull. The 1/23rd, commanded by Lieutenant Colonel Evan Jones contributed 925 all ranks,[2] and was part of the 10,000-strong 'Left Division' commanded by Lieutenant General Sir David Baird. The division included three brigades: Major General Ward's Brigade was made up of battalions of the 28th, 92nd and 95th Regiments; Major General Grosvenor commanded battalions of the 4th, 23rd and 95th; whilst Major General Spencer commanded battalions of the 50th and 79th.

The 1/23rd embarked on the waiting transport ships on 26 July 1807,[3] but the fusiliers found that the usual 'hurry up and wait' procedures had been followed and they were forced to spend a few days at anchor as the final preparations were co-ordinated. Living aboard a vessel was never an experience which drew great favour amongst the fusiliers, but at least the vessels were in harbour rather than subject to the vagaries of the open sea. After a number of days at anchor and having completed all preparations, the force departed on 1 August. The exact destination of the expedition had not been formally announced and it was not until all ships were at sea that orders were finally issued and the true purpose of the expedition revealed – to capture intact the Danish fleet in Copenhagen.[4] The battalion was split between a brig and three troopships.[5] This naturally created cramped conditions and the discomfort of the troops was considerable.

The voyage, in the transports of that day – grimly nicknamed 'coffins', was not the pleasantest of summer excursions. The policy was then to cram as many soldiers and horses into a ship as she would hold, comfort being too ridiculous a thing to be thought of, and the horses being much more considerately tended than the men. It was not strange that

Bentinck, along with plenty others, should be too sick and ill all the way to care much whether he lived or died; that the sea biscuits, as hard as a board and hollow with maggots, failed to tempt the palate.[6] That salt junk was loathsome to his sight, and that even the wooden bowl of grog, the one medicine doled out to all, was rejected with heaving disgust.[7] However, this first trip on the way to war came to an end, like all events in the transitory world.

After they left Harwich, the wind was very light and varied, ultimately delaying the arrival of the British force off the Jutland coast until 6 August. The next day saw the successful meeting up of the differing transports and their escorts in preparation for sailing down the Kattegat toward the Danish capital. On the evening of 8 August with a fresh breeze, torrential rain and bouts of thunder and lightning, the fleet made its way south toward the narrow Oresund straits, dropping anchor close to Helsingør. A commentator observing the fleet remarked on 'beholding of one of the grandest sights of nature and art. The lightning being more vivid than the oldest man on board could remember which enabled us to discern the union of our Fleet.'[8]

The grand statement of a massed British fleet poised off the Danish coast did not mean that hostilities were a certainty. Diplomatic initiatives continued in an effort to break the impasse. Over a period of four days, 6–10 August, Francis Jackson, the British envoy, conducted comprehensive talks with the Prince Regent of Denmark but unfortunately these were ultimately a failure and conflict seemed a certainty. The force remained at anchor for the period 9–15 August conducting preparations for any future landing.

The complexity of an amphibious landing meant that many preparations were required and a number of full rehearsals were carried out. At the same time, the Danes readied themselves for war, the several batteries of Kronborg castle scaling their guns. On the 15th the fleet weighed anchor and, with every gun manned and every sail set, moved past the shores of Zealand. The Danes failed to make any challenge, never mind fire a shot from the heavy batteries guarding the approaches to their capital city. Without interference and in good conditions, the fleet had a smooth passage, anchoring at 8.00 p.m. near the village of Vedbaek, some eight miles north of Copenhagen. The following morning at daybreak:

The boats filled with troops, assembled alongside the respective Ships, and on a gun being fired from the Admiral and a flag hoisted at the Main, the whole pushed off at once for the shore. They kept in line as they rowed, in every tenth or twelfth boat, the colours of a Regiment uncased and blowing open with the breeze. In different parts of the line were boats having field pieces in their bows. The men were ordered to sit down and keep silence. There was some surf on the beach, but not sufficient to obstruct the landing seriously and few accidents happened.[9]

Commencing with the Reserve, the force disembarked and, with minimal noise or confusion, quickly established itself on shore. The landings were observed by a couple of Danish cavalrymen but no opposition was given which allowed an immediate advance to commence toward Copenhagen. Bentinck's recollections were far from precise and he was only able to provide a partial summary of the events but rightly commented on the failure of the Danes to be more pro-active to the British manoeuvres.

On a beautiful Sunday morning, in the June of 1807[10] Bentinck crawled up on deck to see the Squadron drop anchor off Copenhagen. After a brief conference to the leaders, it was decided to sail right up to the harbour and if possible affect an immediate landing.[11] Promptly the men-o'war which conveyed the Fleet took up their positions and led the way with every gun manned and every sail set. Not a shot, however, did they fire and in their astonishment and doubt as to what it all meant, not one iron challenge did the Danes send from the heavy batteries which should have guarded the entrance. So the British sailed up without molestation, took in sail, lowered their boats, and the soldiers crowding into them, were rapidly transferred to the enemy's land without the loss of a single man. Nay, so surprised were the unsuspicious enemy that they sent a flag of truce to ascertain the character and intentions of their abrupt visitors. Then the business proceeded in earnest.

The battalion landed in good style, with the colours uncased and flying in the wind. The only mishap was the unfortunate wounding of a company commander by a Fusilier who tripped with his fixed bayonet. The landing provided Bentinck with a unique opportunity to see with his own eyes:

… the great General who as Sir Arthur Wellesley had already guided the British Arms with the lustre he was destined to heighten as the Duke of Wellington. He acted in this expedition simply as Brigadier General and Commander of the Brigade of Guards. Our old veteran remembers his piercing eye, ready to detect the slightest fault, his spare figure, his quick decided manner, and it must be added, the dislike with which many of his men repaid the strict discipline which he was then even noted as an enforcer. In discipline, he was regarded, according to our informant, as tyrannical and merciless, being liked the least by the men of his immediate command.[12]

The British rested themselves on the beach till night fell and then moved up nearer the city, which lay some distance from the shore. The Fusiliers encamped opposite the Queen's palace.[13] That night was spent in throwing up earthworks, which as the morning broke, began to be needed. For the enemy, quickly making up for their previous inertness, opened a heavy fire upon them from the city walls and outworks. Bentinck was one of the Drummers of our advanced line and heard the thunder of the hostile guns much plainer than he liked.

The garrison of Copenhagen consisted of roughly 13,000 troops, a mixture of well-trained regulars, militia and a university students' home guard. Aside from some movement observed of Danish cavalry, the enemy appeared to be concentrating on preparations within the walls of the city. The British fleet's gun brigs had advanced with the troops along the coast, providing a capability for artillery support to the shore to respond to enemy activity. The Danes soon recognized this threat and at last went on the offensive. A small force of gunboats emerged at mid-morning and attacked the brigs. The troops ashore were close to this action and watched the cannonading between the forces with great interest.

The battalion with its brigade came to occupy a central position in the British line. This allowed the battalion to witness the agreed movement of members of the Danish royal family from the besieged city to Holstein and efforts by Lord Cathcart to gain agreement by the Danish defenders to British objectives. However, the Danes made clear their determination to offer obstinate resistance. The city's fortifications were well constructed but existed to defend a population of 30,000. At this time, due to the influx of many of the population surrounding the city, Copenhagen had increased to a population of around 100,000, crammed into all available buildings and occupying many open areas. It was apparent that any bombardment would be terribly effective and dreadful destruction and loss of life would ensue.

Over the period 21–26 August preparations for the siege continued with heavy rain adding to the discomfort of the troops. Parties of up to 600 men worked intensively in four-hour periods, providing the muscle to erect the batteries and construct the trenches. The Danes mounted occasional cannonading attacks with their gunboats but no significant damage was done to the fleet or the troops ashore. The Danes realized that little could be done from land to cause large-scale damage to the British lines and so concentrated on using the gunboats to open a heavy fire upon the besieging troops. The 1/23rd in particular, some 2,500 yards north-west from the city's outer walls, found themselves the subject of this undesirable attention. Sheltering in the well-kept gardens of large houses of Danish merchants, the troops kept low, pressed behind elm trees and prayed for divine intervention.

The earthworks were drawing swiftly around the environed city, notwithstanding fierce sorties made by the Garrison, in the vain hope of checking the fatal girdle. The British outposts gradually pushed forward, among the villas and the gardens forming the suburbs. Being on duty in one of these outposts one day,[14] Bentinck saw several of our men feasting themselves on peaches, grapes and other fruit, whose fine appearance betokened its growth to some gentleman's garden. Hard dry biscuit and the salted meat in the camp had sent him ravenous for a share in the delicious plunder. So watching for his opportunity, he slipped through a hedge to his front, crept forward among the bushes some 500 yards, and came to a very Eden of a garden. The trees were heavily laden with yellow apples, big plums, and huge bunches of grapes. With eager haste he snatched down as many as he could stow in his pockets and hat, and was staggering off under his load when he caught sight of a rifle, with bayonet fitted, leaning against a neighbouring tree.[15] This scared him considerably. Glancing round, however, and seeing no one, he ran and got the weapon and was about to scramble through the hedge with it, when from a covered walk close to him, there emerged a Danish soldier. He, the owner, had evidently been enjoying himself on the too tempting fruit, sentry though he was, for he was placidly eating an apple. He dropped it with a shout on seeing the intruder, and seeing the latter was but a boy, was triumphantly stepping up to secure both him and the rifle, when Bentinck though naturally frightened, swore that he would shoot him if he took another stride.

Though the Dane could not understand the language, he understood well enough the action that accompanied it. The young drummer was taking aim at his head, and he knew that a boy's finger could pull the fatal trigger as well as a giant's. His evident terror at this predicament, expecting every second a bullet through his brain, struck his boy foe with an idea of something besides his first thought of mere escape – he would drive the Dane before him and take him in prisoner to the outpost. Accordingly, with as much ferocity of face and gesture as his own discomfort made possible, to ensure the Dane understood that he would shoot him first and bayonet him afterwards if he did not get through the hedge and march before him. So, after a vain look round for help the Dane had to comply. Bentinck followed, with the rifle still at the present and in a very few minutes they got back to his comrades, who received them with amusement and reams of laughter.

Bentinck was canny enough to know that the Dane had committed a grave error and, although he himself had done wrong by leaving his post, he was rewarded for his initiative.

He must not have been long in the service or he would of [sic] kept his rifle in his hand, that was the first explicit of any soldiering. When I took him in my Officer gave me five shillings for the rifle and castigated me never to leave my post again, for he might of [sic] taken me instead of me taking him.

This experience gave the young soldier heart and he continued to make use of his initiative, displaying a common soldierly liking for foraging.

On another occasion he was paying a secret visit to one of these alluring gardens when shells from the enemy's batteries began to splinter on the trees and throw up the earth around him, so that he had to make a hurried retreat.[16]

The siege of the city was effective and provisions began to run short. This led to increased efforts by the Danes to run the gauntlet of the besieging troops:

One day the British received word that a very large convoy was on its way from the island quarter, bound for the city. A strong detachment was told off to intercept it. Marching quietly but with alertness, they soon arrived at the road, and took ambush in the thickets along each side of it. In a while the head of the baggage carts came in view escorted by a troop of cavalry. They were sauntering carelessly along, most of them smoking, after the manner of their country, and some of them even singing lustily, as though there was not such a thing as an enemy in the land. Suddenly, a bugle blew; a few rifle shots were fired over their head and a line of red coats gleaming through the bushes on either side of them, cut short their comfort and appraised them that they were prisoners, with no chance of escape except in death. So the whole of the goodly cavalcade was swept off to feed the besiegers instead of the starving besieged and that too without the loss of a man on either side.

All British preparations for the bombardment of the city were complete by 3 September. The defenders thus cut off from supplies, heavily bombarded and losing many men in vain attempts to break through and disperse the foe, the fall of the city could not long be delayed. However, the Danes vowed to continue their resistance and accordingly at 8.00 on the evening of 2 September, the bombardment commenced from the 13-inch mortar batteries together with a few of the new rockets designed by Sir William Congreve, which were fired from the roof of the royal palace at Charlottenlund.[17] Until 2.00 in the morning, the shells were thrown fast and with rapid effect, but the rate slackened and firing eventually ceased by dawn. The bombardment very quickly put several areas of the city, including the university in a blaze.[18] This fearful sight and the obvious accompanying suffering causing much resignation in British hearts.

> Sailors were brought from the ships (where they were too far off to be of material use) to man them [the guns].[19] Jack Tar's delight at being fetched ashore for such work now and then is proverbial. Accustomed to hit ships when pitching unsteadily on the waves, their aim from a stationary gun, at an immovable object, is peculiarly destructive and they began to play havoc with the buildings of Copenhagen. Our old veteran remembers them one morning singling out a stately Church and wagering how soon they could bring it down, for fees gave loose reins to any kind of destruction in those days. In an hour or two afterwards the fine structure fell with a crash heard far along the besieging camp.

The fine structure of the Church of Our Lady, 'Vor Frue Kirke', fell at around 5.00 on the morning of 5 September. This violent action marked a high point in the bombardment and the rate of fire gradually slackened as the daylight grew. A flag of truce was hoisted by the Danes from one of the ramparts shortly after daybreak and a cessation of hostilities was agreed. The strange quiet after such noisy violence let the thoughts of the British troops wander to the spoils of war and what prize money could be expected if the Danish fleet was successfully taken intact. Negotiations began on the morning of 6 September and the articles of capitulation were signed the next day. The destruction in the city was considerable; it was estimated that 1,800 houses were destroyed, 600 of the population killed or wounded and a further 8,000 made homeless.

On 7 September, after the capitulation was signed, the grenadiers from the battalions of the 4th, 7th, 8th, 23rd, 32nd, 50th, 79th, and 92nd together with a flank company of the Guards, eight pieces of field artillery and two or three troops of light dragoons marched with the tune of 'The British Grenadiers' playing and colours flying to take possession of the Copenhagen citadel in the early evening.

The triumphant British found in the dockyard 37 ships of war and a number of gunboats, not all in seaworthy condition but most repairable; 250 bronze and 1,400 iron naval cannon were also seized. Importantly the captured booty included the Danish Navy's entire accumulated stockpile of seasoned naval timber for future ship construction. Two ships captured during construction on the stocks were dismantled and the timber loaded for shipping back to England. In order to make the Danish fleet ready for the trip across the North Sea, 3,000 carpenters alone were drawn from the army and sailors landed from the British ships to work to rig the Danish vessels. The articles of capitulation allowed six weeks for completion of all work on the captured fleet and for the British force to vacate Copenhagen totally. This constraint of time provoked a frenzy of directed activity to clear every serviceable piece of naval equipment or destroy the old or unserviceable ships.

When not engaged in these preparations, the battalion enjoyed the chance to take a decent amount of rest in the suburbs of the city, being able to indulge in sleep without the interruption of a call to arms or the noise of artillery and small arms. Troops were employed to guard properties vacated by citizens during the siege, more concerned about their physical well-being rather their property. The lack of plundering by the British troops was commented on favourably by the Danes, who admired their honesty and discipline, even though they were enemies. All constructed batteries and earthworks were also levelled by the British in an effort to leave minimal trace of the siege on the landscape of Copenhagen.

On 18 October, the battalion embarked upon some of the prizes. On the 20th, with great ceremony, the citadel was given up and all remaining soldiers embarked. The fleet, now consisting of a spectacular 80 warships and some 243 transports, got under way and was fortunate to pick up a favourable breeze on the next morning. Unfortunately the journey home was eventful and more unpleasant for all participants than the journey to war. Tremendously bad weather and formidable winds were experienced on 30 and 31 October. On some ships sails were lost and most of the towed Danish gunboats had to be cut away. The heavy gales of the night of 31 October claimed a number of transports and contrived to prevent many of the fleet from making their way back into Yarmouth. The difficult sands off the east coast of England also caused problems as ships found themselves off course in very shallow water. However, by 7 November, all the transports with men of the battalion on board had finally found their way to Deal. The battalion immediately marched for Canterbury and subsequently arrived back at the barracks in Colchester on 13 November. Leaves of absence were granted across all ranks of the battalion and it quietly resumed the normal pattern of garrison duties.[20]

The expedition had taken four months and been totally successful, achieving the surrender of Copenhagen and all the Danish Navy to His Majesty's arms, with relatively low British casualties. Parliament voted thanks to the Army and Navy. The prize money from the Copenhagen expedition was a tidy sum for all involved but, with the usual frictions of bureaucracy and procedures, it would take some time before soldiers would receive their individual reward. The value of the plunder taken from the dockyard's warehouse alone amounted to £305,666, a significant sum. The British naval gains comprised 17 ships of the line, 17 frigates, 16 smaller vessels and 26 gunboats. An observer called the whole campaign, 'the best stroke that has been done for John Bull for some time'.[21]

The gentle nature of the subsequent garrison duties was enjoyed by the battalion. The size of the garrison meant that duties were light and life was seen as good for all. Due to the strategic requirements of the period, it was not long before this period of calm was to be disturbed. On the evening of 16 January 1808 orders were received for the battalion to march to Portsmouth in order to deploy by sea for foreign service in an undisclosed location.[22]

—————•—————

1. General William Schaw Cathcart, 1st Earl Cathcart (1755–1843). In 1776 he took his place as Lord Cathcart in Parliament and gained a commission in the 7th Dragoons. He fought in America in 1777, before transferring to the 17th Light Dragoons. Returning to the United Kingdom in 1780, he then achieved the rank of lieutenant colonel in the Coldstream Guards. In 1792 he became Colonel of the 29th Foot. He served in the campaigns in the Low Countries 1793–5. He was appointed Colonel of the 2nd Life Guards in 1797 and remained in this position until his death. In 1803–5 he was Commander-in-Chief in Ireland and led the British expedition to Hanover.

Following the success of the Danish expedition, he was created Viscount Cathcart of Cathcart and Baron Greenock of Greenock. In 1812 he was promoted general and served in the allied headquarters during the War of the Sixth Coalition, 1812–14. Elevated to an earldom in 1814, he then served as ambassador in St Petersburg, returning home in 1820. He died in Scotland in 1843.

2. For the Danish expedition, a small rear party of roughly 70 remained in Colchester.

3. Lieutenant John Harrison recalled, they were 'cheered by the loud huzzas of the spectators, which was returned with three times three by the fuzileers'. Royal Welch Fusiliers Museum (RWFM), Accession (Acc.) 1335, Harrison to father, 20 November 1807.

4. For obvious reasons of maintaining the strictest security, the troops were kept unaware of their exact destination, as Lieutenant Harrison commented, 'Everything is kept very secret but it is supposed that we are going to make a great dash somewhere.' RWFM, Acc.1335, Harrison to father, 26 July 1807.

5. A brig sloop had a crew of forty-five to sixty men, whilst a ship sloop had a crew of up to 120 men. Dependent on the mix of troops, equipment and horses, up to 200 men could be transported. Specifically constructed troopships could carry up to 650 personnel, in addition to the crew.

6. Also known as hardtack, made from flour, water and salt. Being hard and dry, if properly stored and transported, they would survive rough handling and extremes of temperature.

7. In the Royal Navy from 1756, the daily issue of grog was a half pint of rum mixed with one quart of water. The purpose was to extend the usage of fresh water by delaying spoilage.

8. RWFM, Acc.1335, Harrison to father, 20 November 1807.

9. Browne, *The Napoleonic War Journal of Captain Thomas Henry Browne*, p. 49.

10. Bentinck's date is wrong.

11. A further historical inaccuracy. The process of negotiation has already been described.

12. At the time, Arthur Wellesley was a knight of the Bath and a major general. On hearing news of the impending expedition he declared his intention not to stay in his appointment as Chief Secretary of Ireland. Wellesley commanded the army's reserve (comprising the 1/43rd, 2/52nd, 1/92nd and elements of the 1/ and 2/95th). On the expedition the Guards Brigade was commanded by Major General The Honourable Edward Finch. A significant engagement undertaken by Wellesley was the defeat of an enemy force at Kioge. He landed an advance guard near Copenhagen on 19 August 1807, conducted a night march and then stormed the Danish positions, taking 56 officers and some 2,000 men prisoner, along with 16 cannon for the loss of only 30–40 Allied troops. By 3 September, he had cleared the island of Zealand of Danish regulars and militia for minimal loss. Wellesley was very much against the bombardment of Copenhagen, hoping that less destructive methods might be successful. He was emphatic in his desire to avoid harming the local people wherever possible. At the end of September he returned to Ireland.

13. The 1/23rd along with the 4th Foot in General Grosvenor's brigade, waited an hour for orders and then advanced parallel to the sea for a mile and took possession of high ground. Around 10 p.m., the battalion arrived in the village of Charlottenlund, taking up positions in the avenues of the royal palace. Piquets were posted to the front during the night, providing sufficient security for an adequate rest but, despite their exhaustion and appreciation of being on firm land, it was an uncomfortable night for the Fusiliers as they lay against their knapsacks on the flea-infested sand of the horse-exercise area in front of the palace.

14. It is possible that Bentinck had relinquished his role as a drummer at this stage and was a private and hence on outpost duty.

15. This may well have been a rifle as the Danish infantry were equipped with a mixture of Danish-produced Model 1785 or 1791 rifles and sharpshooter muskets.

16. It is believed that this heavy shelling occurred on 31 August. After a Danish sortie from the city had been repulsed their batteries commenced a rapid firing of grapeshot and shell from the city walls and outworks.

17. A Danish pamphlet captured by the then Captain J. C. S. Harrison at the conclusion of hostilities highlighted the shock of the British artillery's rockets which, 'civilized nations never made use of before'. Thomas Browne also quotes the writer of this Danish pamphlet. 'But when I saw the air jingling with the never to be heard of inventions, carrying fire thro' the air, not to be extinguished, down upon our dwellings, oh Britain, Queen of Nations, Mother of such noble and manly sons, said I to myself, is this thy work.' Browne, *Napoleonic War Journal*, p. 49.

18. The round tower and the church of the Trinity, which housed the university library on the upper floor, were fortunately saved from complete destruction by the extensive efforts of soldiers, sailors and citizens of Copenhagen.

19. The skills involved in executing a naval bombardment were readily transferable to land.

20. Entertainment on return for the officers' mess included a ball held with the other regiments in Colchester garrison, the 4th and 28th, for selected invitees from the local populace.

21. RWFM, Acc.1335, Harrison to father, 20 November 1807.

22. Snow was on the ground when orders were received on 16 January 1808 that stated, 'The 23rd regiment will march in three divisions, to Portsmouth for embarkation, for foreign service. The 1st division will move by the enclosed route on the 17th, and the remaining divisions on the 18th and 19th. All Officers and men on leave of absence to join the regiment at Portsmouth.' Browne, *Napoleonic War Journal*, p. 68.

Chapter Three

North America and Martinique

———•———

The orders for deployment for foreign service gave the battalion only twenty-four hours before the first troop movement toward Portsmouth was required, resulting in frantic packing, bill paying and issuing of numerous orders including informing individuals on leave to move directly to Portsmouth. Around 15 officers and 100 men were on leave in different areas of England, Ireland and Wales but over a period of three weeks, before the battalion eventually sailed, every single one managed to make his way to Portsmouth harbour. The question of women accompanying the battalion was particularly troublesome. At most six wives for each of the ten companies in the battalion were allowed to accompany the men on a move overseas. The commanding officer had a degree of latitude in increasing this number, but often it came down to the women drawing lots, pieces of paper marked 'To Go' or 'Not to Go'.

The battalion staff were informed that the journey was anticipated to take a minimum of six weeks and the transports were to be stocked accordingly. Officers used their meagre allowance for the baggage and their foreign service to buy tea, sugar, biscuits, some spirits, livestock (fowl, pigs and ducks) and fresh fruit, principally oranges and lemons. The fusiliers prepared in opposite fashion by indulging in the present.

The battalion was not alone in this deployment, being joined by another 3,000 men from the 1/7th, the 1/8th and the 13th Foot. The destination was initially not revealed, but the deterioration of Anglo-American relations after the *Chesapeake* affair,[1] meant that few were surprised when they embarked on the transports[2] to be told they faced an Atlantic crossing and new garrison duties in Nova Scotia, Canada.

The prospect of a posting on seemingly an infinite timeline to a quiet colony where the highlight of garrison duty appeared to be hunting and fishing to provide sustenance, did not appeal to some of the battalion who sought more exciting ventures. Some officers tried their utmost to find ways out of deploying, but for the fusiliers there was no option. The transports weighed anchor on 13 February but within a week, at the entrance to the Bay of Biscay, a transport was reported missing and it was suggested that it had been taken by the French.

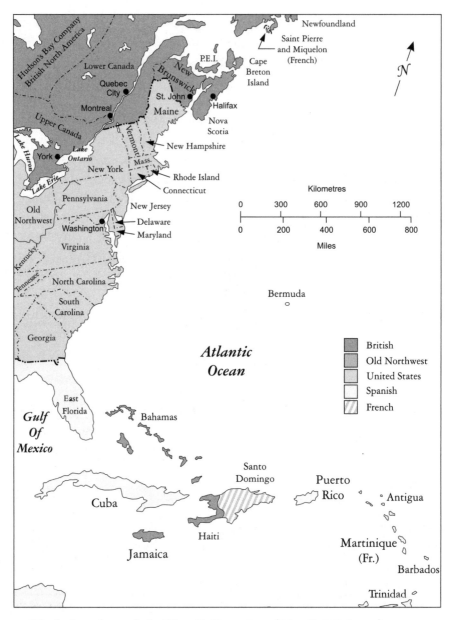

North America and the West Indies, 1809. (*Map © C. Johnson*)

St David's Day is 1 March and it fell during the long sea passage across the Atlantic, providing an occasion for a unique regimental custom for the officers of the 23rd Foot, in many respects a trial for the young and newly commissioned. These junior members of the officers' mess were to be tasked to eat a leek presented by a regimental drummer. The custom was described:

Each Officer is called upon to eat one, for which he pays the Drummer a shilling. The older Officers of the Regiment and those who have seen service with it in the field are favoured with only a small one, and salt. Those who have celebrated a St David's day with the Regiment, but have only seen garrison duty with it, are required to eat a larger one without salt, and those unfortunates, who for the first time, have sat at the Mess, on this their Saint's day, have presented to them the largest leek that can be procured and unless sickness prevents it, no respite is given, until the last tip of the green leaf is enclosed in the unwilling mouth; and day after day passes by before the smell and taste is fairly got rid of.[3]

After a weary voyage of several weeks, including a brief stop at the strategically important location of Bermuda, the convoy arrived at Halifax, the capital of Nova Scotia, on 16 April 1808. Halifax was Britain's principal naval base in North America, commanded by a lieutenant governor, with a well-established garrison, infrastructure, a growing civilian population and further dependencies to be defended, including New Brunswick, Cape Breton Island, Newfoundland and Prince Edward Island. The battalion was given the responsibility of defending the approaches to Halifax by garrisoning a number of outlying forts. On 13 May, much to the surprise and delight of the battalion and the inhabitants of Halifax, the lost transport arrived in the harbour, six weeks after being posted 'missing', having had a particularly slow and meandering trip across the Atlantic.

The battalion was split amongst a number of different locations. Battalion headquarters was located at the Fort of St Laurence at Annapolis Royal, on the far side of the province. Troops were also stationed at Digby on the shore of the Bay of Fundy and the western side of Halifax harbour. On 10 August at Annapolis, the new governor, Lieutenant General Sir George Prevost, inspected the battalion, which on parade consisted of 23 officers and 744 non-commissioned officers and men.[4]

For Bentinck garrison life with the battalion was generally agreeable, though with some unpleasant aspects:

We spent almost a year in Canada, in various places.[5] It was very pleasant for the men. Those of good conduct could at any time get leave to go fishing or have hunting excursions; fish swarming in the rivers and plenty of wolves, deer and rabbits in the woods to be had for killing.[6] Being on the border of the United States, many soldiers here deserted. On a narrow river which divided the two territories,[7] ferry boats were kept at certain places and the ferrymen were quite as willing to take over a deserter as they would anybody else and once on the opposite bank, the absconder might shake his fist at a pursuer. But the punishment was terrible if he chanced to be caught.

An indication of the importance attached to the recovery of deserters is this note, written by Major Thomas Pearson, a detachment commander of the 23rd Foot:

> For the apprehension of the above deserters, so that they may be lodged in any place of safe confinement, or any party bringing the above men to Halifax, shall receive the following reward; three guineas, by regulation; three pounds, ten shillings, currency from the Treasury of the Province; and two guineas and a half for each man, to be given by the regiment on their arrival in Halifax.[8]

The harsh punishment did not stop soldiers attempting to desert, as Bentinck commented:

> One man, who had tried it on before was overtaken before he could cross and was sentenced to receive 999 lashes.[9] Flogging was then done by the Drummers. It was the duty our friend most dreaded, for if they did not fetch blood soon enough or copiously enough, the Officer would call out, 'That Drummer is not doing his duty,' and if he failed after that, his cat was given to another and he came in for a taste of it. They were expected to make the blood run out of the poor fellow's legs; and before they had been at it long too. The deserter above mentioned never came out of hospital after his punishment.

Despite desertions by individual soldiers, the battalion was quite appreciative of its frontier life in the colonies rather than the monotony of serving in an English garrison. However, many of the officers were restless as they saw how slow promotion was for those serving in this foreign posting and regretted missing out on the expedition to Spain. In the autumn the prospect of more active duty returned and was much favoured by the bored officers. A number of rumours had spread about an expedition to seize some of the French West Indies territories. This provided excitement but, at the same time, there was a noticeable reluctance across all ranks, for service in a location renowned as the graveyard for British troops, with its ever-present yellow fever and malaria, was feared. As usual the exact destination was kept secret but the rumours continued. It was observed that,

'Many are the speculations. Martinique, Cayenne and the city of Saint Domingo are mentioned; however the object of the attack is a profound secret, perhaps wishing to keep our neighbours on their guard and put them to expense.'[10]

In November 1808 part of the battalion was issued with the new Baker rifle and orders were given for an expedition, mounted from Halifax, to capture the French-held island of Martinique. The British had been fortunate to intercept despatches sent by the French governor of Martinique, Admiral Louis-Thomas Villaret de Joyeuse, which provided a comprehensive account of the poor defences of the island, and an order of battle revealing a garrison of only 2,750 regular troops and 3,500 lower-quality National Guardsmen. A joint Navy/Army expedition was suggested and the Nova Scotia garrison provided a force of a company of Royal Artillery, and three battalions of infantry: the 1/7th, 1/8th and 1/23rd. Each battalion was to leave but one company, consisting of an amalgamation of married men and invalids, in order to continue the necessary garrison duties.

On 6 December the Martinique expedition convoy departed Nova Scotia. On 21 December the convoy crossed the line of the Equator for the first time and reached the relative shelter of Carlisle Bay, Barbados, on 29 December. A parade state for the 1/23rd on 1 January 1809, aboard the ships in the Bay, showed 35 officers, 43 sergeants, 37 corporals, 18 drummers and 853 privates. The health of the troops was a great concern and strict orders were given to ensure that the men bathed regularly, avoided being out in the heat of the day and had fresh fruit at least once a day. However, these rudimentary attempts at health and hygiene in these tropical locales could not stave off all infections and diseases. The more time the expedition spent at anchor, the more illnesses slowly spread amongst the battalion.

The fame of the West Indies for being a location often fatal to the health of the European was well warranted. A battalion subaltern visiting the renowned Nancy Clarke's hotel for dinner was grabbed by the owner on entering the hostelry. 'She took hold of a button of my regimentals, looked me in the face and said "What Regiment do you belong to?" On me telling her the 23rd, she replied, "Twenty third, Twenty third, Ah me show you plenty of Twenty third in Church-yard dere." The Regiment had been in Barbados about ten years before, and had lost many men and Officers by the fever.'[11]

Despite the best efforts of a British fleet, which had been blockading the island of Martinique for a couple of months, French reinforcements of men and materiel had been safely landed earlier in December. This placed more pressure on the British expedition to achieve its aims quickly before further reinforcements could be received from France. However, over a period of two weeks there was

Martinique, 1809. (*Map © C. Johnson*)

significant debate and procrastination amongst the British generals over the course of action to take. It was feared that the defences, centred on the formidable Fort Desaix, were now too strong and that a deliberate attack could only end in defeat and the suffering of a great number of casualties.

The organization of the force of 10,800 was decided upon and an order of battle issued. The land force was formed into two divisions, further split into brigades with an according amount of artillery attached. The 1/7th and 1/23rd, together with five companies of the 1st West India Regiment, were formed as part of the First Division into the Fusilier Brigade under the command of Major General Hoghton. However, it was not until 29 January that the expedition sailed for Martinique. In the early hours of the 30th, the landing commenced, with the British force split between the First Division landing on the east coast and the Second Division on the south coast.

The landing of the battalion took much longer than had been planned and eventually, after many delays, the growing light was used to march inland four miles to the banks of a river where rest was taken. The next day the advance continued toward heights which were deemed to be vital ground. Occasional sightings were made of the enemy upon forward hill features or to the flanks, but they remained at a distance, carefully watching developments.

The French, although not contesting the landings, had not wasted too much time, conducting deliberate defensive preparations on the two hill features. On Mount Bruneau, a strong force had been positioned with orders to cause as much attrition to the British as possible. The position benefited from a river to the front which provided quite an effective natural obstacle. Two artillery pieces were deployed on the left flank of the position, giving maximum effective fields of fire across the forward slopes. Despite being without any significant artillery support and noting the amount of French preparations, the British decided on 1 February to conduct a frontal attack on the French position. As the sweating troops advanced up the slope toward the French it could be seen that the enemy had chosen the location well, carefully positioning their forces, making best use of the ground and the cover afforded by sugar-cane plantations.

The dense natural vegetation hid many of the French and even in some areas afforded some element of protection from musket fire. The advancing British troops were only able to return snatched shots at a barely identifiable enemy. The French immediately exploited this advantage and concentrated a rapid succession of volleys in an attempt to turn the staggering advance into a retreat. However, the British troops, although taken at a great disadvantage, continued to scramble forward, intent on closing upon their foe. The seriousness of the situation resulted in the battalion being ordered to advance with a controlled, steady rate of fire, closing the distance with the French on the top of the hill. Once the enemy were some fifty paces away, the order was given to charge and, with an immense cheer, the men rushed with bayonets fixed at the remaining enemy, driving the French off the high ground in confusion.[12]

> The French strongly posted in the cane-breaks opened a deadly fire on their scarlet-clad opponents and the latter could only return random shots at their unseen enemy. Thus taken at a great disadvantage, although stronger in number, our men were swept by volley after volley as they scrambled forward to clear the jungle. Several of Bentinck's comrades were smitten down in their attempts to have the French driven off. Being weak in numbers compared with the British, the enemy could only keep up a skirmishing kind of warfare, favoured by the bushy nature of the country.[13]

The next day the battalion participated in sweeping the French from the heights of Sourier, sustaining further casualties. The closer the British got to the main French defensive position the more determined the efforts to deny their advance but the British resolutely drove the enemy back.

> At last, the French were reduced by fever and fighting to little more than 1,000 men. These defended the approach to the town with great gallantry. The red blazes from their muskets played as unflinchingly and so nearly as to dazzle the eyes of the British, who as before had to fire at random into the dense jungle in which the foe was posted on every bund. A general charge with the bayonet effected some clearance, but at a great sacrifice, as our men had as much as they could do to force a way through the cane-break and many were actually put to the bayonet as they were fast entangled in the immense briars and creepers. The combat was muzzle to muzzle.
>
> The Company Bentinck was in, less than 100 strong to commence with, lost 35 men and Officers out of that number.[14] Several other Regiments got it quite as badly, but after some hours obstinate fighting the enemy was driven from every position and finally beaten.

By 4 February the French forces had nearly all either surrendered or withdrawn into the main position, Fort Desaix. It was a formidable defensive position, with more than 60 heavy guns, 40 field guns, 14 mortars, 6 howitzers and a garrison of at least 2,000 regular troops. Substantial investment works were required by the British and all available troops and sailors were concentrated on the siege with construction of gun and mortar batteries beginning forthwith.

The Sailors had been brought ashore to man the guns and do occasional hand to hand fighting, which they addressed greatly, not troubling to load their muskets when once discharged, but laying about the French with the stock, a tree bough, or their fists, as chance or inclination might dictate.[15] Our black soldiers were their special aversion, for their laziness and cowardice.[16] These fellows pretended to be ill by the dozen when any heavy guns were to be moved forward or hard trench work was to be done. They were able to duck and run with amazing dexterity when shots began to play short with their precious carcasses. The sailors whacked these cowards and idlers whenever they could catch them in their failings and some were even shot because they took to throwing their ammunition away so they might not be able to go into action.

The conduct of the siege also provided an experience that Bentinck would not forget and:

… an illustration of the reckless bravery which characterised our troops from the old war scarred warrior down to the youngest recruit. While investing Fort Desaix a French force issued from it one day with the evident intent of making a smart dash through our lines.[17] Our troops were too wary to be caught napping and in a moment they were under arms and not vulnerable to an attack. The bugles rang out the advance and the French, on seeing this, hesitated and then halted. But there was true mettle amongst the French, only not enough of it. A big drummer sprang from the ranks and beating the pas de charge[18] came boldly on towards the advancing foe, then less than 100 yards from them. When he had got about half that distance, looking back and hurrahing at his still wavering companions, one of Bentinck's companions, a noted shot in the Company, turned and said to him, 'Bentinck, you want a new pair of drumsticks don't you?' 'Aye, I could do with 'em, why?' replied the lad. 'Because you shall have 'em, by God,' answered the soldier, levelling his musket at the French drummer, so gallantly advancing. As the red flash burst from the piece, the latter threw up his arms, fell flat on his face and the fatal drum sticks dropped from his nerveless grasp.[19]

'Run and get them,' shouted his slayer to Bentinck. Like a tiger's cub excited with the taste of blood, the little drummer, forgetful of the French muskets, of all but the French drumsticks, put down his drum and ran like a deer to the dead Frenchman. Nor is it surprising that he came back quite as fast, for as he stooped to pick up the coveted sticks a hostile bullet whizzed past his ear, followed by another and another and another as he sped back with his trophies, escaping from the ordeal without a scratch. The French then fell back into the fort.

The French continued to defend the fort with gallantry but the conditions within meant that disease was starting to be a significant problem, reducing every day the number of fit men able to man the defences. They continued to fire upon the British encampments with both shot and shell but could do little to delay the natural conclusion to the siege. On the evening of 19 February, the bombardment of Fort Desaix commenced from six different points, using 14 heavy guns and 28 mortars.

At 9.00 on the morning of 24 February, three white flags were raised on the fortress. Immediately fire from the attacking batteries ceased and terms were negotiated. The French garrison of roughly 2,000 men fit for duty and 500 sick and wounded surrendered, along with 140 cannon. Four regimental eagles were captured by the British. The battalion proudly took into its possession the eagle of the 82nd Regiment of Infantry.[20] Transports were prepared for the defeated French, who marched on the evening of 25 February with full honours down to ships for a passage home.[21] Their behaviour was commented upon:

> The French troops immediately on being embarked, though having so shortly before parted with their Eagles, were seen laughing and singing and dancing on the decks, just as they would have done in any little cabaret near Paris, and in observing this, we could hardly refrain from envying their happy frivolity.[22]

Accounts by different members of the 1/23rd of casualties incurred on the expedition appear to overstate the actual numbers. Total British casualties stated by Lieutenant General Beckwith for the duration of the expedition were 561. In the period 1–27 February, 144 of the battalion were admitted to hospital: 88 with gunshot wounds, 9 with fever, 44 with fluxes and 3 with general injuries. It is interesting to note that 5 fusiliers died of their gunshot wounds and 1 from flux, and 86 of these casualties were still in hospital at the end of the month. The phlegmatic Captain Hill commented later in a letter home that, in this expedition, the Light and Grenadier Companies alone, 'between us lost 50 flankers killed and wounded; you may easily guess that we must have been in the thick of it'.[23] The battalion embarked on transports destined for Nova Scotia on 9 March. The wounded and sick were carried on a specially requested hospital ship but it was unable to stop the shadow of death falling on a number of fusiliers on the long and uncomfortable journey.

The troops left behind on garrison duty in Nova Scotia had not fared much better in regards to health. A particularly harsh winter had been endured and dysentery had spread amongst them. The returning troops were severely weakened and all efforts were undertaken to recover their fitness. This unhealthy mix caused considerable challenges for the officers. One commented:

> The state of our Regiment at present is deplorable, dysentery or a complaint something like it has got among the men and we have 320 sick; the expedition has cost us near 70 men buried since we left this place last winter. The sick we brought back either very shortly died or recovered, the principle part which have fallen ill since, in my opinion have caught it by infection.[24]

Not long after the battalion returned to Halifax, the troops that had been engaged in the Danish expedition received their prize money, arising chiefly from the sale of the immense fleet of ships and the accompanying equipment surrendered. Privates received £3 13s 6d each, this being the first prize money that many had ever pocketed, which greatly pleased them and set a tone for their future desires of involvement in active service.

News of the capture of Martinique eventually reached Britain. A number of institutions were generous in bestowing charity to the troops who had fought for possession of the island. The Patriotic Fund at Lloyds granted a sum of £850 to the wounded of Martinique. The Grenadier Company of the 1/23rd, which had been the most heavily engaged and suffered the greatest number of casualties across the battalion in the expedition, was given £250 of this. This sum was used to erect a memorial in a church in Halifax.[25]

---

1. In June 1807 the USS *Chesapeake* was engaged by the British frigate *Leopard* and boarded in the pursuit of British deserters. The substantial tensions emanating from this incident prompted Viscount Castlereagh to reinforce the colonies to make them more defensible.

2. *Lord Collingwood, Robert, Sea Horse, Traveller, Albion* and *Harriot.*
3. Browne, *Napoleonic War Journal*, p. 73.
4. Three sergeants, one corporal, four drummers and 192 privates were from Wales.
5. Troops were rotated between posts to alleviate the monotony.
6. In particular, some of the officers revelled in this life. 'I bought fishing lines, and used to occupy myself and the crew of my boat in fishing for my little garrison. We caught fish in the greatest abundance, and the men were capitally supplied with it. The fish we caught were Cod, Haddock, Macharel and Halibut and a large and coarse species of Turbot. Crabs and Lobsters were also in the greatest abundance.' Browne, *Napoleonic War Journal*, p. 78. Officers enthusiastically recorded their pastimes as including shooting, fishing and farming, whilst some purchased land and cultivated it to produce additional rations.
7. This is most likely the St Croix River.
8. Graves, *Fix Bayonets!*, p. 117.
9. In this period, the maximum number of lashes that could be inflicted on soldiers in the British Army was set at 1,200. Such a number could obviously kill or disable a man and the number of lashes sentenced usually varied from 100 to 1,000. Oman noted that 1,200 lashes were only inflicted nine or ten times over the period 1809–15 and that 1,000 lashes were only administered about fifty times. Oman, *Wellington's Army 1809–1814*, p. 239. Lieutenant Colonel Ellis, as the commanding officer of the 1/23rd, used a mixture of discipline and humanity. In the period October 1808–June 1809 there were thirty-two regimental courts martial 'by which 101 men have been tried, five Sergeants and three Corporals reduced, 36,550 lashes sentenced and 5,950 inflicted'. From National Archives, War Office 27, vol. 94, Inspection Report, 1/23rd Foot, 27 June 1809.
10. RWFM, Acc. 3777, Hill to mother, 29 November 1808.
11. Browne, *Napoleonic War Journal*, p. 93.
13. Casualties in the 1 February action amounted to 1 sergeant and 14 rank and file killed, and 1 sergeant and 5 rank and file missing, with 81 all ranks wounded. It was estimated that the French suffered around 400 casualties.
13. This passage may refer to the determined efforts made on 2 February by the Fusilier Brigade to capture two redoubts to the front of Fort Desaix. Each redoubt was held by a French detachment of 150 men with three 12-pounder guns. The 7th Foot led the attack but suffered substantial casualties from artillery and was covered in its withdrawal by the Grenadier Company of the 23rd. 'At this point Lieutenant General Beckwith approached Ellis to ask whether his men could take the French position. "Sir," replied Ellis, "I will take the flints out of their firelocks and they shall take them."' From the Journal of Lieutenant J. Harrison, quoted in Broughton-Mainwaring, *Historical Record of the Royal Welch Fusiliers*, p. 122. But an unexpected deep ditch, high palisades and a lack of ladders provided an insurmountable obstacle. An attack the next day was successful as the enemy had withdrawn from the position overnight, spiking and dismounting their guns in the process.

The French decided that they should concentrate on defending the principal position, Fort Desaix.

14. It is not clear which company Bentinck served in during the Martinique campaign.

15. On 6 February the French, seeing the limited effect their bombardment was having on the British preparations, decided to go on the offensive and they mounted a raid from Fort Desaix aiming to destroy some of the newly constructed earthworks. This occasion presented an opportunity for the sailors to participate in hand-to-hand fighting, which they did with the greatest of fervour. This action, together with the sailors' hard work at assisting with preparations for the siege, created a close relationship between the sailors and the fusiliers, one which resulted in Captain Cockburn, RN, being gifted a Royal Welch Fusilier sword as a special souvenir. This sword is now in the possession of the Royal Welch Fusiliers Museum, Caernarfon Castle.

16. These soldiers were from the West India Regiment. Soldiers were natives from the islands whilst Europeans provided the officers.

17. This is possibly a reference to a French sortie from Fort Desaix that occurred on 8 February 1809.

18. A rapid drum beat favoured by the French, also known as 'Old Trousers' in British Army slang.

19. The battalion had a rifle company at the time and from a distance of 100 yards, this would have been quite achievable.

20. This eagle is on show today in the Royal Welsh Fusiliers Museum.

21. A subsequent court of enquiry sat in Paris to determine the causes of the surrender of the governor, Admiral Villaret Joyeuse, and his neglect of duty in not preparing the defences to a suitable standard. He was stripped of his rank and honours.

22. Browne, *Napoleonic War Journal*, p. 108.

23. RWFM, Acc. 3777, Hill to mother, 30 April 1809.

24. Ibid.

25. This church is in fact St George's Anglican Church, which in 1801 was built on the site of a Dutch Lutheran Chapel. The chapel was badly damaged by fire in 1994 but has since been rebuilt. The 23rd Foot Grenadier Company memorial has been restored as well as possible. It lists a corporal and two privates who were killed at the heights of 'Sowrier' on 2 February 1809.

Chapter Four

Deployment to the Peninsula

———•———

The battalion returned to Halifax from Martinique in April 1809. Over the winter of 1809–10 it fulfilled outpost duties and the slow pace, and the better weather of the spring and early summer of 1810, together with the efforts of the officers allowed the fusiliers gradually to regain strength and health. This was very timely because in August 1810 the battalion received orders to proceed to Lisbon in Portugal and to take the field against Napoleon's marauding troops.

The 1/23rd was sent at a time when a French army under Marshal Masséna had forced Wellington's Anglo-Portuguese army to retreat to the formidable entrenched Lines of Torres Vedras. Constructed in remarkable complete secrecy, the defences stretched from the sea across to the River Tagus to the north of Lisbon. Despite Wellington's retreat, news of his ability had passed across the Atlantic and his operations were held very high in estimation. He had succeeded in defeating the French at Busaco in September and the retirement into Portugal was but the next stage of his plan to thwart the numerically superior French.

The British could use Lisbon and the Royal Navy to bring in supplies of men and materiel whilst the French, unable to break the chain of these fortifications, were forced to halt. They now suffered from being at the end of a very long supply route, scouring the local scorched-earth countryside for food but unable to gather sufficient strength to mount a further offensive. Wellington gained the time he needed. The 1/23rd was but just one of the many battalions sent to reinforce the Peninsular army.

On 11 October, the battalion embarked on the transports *Regulus* and *Diadem*, in anticipation of another torrid time afloat. However, the Atlantic crossing proved to be much fairer than anticipated. The battalion had learnt much from the trials of looking after a great number of sick on the return journey from Martinique. Accordingly, a great emphasis was placed by the commanding officer and his company commanders on the care of the men and the conditions they lived under whilst on the transports.

The 1/23rd in Spain and Portugal, 1810–11. (*Map © C. Johnson*)

The crossing took a respectable four weeks, the transports arriving at the mouth of the Tagus estuary on 11 November. On disembarking the day after next at Lisbon, the *Regulus* had only three men sick; the *Diadem* was slightly worse off with twenty in all sick. This fact was attributed by some officers to the order passed prior to embarkation that all meals where possible were to be eaten on the open deck.

However, there were still deaths on the voyage:

One of Bentinck's Comrades died on the sea passage and after the custom in troop ships, was sown up in a sack, almost before he was cold, with a cannon shot at his feet to sink him. He was then tilted off a plank into the sea, with a complete absence of ceremony. His widow proved herself to be worthy of a soldier's wife, for she married another soon after they landed.[1]

The Regiment sailed to Lisbon, the capital of Portugal, landing near Black Horse Square,[2] so called from the colossal bronze statue which ornamented it and formed the sighting point for vessels coming into the harbour. The French, who had been in the city just previous to the arrival of our forces, were offered an immense sum of money if they would respect this work of art, but as usual, they were bent on destruction and irreparably injured it.[3]

The British were billeted in the immense convents that abound in the city.[4] The inmates had of course fled before the French held the place. These sacred buildings were rich in architecture; in images of saints, carved in both wood and stone, in splendid furniture for their state apartments and in pictures of rare value. Most of the moveable things had of course been carried off by the French. Much of what was left behind the slothful neglect of the Portuguese Supply Department forced our own soldiers to destroy.[5]

Having no fuel of any kind served out to them, even so much as to cook their meals with, they burnt up carved work and polished mahogany like dried sticks. Even the wooden saints were powerless to protect themselves from their red-coated Protestant allies. 'Fetch Saint Antonio here,' the cook would cry out as his fire got too low; or 'Help me on with Saint Nicolo, Bentinck,' and by their grins as the helpless 'Saint' crackled into flame they might have been mistaken for a pair of gnomes cruelly tending him in purgatory.

After only three days in Lisbon, the battalion commenced its march on 16 December north-east toward the Lines of Torres Vedras to link up with its parent brigade, the Fusilier Brigade and parent division, the 4th.[6] The experience of war and activities of the French were very apparent:

> After a few days, the British marched into the interior, to a village called Assan Bouya,[7] within about three miles from Villa Franca, where a strong French force was lying. Their route lay through the ruins of a beautiful country. The vines, the orange groves, the wild flowering shrubs, it is true remained; but once stately mansions were dismantled, their lovely gardens a trampled wreck; peaceful farmsteads upheld their blackened skeleton walls in mournful protest against the wanton havoc that had left them thus; entire villages were roofless, windowless and bare. Weeping and wondering children wandering up and down, while the men lent in helpless fury against their empty doorsteads.[8]
>
> It seemed as though the French could behold nothing pleasant without destroying it. Besides this devastation of dwellings, they had burnt all the corn stacks they could not carry off, driven with them all the cattle they had not used and trampled down the rising crops, so the country was a complete waste.[9] The only commodity they had left was wine, perhaps in the hope of needing it again for themselves if returning to the district. Being the chief produce of the country, it was of course very cheap. Our men got as much as they could well carry at two pence a pint.

The French had retreated from the positions they had occupied for six weeks and subsequently moved into cantonments. The heavy and prolonged rains of the recent weeks made it impossible for any offensive operations to be undertaken. Hence the allied army was also ordered into cantonments for the winter months, the battalion establishing its quarters at Azambuja on 19 November.

> Not long after arriving at Assan Bouya, one of the Fusiliers – not Bentinck's Regiment, but the 7th – attempted to desert to the enemy at Villa Franca. One of our light Hussars caught him before he reached their lines and brought him back. He was at once tried by a General Court Martial and sentenced to be hung. The following morning he was accordingly taken outside the village, all the troops were paraded to witness the final punishment, in order that they might take warning by it and were formed up around an olive tree that stood on the plain. In a few moments, the unfortunate fellow was strung up to a branch

and left dangling there as a reminder of the fate of all captured deserters.[10]

There was little information on the prospect of future operations, which caused some consternation. Captain Harrison commented, 'We are kept in such obscurity respecting the arrangements and plans of the Army, that it is almost presumption in me to offer a description that you will get more minutely and perhaps more correctly detailed in an English paper, to which we are obliged to refer to sometimes. In fact, everyone here is ignorant of the intentions of the enemy and our Commander. All we can do is to keep ourselves and our men prepared to move in any direction at a moments notice.'[11] The impasse was broken by the French lack of supplies and a need to take drastic action. Harrison reported that French prisoners had 'described their Army to be in great distress. Spirits they can't get and have not had any for some time, Provisions scarce, and clothing getting very bare. Shoes are very much wanting.'[12]

On 19 January, a French raiding force had attacked the village of Rio Maior, falsely believing a well-stocked magazine of provisions to be present. The battalion, as a unit stationed nearby, was one of the first to react. The fusiliers fought off the marauding French, who were disappointed in their search for the magazine. The French, acknowledging the wasted effort, tried their best to extricate themselves with minimum casualties but ended up losing a handful of men killed and wounded, together with twenty captured. The 1/23rd was unfortunate to lose Captain Mercer and three men killed in this minor action.

To prevent a further excursion by the enemy, the Fusilier Brigade was moved on 24 January to occupy the village of Aveiras de Cima, about five miles to the west of their previous position. Heavy rain then rendered the roads impassable and, once it was clear that no major operations could be mounted by either side, the battalion was able to settle into a quiet defensive routine.

During the winter in cantonments officers and men fell prey to various illnesses, particularly dysentery, with the battalion providing an unfortunate number of nearly 300 inhabitants for the hospital. Throughout the long campaign in the Peninsula, the health of Wellington's army was always fairly poor with those battalions which had previously served in the Walcheren expedition of 1809 being especially pitiable. At times during the campaign the 1/23rd, with nearly a thousand men on duty in the Peninsula, could only muster 400 men due to the degrading effects of disease.

The distressed circumstances of the country meant that fresh food was terribly difficult to procure and expensive. The battalion was not assisted by the long bout of general inactivity. Although occasional fine weather allowed some exercise, the winter in cantonments was long and tedious and the fusiliers actively sought out alcohol, with the usual consequences. Eventually, in early March, the French took the decision that, with their supply lines over-extended, little could be achieved by holding their ground and a cleverly organized retreat took place with the allies in pursuit.

The country to be marched over was mountainous and beautiful to the observer, but the roads, generally constructed with large stones, and the required fording of many streams as a consequence of recent heavy rain, made it peculiarly hard going for the pursuers. The weather throughout the period of the pursuit was unpleasant, with grey, overcast skies, frequent precipitation and occasional heavy downpours. The lack of food and general French tactical skill added to the challenges as Bentinck related:

> When the British had lain in this village about two months, receiving reinforcements and by holding the enemy in check at this point giving our other forces time to make head against them, their Garrison in Villa Franca bethought themselves that it was time to 'move on.' They were protected from us by a small river,[13] on which their sentries were posted night and day. The hostile sentries were almost within musket shot of each other, but after the first duty, by tacit understanding, ceased to punch bullet holes into each other.[14]
>
> One fine morning our sentry noticed that his French counterpart on the bridge kept in one attitude a remarkably long time. Growing curious, he at length shouted to him, but no word, nor motion, did the Frenchman send back in reply. Our sentry began to sniff a rat and going nearer to his supposed foe took a long and careful aim at him. His bullet produced no change, though he felt certain it had hit its mark. No foe popped up his head to see why the stillness of morning was broken, but one or two of our men came out and venturing up to the rigidly erect French sentry found him literally a 'man of straw.'
>
> The French had evacuated the town and struck up this ingenious 'dummy' to delay as long as possible all information of their movement.[15] The British were at once astir. They left Assan Bouya and took possession of the more advanced and stronger town given up by the enemy.[16] Only staying there a couple of days to strengthen it, they left a small garrison in charge and pushed on after the French to Pombal, a couple of days march.[17]

Here, at Pombal, the enemy issued forth to meet them, made a spirited attempt to drive them back but being pounded with field artillery and well peppered with musketry, they never crossed bayonets but retreated into the town, leaving the British encamped on the plain in front. Next morning the latter were surprised to see the town burst forth into flames.[18] The French, carrying on their usual mode of warfare had set it on fire when they had done with it and had gone out from the other side of the hill in full retreat. Our forces at once pursued, marching through the blazing town, the soldiers carrying their cartouche boxes under their greatcoats to prevent them being exploded by the sparks which rained down on them like a fiery shower. Finding that the enemy had used his legs too well to be easily overtaken, our troops cut across the country to Alavanza,[19] a small fortified town about a day's march off. The Division had all this time been commanded by General Cole,[20] Wellington the Commander-in-Chief, being busied elsewhere. The French in this district were under Marshal Soult.[21] They kept the British out of Alavanza for three or four days by fierce cannonading and threatening demonstrations, but on our troops receiving reinforcement and preparing to storm the place, they left it and again retreated.[22]

The French retreated in an increasingly poor state, with dead and dying soldiers and followers and exhausted horses left behind. Furthermore, the local population were treated with indescribable cruelty. Soult's capture of the key fortress city of Badajoz caused the course of the Allied advance to be changed by Wellington who perceived it important to regain control of the fortress.[23] The battalion, as part of the 4th Division, was pushed hard in chasing the fleeing French.

Hotly pursuing, the British followed, and in a few days came up with them at Elvos.[24] Again came the order to storm and again did the foe evade it by retreating to Campo Moyo.[25] Almost as soon as the front British ranks were in sight of the town, the French issued forth with cavalry and infantry to meet them, and made a spirited attempt to drive them back. Fortunately, the Fusilier Brigade was accompanied by detachments of the Royal Artillery who took great delight in pounding the advancing French, who were also fair peppered with accurate musketry by the jovial Fusiliers. The Infantry never got to cross bayonets with each other as the French, under the weight of accurate fire, turned and retreated into the town, with its clearly prepared defences nine miles off and again did Cole's Division press forward on their traces.

The pace of the pursuit and the extended supply lines meant that provisions grew scarce and the number of stragglers began to grow. On 22 March, after 110 miles of hard marching in six days, the battalion consolidated at Portalegre alongside other elements of the 4th Division.[26] Two days later all available troops were sent to attack the French, who were in the process of withdrawing from Campo Maior. Although some French were hunted down, the Allied forces were not particularly well co-ordinated and the majority of the French managed to flee successfully.

As soon as the first British troops reached Campo Moyo our forces fell on the enemy's outposts, and drove in a swarm of skirmishers posted in the groves before the town and soon the fierce thunder of cannon on both sides gave token of a less bloodied encounter than hitherto. An immediate assault was ordered. The Divisions were told off and amid the roar of the heavy guns and a continuous crackling of musketry dashed gallantly at the place, burst into it and drove the French fighting out of town. Intimidated by the fury of the onset, they gave way on every side but one or two Battalions of veteran troops kept well together and by turning at bay from time to time kept their pursuers well in check. This gave their less resolute comrades the time to affect a safe and tolerably fair retreat.[27]

Had we possessed an efficient cavalry force the case would have been a bad one for the enemy. But there was on this occasion only the 13th Light Dragoons in the field. These again and again rode at them, trampled crowds of stragglers under foot and brought back droves of prisoners.[28] Their long straight swords[29] made terrible work on the scattering French, thought Bentinck, as they galloped at full pelt amongst them. The gashed bodies were so thickly strewn across the ground that Bentinck could hardly keep clear of them. He was unused to the havoc made by cavalry and found this first lesson more than his stomach could take.[30]

The French, however, made good their way into Badajoz, nine miles distant – this famous stronghold whose subsequent capture formed the most desperate enterprise affected by the British during the whole war and even caused the 'Iron Duke' to weep for the blood so fearlessly given by so many of his gallant soldiers.

After driving the French to Badajoz, our gallant force returned to Campo Mayo.[31] The inhabitants had been so terrified by the violence they had suffered from the French that they had dreamt the latter could not be beaten, but mistook the British for them returning. The poor inhabitants, thinking of the need to conciliate the troops in the flash of victory, crowded the walls and cried out 'Viva Francais, Viva Francais.' On perceiving their terrible blunder they were more frightened still, thinking the British would surely make them smart worse than their foes had ever done, so changing their tune they shouted, 'Viva Anglais, Viva Anglais,' with even greater fervour than before. It is needless to add that it made no difference in their considerate treatment by our leaders.

The battalion had little more than ten days in Campo Maior, recovering from its exploits, before new orders were received and they were on the move again in pursuit of the retreating French.[32]

—————•—————

1. A common and indeed pragmatic practice.
2. Black Horse Square is more commonly known as Praça do Comércio.
3. The countryside surrounding the city had been deserted by its inhabitants, as a consequence of the scorched-earth policy. Subsequently Lisbon was pretty well crowded and becoming filthier and filthier in such conditions. Many of the wealthiest families had decided to flee to Brazil following the example of the royal family.
4. The battalion was initially marched to a camp in the Prince's Park in the suburb of Belém.
5. This lack of basic supplies and the poor state of the supply department caused difficulties for the battalion officers seeking to obtain equipment for the future campaign. 'All provisions are very dear, wine and fruit only reasonable. Our horses feed on barley and only some bad straw, so it is not to be wondered that at their looking ill. Our Cavalry is much wasted, many horses are unserviceable and the others half starved. It is some consolation that the enemy is as badly off and much more numerous.' RWFM, Acc. 1335, Harrison to father, 27 October 1810. (Harrison came to Portugal direct from the UK so this letter predates the arrival of the main body of the battlion from North America.)
6. 1/23rd Foot, 1/7th and 2/7th Foot formed the Fusilier Brigade, the two other battalions being Peninsula veterans, who wasted no time in calling the 1/23rd Foot 'Johnny Newcomes'. The brigade commander was 'Ned' Pakenham who had

previously commanded the 1/7th in Nova Scotia and was well versed in the character of the 1/23rd and a firm friend of Lieutenant Colonel Ellis. The fourth element of the brigade was a company of the Brunswick Oels Jaegers, more commonly known as the 'Black Legion', a foreign unit formed by the Duke of Brunswick, nephew of King George III. The brigade was part of the 4th Division, which was commanded by Major General Galbraith Lowry Cole. Command of the brigade changed twice early in 1811, with first Major General William Houston being appointed. He subsequently moved on to command the new 7th Division and was followed by Colonel William Myers, who moved up from commanding the 1/7th Foot.

7. Azambuja, about fifteen miles south-west of Santarém. Harrison wrote of its attractiveness, 'the confusion of mountains to the north, towering over the tops of each other, composed of the kind of granite which the reflection of the sun renders most pleasing to the eye. To the south, within a mile runs the noble Tagus, the banks a rich fertile plain of meadowland to a great extent. To the East and West are the gradual terminations of the mountains towards the river. If a few magnificent buildings were interspersed about the country, nothing is wanting to complete the delightful scenery of nature.' RWFM, Acc. 1335, Harrison to father, 27 October 1810.

8. This passage most likely refers to the march from Sobral to Azumbuja. It was commented by Captain Hill that, 'The country is dreadfully ravag'd, I saw nothing except a few pidgeons left about the villages; the floors and rafters taken out either to burn or make huts. All the inhabitants had retire'd before our army, so that what a few months before had been a fine country is literally now a desert, with the exception of the roofs of the houses.' RWFM, Acc. 3777, Hill to mother, 21 November 1809.

9. Harrison commented that the French left everything in, 'a most dirty and filthy description'. RWFM, Acc. 1335, Harrison to father, 26 November 1810.

10. Research by Donald Graves (*Dragon Rampant*, p. 121) suggests that this individual was Private Matthew Power of the 1/7th Foot. It has been calculated that, between 1808 and 1814, Wellington executed at least 112 soldiers for such offences as desertion, mutiny, gross insubordination, and the murder and robbery of civilians. The quote is from Oman, *Wellington's Army 1809–1814*, pp. 243–4.

11. RWFM, Acc. 1335, Harrison to father, 26 November 1810.

12. RWFM, Acc. 1335, Harrison to father, 9 February 1811.

13. Rio Maior.

14. Harrison commented on this when touring the piquets to see for himself, 'the right of our advanced position to the bridge over the River Rio Maior, which divides the contending parties. On the bridge are posted a French and English sentry within a few paces of each other. On the right and south of the bridge is near two miles of flat ground, chiefly vineyards and Indian corn fields. This is occupied by a chain of double videttes of each Army, and all the formidable passages of the Rio Maior to the northward are protected by strong piquets. I very distinctly saw Santarem on the opposite hill from whence I viewed this truly beautiful scene. There was one plan of attack formed on our side, but from the nature of the ground and advantageous

position of the enemy, it was relinquished, therefore we are at a loss to know how this affair will terminate, or which side will strike the first blow.' RWFM, Acc. 1335, Harrison to father, 21 December 1810.

15. This most likely refers to the French evacuation of the town of Santarém overnight. Towards the end of February Masséna's situation had become critical. Masséna had noted the careful gathering of British reinforcements, his supplies were almost exhausted and foraging was not finding adequate quantities of food. The fatigue, weather and lack of supplies had created an outbreak of disease, with nearly 20,000 men being lost. Prisoners caught foraging confessed that clothing was very bare and shoes much in wanting. The Anglo-Portuguese force benefited from shorter lines of communication and was steadily becoming stronger. Deciding that he was unable to gather sufficient supplies to defend effectively against such numbers, Masséna skilfully conducted the withdrawal of his troops over 3–5 March, assisted by ruses such as the one described. Wellington did not know of the French withdrawal until the morning of 6 March and it was not until 8 March that he decided Masséna was in full retreat. Adroitly, Harrison made the observation at the end of 1810 that, 'the French are surrounded in every quarter and I should think would require a very deep ruse de guerre to effect their entire escape from the country'. RWFM, Acc. 1335, Harrison to father, 26 November 1810.

16. Santarém.

17. On 6 March the battalion entered Santarém, on 7 March Golegao, 8 March Thomar and 10 March Pombal, after a day's thirty-mile march, each time closely pursuing the enemy. At Pombal the French conducted a defensive action, long enough to set fire to the principal buildings and retreat to the relative security of nearby heights, benefiting from a river and marsh to their front. The limited supplies and the fatigue of the men led Harrison to comment that the battalion, 'had no meat for two days before or spirits, only a small portion of biscuit and water to support us. Our men are almost barefoot and a great deal fragged.' RWFM, Acc. 1335, Harrison to father, 17 March 1811. This fatigue and the lateness of the day prevented any further offensive action.

18. This event took place at Condeixa.

19. Possibly Cazal Nova.

20. Sir Galbraith Lowry Cole (1772–1842). Commissioned as a cornet in the 27th (Inniskilling) Regiment of Foot and served in the West Indies, Ireland and Egypt. In 1806, as a brigadier, commanded the 1st Brigade in Sicily and at the Battle of Maida; 1808 promoted major general and then served throughout most of the Peninsular campaign, commanding troops at Albuera, Salamanca, Vitoria, Pyrenees, Nivelle, Orthez and Toulouse. Member of Parliament for Enniskillen in the Irish House of Commons 1797–1800, 1823 Governor of Mauritius, 1828–33 Governor of the Cape Colony. He was invested as a Knight Grand Cross, Order of the Bath in 1815.

21. Nicolas Jean-de-Dieu Soult, Duke of Dalmatia (1769–1851). Enlisted as a private in the French infantry in 1785. Within six years he had been promoted sergeant and subsequently distinguished himself as an officer at the Battle of Fleurus in 1794, for

which he was promoted to be a brigade commander. He then fought for five years in Germany and Switzerland, commanding a division. In 1804 he was made a marshal and commanded a corps at Ulm and Austerlitz and participated in the Battle of Jena. Napoleon appointed him to conquer Spain in 1808 and until 1814 Soult was engaged in the Peninsular campaign, culminating in defeat at the Battle of Toulouse. At Napoleon's first abdication he declared himself a royalist, acting as Minister of War for a number of months, until the return from exile of Napoleon whereupon he declared himself a Bonapartist and acted as the Emperor's chief of staff in the new campaign and the decisive Battle of Waterloo. On the restoration of the French monarchy he was exiled, but returned in 1819, again being made a marshal of France in 1820. He then served in a variety of political appointments including as Prime Minister and Minister of War. Ever the political opportunist, in 1848 when Louis Philippe was overthrown, Soult declared himself a republican.

22. No mention is made of a French rearguard action at Redinha, north of Pombal, where the battalion participated in its first proper engagement. No casualties were sustained but many were exhilarated by the action and the ordered advance of both the infantry and the cavalry.

23. On 11 March 1811, French forces occupied Badajoz after the surrender of the Spanish garrison.

24. Elvas.

25. Campo Maior.

26. Muster state of the battalion was 32 officers, 25 sergeants, 13 drummers and 503 rank and file present and fit; 4 sergeants, 3 drummers and 128 rank and file on march from Aveiras de Cima; at Belém, 3 officers, 8 sergeants, 4 drummers and 40 rank and file.

27. An anonymous letter by an officer from the battalion provides a succinct summary of the engagement. 'The enemy's artillery played on us in high style, and many shot passed close to me. Our first line lost about 20 men killed and wounded. To have seen us deploy and march in line, as we did, you would have been highly pleased. I never saw better. The troops in the highest spirits, and to do justice to the Portuguese, they equalled us. When our first line had approached within about 400 yards, without firing but marching as steady as a rock, in ordinary time, the enemy's infantry began to retire, in double quick time, and the artillery and cavalry followed their example' Letter dated 17 March 1811, in Cary & McCance, *Regimental Records of the Royal Welch Fusiliers, 1689–1815*, p. 237. At the end of the engagement it was found that some 3 French officers and 140 men were captured, with their losses estimated as being 250 killed and wounded. The British lost some 40 soldiers killed.

28. The 13th Light Dragoons were guilty of indulging in a seven-mile pursuit of the broken French cavalry, which only ended when the French reached the safety of Badajoz. Despite them meeting the French artillery convoy, only a couple of guns were captured. The British and Portuguese forces lacked sufficient combat power to defeat the French, who took advantage of the lack of an attack to march away to Badajoz, providing an important 2,000 reinforcements to the garrison.

29. An error, the swords would have been the curved 1796 light dragoon sabre.

30. This accords with comments made by a British light dragoon, George Farmer, who examined the appearance of French casualties injured by British swords designed for the cut and slash, remarking, 'the appearance presented by these mangld wretches was hideous ... as far as appearances can be said to operate in rendering men timid, or the reverse, the wounded among the French were thus far more revolting than the wounded among ourselves'. *United Service Journal*, 1840, Volume 3, p. 370.

31. The endless marching had taken its toll on both equipment and the men, who were exhausted. Lieutenant Farmer spoke for all of the battalion when he commented that he had 'not a shoe or stocking to my feet, nor a farthing to purchase them'. RWFM, Acc. 5257, Farmer to brother, 3 April 1811.

32. The men were engaged in repairing basic equipment to prepare for future marches and anything the locals could provide, although limited, was seized upon. The lack of decent shoes meant that many pairs simply fell apart after only a few marches, whilst the local boots were 'very clumsy and of a dirty buff colour; their rough seams made their wearers hobble like so many cripples'. J. Emerson, 'Recollections of the Late War,' in W. H. Maxwell (ed.), *Peninsular Sketches* (2 vols., London, 1815), Vol. 2, p. 208. The cost of frequently purchasing shoes was exorbitant for most officers and all of the soldiers. So instead of shoes, soldiers resorted to wrapping cloth around their feet or, in some cases, simply going barefoot.

Chapter Five

Battle of Albuera

———•———

Following consolidation at Campo Maior, the 4th Division participated in a very efficient siege of the French-garrisoned city of Olivenza, which fell but six days after investment. This was a key preliminary step for the siege of Badajoz, which had now been held by the French for nearly a month. Its key location allowed tactical domination of the central road from Portugal into Spain, achieving significant interdiction of key lines of communication. It also meant that any Allied advance into Spain could be quickly blocked whilst a threat of a limited offensive into Portugal could be maintained.

Wellington ordered the siege of Badajoz to commence in late April but troop manoeuvres and the general scale of work required for a credible investment of the fortress took time. For the investment operation, the battalion was deployed in a village south of Badajoz and during this period received a much needed draft of 9 officers and 203 men from the 2nd Battalion.

After the capture of Campo Maior and the smart action which followed it,[1] the British force with which our friend Bentinck served, prepared for action. Marshal Beresford's[2] Corps,[3] crossed the River Guadiana[4] with the hope of taking the great fortress of Badajoz, which gave the French command of the southern provinces of Portugal. That night, of the 11th May 1811, our main body kept out of sight and danger behind an adjacent hill, whilst strong working parties crept up to within about a quarter-of-a-mile from the walls and commenced silently and rapidly throwing up earthworks.

The investment of Badajoz commenced on 8 May and by 11 May the embankments were sufficient to allow the bombardment of Badajoz to begin but the French counter-battery fire was very effective, as Bentinck alludes to, with four of the five guns in the breaching battery dismounted overnight. The execution of the siege encountered other problems too. The only suitable encampment area with sufficient wood and water for the troops was nearly five miles from the town and the duty of manning the outposts and constructing the trenches was undertaken by two brigades for each twenty-four-hour period, the remainder conducting administration. The Allied cause was also not helped by the siege train being of poor quality and consisting of much old equipment. There was general anger amongst the British troops over the performance of the equipment and the mismanagement of the siege.[5]

> No wonder every man wrought hard, for as soon as the gathering light in the east made them visible, the French opened upon them from every battery within reach, with the earnest endeavour to destroy both them and their dangerous work. Our sappers were withdrawn for the day, picked marksmen only being left behind the ridge they had thrown up, for the purpose of popping off the enemy's gunners. The following night our spade men again went out and by morning had made certain trenches tenable, then the siege went rapidly on. A breaching battery was erected, but the guns being made of brass soon became useless. Others were sent for, but an event was about to happen that postponed their arrival.

The relatively slow process by which the investment occurred and the lack of decisive progress in creating the conditions for assaulting the fortress led to some sensational developments. By 8 May, Soult had assembled some 24,000 men and set off from Seville to lift the siege of Badajoz. This movement was reported and rumours of a relief force reached the besiegers. On the late afternoon of 13 May, just as the battalion was parading in order to march to the trenches, 'A mysterious report was whispered through the camp that Soult was approaching by rapid marches, with a large force to raise the siege. This so unexpected and sudden piece of information, you may easily suppose, excited our astonishment not a little.'[6]

When the movements and size of the French force under Soult were confirmed, orders were issued for the immediate withdrawal of mortars and heavy cannon. The fusiliers received the morale-sapping instructions to destroy in a few hours what had been the labour of so many hands for more than a fortnight. Subsequently orders were issued for redeployment toward the village of Albuera where several roads intersected, the most important being the royal highway between Badajoz and Seville. It was deduced that the French would pass through this location.

Marshal Beresford, who was commanding all Allied troops, issued orders to manoeuvre some of his forces in that direction and to be in a position to block, or at least delay the enemy. The 2nd Division began its redeployment before daybreak on 14 May. The 4th Division, with the battalion as part of its Fusilier

Brigade, was given instructions to be ready to march at a moment's notice and continued in this state of uncomfortable anticipation all day. The 4th Division was left to provide a reduced manning of the besieging positions around the citadel, yet poised to move rapidly to link up with the 2nd Division. This uncertainty was not enjoyed by the battalion as the men were exposed to dreadful weather and unsure if they would be tasked to remain in place or to re-join the main Allied force.[7] A further dull but important and time-consuming task given to the battalion was to accompany the valuable equipment of the siege train and other stores to Elvas.

In the early hours of 16 May the order did come to link up with the 2nd Division in the vicinity of Albuera. It required an immediate move in the hours of darkness and consequently the difficulties of command and control were considerable and confusion abounded as heavy rain hindered attempts to form up the battalion. Four sentries could not be found amongst the dense corn and were left, but were subsequently able to make good their retreat with the use of some initiative and rejoined the battalion before daylight.[8] The 4th Division, which the battalion marched with, also had the misfortune to take the wrong route, which added to the time taken to reach the battlefield. The result was that the 4th Division arrived after key positions had already been occupied.

> The army had not invested the place a week when about Two O'clock one morning – May 16th – a Light Dragoon rode in to the 4th Division with orders to its General, Sir Lowry Cole, to march at once to Albuera, as Marshal Soult was advancing with a large army to drive away the British from Badajoz. Our friend Bentinck had been on duty in the trenches shortly before this message arrived, where the Colonel of his Regiment, the 23rd Royal Welsh Fusileers, had been shot in the head within a few yards of him.[9]
>
> Hurriedly the weary soldiers were roused from their sleep by the sharp blasts of the bugles and without a moment's pause for breakfast or anything else, poured like a scarlet stream in the direction of the hostile host. Their march was a long one, for it was near Seven O'clock when they came in sight of the dense woods which had concealed the enemy's approach. Marshal Beresford, with all the troops from immediately before Badajoz, and General Blake,[10] with a reinforcement of Spaniards and Portuguese from Cadiz, were already there and the battle had begun.
>
> The French army consisted of about 25,000 infantry and 5,000 cavalry; the allies had less than 2,000 horsemen, but about 27,000 foot,

though many of the latter were Spanish and Portuguese regiments, who
generally did more harm than good, by fleeing when the crisis came.[11]
The 4th Division, in which our old soldier served, had two Brigades in
the field, one of Portuguese, under General Harvey;[12] the other
composed of the 7th and 23rd Fusileers.[13]

Conspicuous by his height, among the men of our friend's Company
was a huge Irishman. As they were coming into the fight in the morning
this fellow either was or pretended to be so sick as to be unable to
proceed, but Major Kenrick, who since Colonel Ellis was wounded at
Badajoz had commanded the regiment,[14] swore that ill or well he would
do to be shot at, told them to put him on a baggage donkey that by
some chance happened to be near, and the big fellow, with his feet
trailing on the ground, was trotted up to the front, amid the laughter of
his comrades. Notwithstanding his size, he was one of the few un-hit
throughout that bloody day, and ever afterwards went by the nickname
of 'Field Marshal,' from his having ridden up to action.

Beresford judged the village of Albuera to be vital ground and the German
Legion Brigade was given the critical task of holding the village. The 2nd Division
was placed on some of the high ground to the west, the Portuguese Division to
the north and the Spanish to the south. The cavalry was positioned on the flanks
and thirty-two artillery pieces were stationed along the defensive line.

According to a number of our men as we were but few, we estimated
them about five to one. Their cavalry and Lancers overpowered us in
numbers. They got a great advantage over us for they got arranged for
action before we got there. They had crossed the river and got on the rise
of the Plain, there was one part of our Army got there before us and they
cut them up before we could get there to assist them. Our orders were to
group as quick as possible but before we got there they had done their
mischief and they thought of serving us the same but they was mistaken.

Soult was unsure of Allied dispositions but on a ground reconnaissance had
noted a weakness in the tactical positioning of the Allied defensive position on
the right flank. A combination of woods and dead ground would allow a force to
move with cover toward the Allies and high ground to the south overlooking the
Allied position could be used to launch an attack. Soult commenced with a feint
attack toward the village of Albuera and then concentrated on trying to roll up the
Allied right flank. It was at this point that the 4th Division was arriving on the

battlefield and the nature of the ground afforded them a grand view of the battle evolving on the plain in front of them.

When the 4th Division arrived, the French attack on Albuera was being beaten off and the division was positioned by Beresford behind the 2nd Division. The French had successfully infiltrated toward the Allied right flank and launched a strong attack supported by artillery.

> As they came in sight of the battlefield, a dense mass of lancers, which had been hurled upon the front Division, were trampling and spearing all before them.

The Spanish troops were able to hold the French for a time, allowing the 2nd Division to be brought up. As the division moved to replace the Spanish in the line, the French took the opportunity to attack Colborne's Brigade of the 2nd Division, which was exposed in line formation. French cavalry and lancers decimated Colborne's Brigade, with 1,248 of its 1,648 men killed, wounded or captured. The 1/3rd and 1/48th were nearly destroyed and lost their colours. Beresford was quick to reinforce the flank with the brigades of Hoghton (1/29th, 1/48th and 1/57th Foot) and Abercromby (2/28th, 2/34th and 2/39th Foot).

The 4th Division was at this time positioned about a mile and a half away and the lack of orders and information from Beresford had made its commander, Major General Cole, anxious. Eventually, after a heated discussion with one of Beresford's staff, Cole decided to advance his two brigades of some 5,000 men across the mile and a half of open ground toward the heights and the fighting. Such a move would expose his right flank to cavalry and consequently Cole ordered the advance in a protective formation, battalion columns in echelon from the left – that is with the line of units staggered back from the left to the right.[15]

The troops advanced rapidly but unfortunately the fog and rain cleared, allowing French artillery to engage them accurately. The artillery tore into the nine regimental blocks of the advancing troops but the 4th Division was resilient. Despite numerous casualties they closed with the French and moved into line, all the time under ferocious artillery fire. Members of the 1/23rd have left various accounts[16] of what followed, in addition to Bentinck's recollections:

> Just in the nick of time to save a remnant of their comrades the 4th Division dashed forward, cheering as they ran. Jets of flame sparkled along their serried line as they neared the foe; saddles were emptied fast, and a steady rush with the bayonet drove the French masses back. But the latter were not beaten.

We will quote the words of Napier, for the best description of the events following this critical juncture, and of the triumphant conclusion finally achieved by the gallant 4th Division and the Fusilier Brigade, when the day seemed all but lost.[17]

'Such a gallant line, issuing from the midst of the smoke, and rapidly separating itself from the confused and broken multitude, startled the enemy's heavy masses, which were increasing and pressing onwards as to an assured victory; they wavered, hesitated, and then vomiting forth a storm of fire, hastily endeavoured to enlarge their front, while a fearful discharge of grape from all their artillery, whistled through the British rank. Myers was killed; Cole, and three Colonels; Ellis,[18] Blakeney,[19] and Hawkeshawe, fell wounded, and the Fusileer battalions, struck by the iron tempest, reeled and staggered like sinking ships. Suddenly and sternly recovering they closed on their terrible enemies; and then was seen with what a strength and majesty the British soldier fights. In vain did Soult, by voice and gesture, animate his Frenchmen; in vain did the hardiest veterans, extricating themselves from the crowded columns, sacrifice their lives to gain time for the mass to open out on such a fair field. In vain did the mass itself bear up, and fiercely striving, fire indiscriminately upon friends and foes, while the horsemen hovering on the flank threatened to charge the advancing line. Nothing could stop that astonishing infantry; no sudden burst of undisciplined valour, no nervous enthusiasm weakened the stability of their order; their flashing eyes were bent on the dark columns in their front; their measured tread shook the ground; their dreadful volleys swept away the head of every formation; their deafening shouts overpowered the dissonant cries that broke from all parts of the tumultuous crowd, as slowly and with a horrid carnage it was pushed by the incessant vigour of the attack, to the farthest edge of the hill. In vain did the French reserves joining with the struggling multitude, endeavour to sustain the fight; their efforts only increased the irremediable confusion, and the mighty mass giving way like a loosened cliff, went head long down the steep hill. The rain flowed after in streams discoloured with blood, and fifteen hundred unwounded men, the remnant of six thousand unconquerable British soldiers, stood triumphant on the fatal hill!'

The Fusilier Brigade stopped on the crest of the hill some seventy paces from the French and a vicious exchange of musketry fire occurred for nearly twenty minutes.

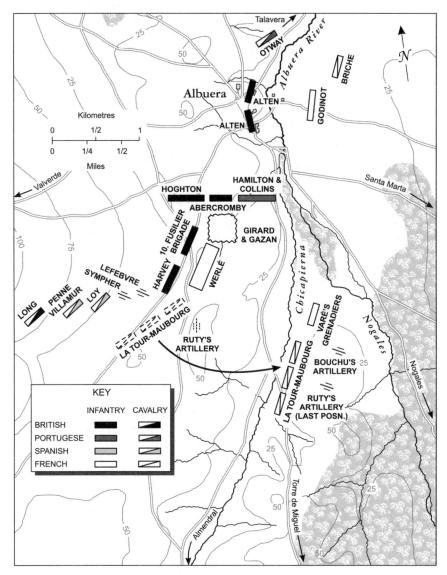

Last phase of the Battle of Albuera. (*Map © C. Johnson*)

As fast as gaps appeared in the ranks, they were filled by vengeful comrades closing them, masking the thinning of the line. The fusiliers gradually pushed the French back and linked up with Hoghton's Brigade of the 2nd Division, as well as being reinforced by Hamilton's Portuguese Division and some Spanish troops.

The French then launched firstly their lancers, followed by dragoons. For some of the battalion, it was the first time that they had experienced the formidable

French lancers but both the division and the battalion's formations were well balanced to meet a cavalry attack.

Gathering another Regiment to their support the enemy turned and made a more furious charge, but this time we were strong enough to receive them. Throwing his men into squares,[20] General Cole held his ground without a backward step, and again poured forth a murderous fire upon the assailants. Our friend Bentinck, and many others besides him, quaked as they for the first time beheld the fierce lancers gallop up to the very square in which they stood, spearing down the front-rank men within three yards of them. Many a Fusilier received his death thrust there, but as fast as they fell the gaps were filled up. Bentinck and his brother bandsmen dragged inside the square those who were only wounded, to be carried off when there was time to the rear.

'Our Officers stood at each flank, the Colonel sat on his horse within the square, calling out to his men to receive the charge with their bayonets and not fire a shot until the enemy turned their horses from them, lest they might break in when our muskets were empty. Again and again they came at the squares, but not one did they break, and as each time they recoiled like a wave from a rock, our parting volleys followed them, avenging the loss their onset had inflicted.'

During one of these charges one of Bentinck's comrades, who had formerly been captured by the French, but had contrived to escape, recognised one of their Lancer officers as the Governor of the Prison in which he had been confined, a man of great harshness towards the prisoners under his care. Swearing a vengeful oath, the Fusileer twice took a long aim at this officer as he came forward, but the speed at which he rode prolonged his life; not for long, however, for as he charged a third time his late prisoner reserved his fire until within a horse's length, and then shot him through the head, bestowing a malicious kick upon the body as it rolled dead at his feet.[21]

The 4th Dragoon Guards,[22] posted close to Bentinck's company, had recently returned from India, and several of their trumpeters were blacks. One of these poor fellows as he sat on his horse a little out on the plain, had his head swept clean from his shoulders by a French hussar, who stuck it on his sword crying out as he sped back that he had 'killed an English Devil.'

'The most desperate combats centred round the colours, which the

French horsemen sought to capture, and our men to retain. Several times they were cleft from their poles by the swords of the French hussars, but were as promptly stuck on the long pikes or halberds which at that time our sergeants carried instead of firearms. At length, after five of its bearers had been slain, one of our colours was taken, and with loud 'hurrahs' the French hung it on a tree within their lines, in taunting triumph.'

The colour of Bentinck's company was only saved from similar disgrace by the daring of one of the Sergeants, who after a French trooper had cut down the man who bore it and run through the body a Lieutenant who then seized it, ran after the Frenchman as he was riding away with it, shot him from his saddle with a firelock he had snatched from a soldier, and thrusting the tattered flag within his coat, regained his square amid the cheers of the whole Regiment.[23]

At the conclusion of the attack on the hill, the French came within fifteen paces and it was a determined bayonet charge that broke the enemy and caused them to retreat in disorder. A cavalry counter-charge followed but the 4th Division was too determined to give up the ground that they had so resolutely gained. The French faltered and then very rapidly disorder spread and they broke. The battle had ended.

During the day all the Captains but three were killed or wounded in the Regiment, nearly all the Lieutenants, and some 700 out of the 990 who went into battle. The two Generals of the Division, Cole and Myers, were both hurt.[24] The Sergeants had to command the Companies and there was commissions granted to the Sergeants that commanded the Companies that day.[25] This havoc was not caused by cavalry charges alone, fierce and numerous as they were; but chiefly by the artillery which cut clear lines through the unflinching ranks. We were very short of cavalry in the chief part of the day. The 2nd battalion of the 7th Fusiliers was cut up so that what few was left was sent into the 1st.[26] The band came home to England to raise another battalion.

The principal reason for the number of Allied casualties would appear to have been the tactical positioning of the battalions and brigades which gave the French the widest opportunity to bring a high volume of both artillery and musket fire to bear against the exposed troops. The desperate advance by the 4th Division upon the French forces on high ground was a huge gamble and the near hand-to-hand combat of so many men contributed to making it a terribly bloody affair.

The French retreated late in the evening and then we got some water for our own wounded men to drink. After the action was over our own provisions came late in the evening and our Corporals went to fetch them. When they asked them how many they had they did not exactly know but they told them a great deal more than there was. So that we all had enough. We kindled the fires with the broken stocks of the rifles and the broken gun carriages. We made ourselves very comfortable amongst the dead. The Doctors was very busy dressing the wounded and women carried the lantern for them. We stopped the next day to see how many men we had present.

The losses to both sides were considerable, Allied losses being 5,916 with very likely a similar French figure. Battalion casualties at Albuera were: 2 officers and 1 sergeant and 73 rank and file killed; 13 officers, 12 sergeants, 1 drummer, 232 rank and file wounded; 1 sergeant and 5 rank and file missing. The unwounded were surprised at their good fortune. Two officers and 35 men subsequently died of their wounds.[27]

In the immediate aftermath of the battle, both sides, although possessing a modicum of relatively unscathed reserves, were too exhausted to conduct a further engagement. The French withdrew before dawn on 18 May southwards toward Seville, hindered by the numbers of wounded and occasional skirmishing. The Allies returned to the blockade of Badajoz.[28]

Thus did the Division of our old soldier, Bentinck signalise itself with glory at the memorable battle of Albuera, speaking or which, Soult, the French commander, afterwards did say that 'in the whole course of his military service he had never witnessed so desperate and sanguinary a conflict'.[29]

It was an opinion that was supported by Bentinck, who said,

It was the most severe action we had all throughout our time in the Peninsula.

———————

1. The successful siege of Olivenza.
2. Beresford, General William Carr (1764–1854). He served under Sir John Moore throughout the Corunna campaign of 1808–9. Because of his outstanding gifts as an organizer, he was selected by Wellington in 1809 to train the Portuguese Army. In that capacity he raised the famous *caçadores* regiments which earned Wellington's

praise. On 2 March 1809 he was promoted marshal in the Portuguese Army. He served as the Master-General of the Ordnance from 1828 to 1830.

3. The force consisted of two divisions, the 2nd and 4th with accompanying Portuguese and Spanish troops, to provide a total of some 27,000 men.

4. At this time it formed the border between France and Spain.

5. Private Richard Roberts provided an interesting recollection of this Badajoz siege: 'We next sat down before Badajoz, and raised an entrenchment camp, erected batteries, and commenced the siege in due form. It was not, however, destined to fall into our hands at once. The effect of our guns, however, fell short of our expectation. We were sacrificing time, ammunition, and many valuable lives, to little purpose.' Roberts, 'Incidents in the Life of an Old Fusilier', No. 1, p. 21.

6. RWFM, Acc. 1335, Harrison to mother, 24 May 1811.

7. It was indeed a difficult period for the battalion as Harrison related, 'to our no small astonishment we remained in this unpleasant uncertainty all the day of the 14th, that night and the following day, during which our poor fellows were exposed to dreadful weather, and not more than a blade of grass to cover them.' Ibid.

8. The total strength of the battalion at Albuera has been estimated as 733, made up of 41 officers and 692 other ranks.

9. This is incorrect. No officers from the 23rd Foot were killed or injured during the few days of siege operations. However, Lieutenant Colonel Ellis was shot in the head during the successful siege of Badajoz in April 1812.

10. Lieutenant General Joaquín Blake y Joyes (1759–1827). Born to a wealthy Irish father and a Galician mother, he joined the Spanish Army, seeing action at Gibraltar and Minorca in his youth. He fought through the war with France commencing in 1793, and by 1808, at the start of the Peninsular War, was a lieutenant general. After the war, in 1815 he was made Chief Engineer of the Spanish Royal Army.

11. At Albuera, Marshal William Beresford commanded an army of about 35,000 British, Portuguese and Spanish troops. There were 10,603 British and Germans, 10,201 Portuguese and some 14,552 Spanish. The comments on the capabilities of the Spanish and Portuguese troops are unfair. The Portuguese had a good combat record and Albuera generally reinforced this. The broad organization of the Anglo-Portuguese force was: 4th Division, Major General Lowry Cole; 2nd Division, Major General William Stewart; Portuguese division, Major General John Hamilton; there was also a light infantry brigade of the King's German Legion and an independent Portuguese brigade; plus artillery and cavalry. The French force, led by Marshal Soult, was smaller, 22,856 men in total, but superior in terms of quality and experience. There were roughly 19,000 infantry, who were seasoned troops with a confident commander, General Jean-Baptiste Girard. A strong cavalry force of around 3,000 sabres was commanded by Lieutenant General Victor La Tour-Maubourg, while Brigadier General Charles de Ruty had some 30 artillery pieces.

12. Brigadier William Moundy Harvey. Commissioned in the Marines in 1794, transferred to the 1st West India Regiment in 1797 as a captain. He served in the

Portuguese Army 1809–13, initially as the Colonel of the 6th Infantry Regiment and subsequently as a brigade commander. He died in 1813 on a passage back home.

13. Commanded by Sir William Myers.

14. No officer named Kenrick served in the battalion. Lieutenant Colonel Henry Ellis was in command at Albuera. Henry Walton Ellis was born at Cambray in 1783, son of then Lieutenant Colonel John Joyner Ellis RWF (subsequently Major General John Joyner Ellis, of Worcester), who purchased a commission for him as ensign in the 89th Foot on 26 March 1783 when he was only a few weeks old. The 89th Foot was disbanded later in 1783 and the baby Ellis was placed on half pay until 21 September 1789 when he was put back onto full pay as an ensign in the 41st Foot. He transferred to the 23rd Foot as captain-lieutenant on 3 September 1795. Promoted captain 20 January 1796, major on 23 October 1804, lieutenant colonel in command 23 April 1808 (aged 25) and colonel 14 June 1814. He was nominated KCB on 2 January 1815.

During his service he was wounded eight times, including the Helder expedition in 1799; at Alexandria in 1801; Albuera where he was shot through the right hand; he received a musket ball in the head at the capture of Badajoz; suffered a grazed temple at Salamanca; a musket ball through the cheek in the Pyrenees; and damaged an eye at Orthez. At Waterloo he was mortally wounded by a musket ball and expired on 20 June. He was buried in the cemetery next to the church of Waterloo. The cemetery was closed between 1955 and 1975. It is assumed that Ellis's body was not found but the triangular stone inscribed in English and French with his details was moved to the Wellington Museum. In 1839, the officers of the Royal Welch Fusiliers placed a handsome marble slab in the church at Waterloo.

In addition, the regiment erected a massive memorial to him in Worcester cathedral, his home city, where citizens had presented him with a splendid silver cup in appreciation of his service on 26 December 1814. This cup and his medals are held in the regimental museum. The memorial in Worcester Cathedral reads: 'In memory of Colonel Sir Henry Walton Ellis, KCB. A native of this city, who, at an early age, entered the 23rd Regiment or Royal Welch Fusiliers, then commanded by his father, Major General John Joyner Ellis, and afterwards led on to honourable distinction by himself, during seven years of unexampled military renown, having received eight wounds, and rendered services as important as they were brilliant in Holland, Egypt, the West Indies, America, Spain, Portugal and France. He fell by a musket-shot at the head of his Regiment, almost in the glorious moment which announced victory to Great Britain and peace to Europe on the memorable plains of Waterloo. He died of his wound on 20 June 1815 aged 32 years. His loss was lamented and his worth recorded by the illustrious commander Wellington, in words that will perish only with history itself! This monument was erected by the officers, Non-commissioned officers and privates of the Royal Welch Fusiliers as a tribute of their respect and affection to the memory of a leader, not more distinguished for his valour and conduct in the field than beloved for his every generous and social virtue.'

His medals are: Army Gold Medal engraved Albuera with clasps Badajoz, Salamanca; Army Gold Cross Albuera, Badajoz, Salamanca and Vitoria with clasps Pyrenees, Martinique, Orthez and Toulouse; Waterloo Medal; and Sultan's Gold Medal for Egypt 1801.

15. Captain Hill 'conceived the depth of the columns as nine ranks. The distance of the enemy's second line or column was about 60 yards and in their rear again some cavalry was found.' RWFM, Acc. 3777, Hill to mother, 22 May 1811. This tactical positioning was intelligent and it placed Beresford and the 4th Division at a great disadvantage as it pre-empted the likely tactic of feeding troops piecemeal into the battle.

16. Harrison provided one detailed account: 'our Division advanced in contiguous columns of Battalions at quarter distance till within about musket shot of the French, when we closed and deployed our first company of the Battalion. In this situation we remained for some time, and some Spanish cavalry were driven in, who I am sorry to say figured shamefully. The French cavalry who were now in great force and looked very formidable, elated with the little success over the Spaniards, advanced au pas de charge on our line, but observing us so unshaken and so little dismayed at their fierce appearance, when within about one hundred yards, they wheeled about and we saluted their "derriers" with a smart fire. Their Infantry's formation was covered by their field pieces which kept up a heavy fire with grape shot and round shot on our line at a very short distance. I am sorry to say some time elapsed before these noisy gentlemen were answered by our artillery on the left of our Brigade. At this time, the Brigade on our left, the 3rd, 48th and 66th, were warmly engaged. Some Cavalry arriving on our right to divert the attention of the enemy's cavalry, our Brigade advanced at a steady pace reserving our fire and leaving the Portuguese brigade to join our second line. The French Infantry were formed on an eminence and we had every disadvantage of the ground. They soon opened their fire. We returned it handsomely, came down to the charge and cheered. They faced about after a few paces and with others coming to their assistance, the contest soon became general and a most determined fire kept up on both sides, so near almost as to be muzzle to muzzle. They again drew us on by showing us their backs, and we twice repeated our former treatment. This work lasted some time, they continuing to bring up fresh Regiments, our Brigade being much broken by its loss, not above one third of our men were left standing. Their Infantry flanked our Battalion on the left and were coming in on our rear, their Cavalry at the same time making a desperate charge on our right and rear and I assure you that we had enough to do. At this juncture I met with my reward for the day, and the Portuguese Brigade coming up, our people gradually retired from the scene they had supported with credit to themselves and honour to their country.' RWFM, Acc. 1335, Harrison to mother, 18 May 1811.

Just as the Fusilier Brigade carried the heights opposing them and drove off the two French infantry columns in disarray they were attacked in the front by cavalry, 'who, receiving the fire of all our companies, put themselves in order and prepared to charge, thinking the whole unloaded. The spurs were in the horses' sides, they were coming on, the Grenadiers then fired on them at about 15 paces distant and the file fire recommenced from those who had first fired, when they went to the right about and galloped off. It was nothing but the steady, determined attack of the Infantry on the right that saved the day. Had they been broken we should have been annihilated.' RWFM, Acc. 3777, Hill to mother 22 May 1811.

17. General Sir William Francis Patrick Napier (1785–1860), author of the *History of the War in the Peninsula and in the South of France from 1807 to the Year 1814*. The famous passage that follows is taken from Volume 3.

18. During the battle Lieutenant Colonel Ellis was shot through his right hand and lost the ends of his third and little fingers.

19. Lieutenant Colonel Edward Blakeney (1778–1868) was the commanding officer of the 2/7th Foot. He was subsequently severely wounded at Badajoz and commanded the 1/7th Foot in North America and France 1814–15. He ultimately became a field marshal in 1862.

20. The 4th Division advanced in battalion columns echeloned from the left. It is unlikely that squares were formed.

21. This is very unlikely to have happened. However, during the retreat to Corunna in 1809, at the village of Cacabellos, a Rifleman Plunkett made his name in the history of the regiment when, lying on his front, he shot and killed the French General Colbert with a shot to the head using a Baker rifle at an incredible range said to have been 800 yards, though this is certainly exaggerated. The true range was probably between 200 and 400 yards.

    Interestingly Roberts also commented on a similar event, 'Under cover of the guns, they had a marksman sitting, who picked off our officers one after another. I kept him in my eye, but I had no means of popping him over in the heat of the onset. I saw him take aim at Sir William Myers, who in an instant dropped from his horse. I then made bold to warn Colonel Ellis of his danger, and expressing my fear that the next shot was intended for him, I said I would strive to flank him on the left. I did so; the man tumbled over, and he did no more execution that day at least.' Roberts, 'Incidents in the Life of an Old Fusilier', No. 1, pp. 11–12.

22. In fact the 4th (or the Queen's Own) Regiment of Dragoons, commanded by Major Burgh Leighton and part of the Heavy Cavalry Brigade.

23. This account has to be seen as inaccurate. The British force lost five colours in all – the King's Colour and the Regimental Colour of both the 2/48th Foot, and the 2/66th Foot and the Regimental Colour of the 3rd Foot (Buffs). However, the last of these was recovered on the battlefield by a soldier from another regiment, which left a total of four colours in French hands.

24. Lieutenant Colonel Sir William Myers (1783–1811) commander of the 1st Brigade (1/7th, 2/7th and 1/23rd Foot), one of the two brigades in the 4th Division. General

Cole received a relatively superficial wound to his thigh. Whilst advancing up the hill toward the enemy, Myers's horse was shot from under him. He continued on foot until another charger could be found when he was struck in the area of his hip by a musket-ball which then passed through his intestines. He did not fall from his horse but was eventually carried away to receive attention. He subsequently died of his wounds at Valverde on 17 May 1811.

25. It took over a month for the actions of sergeants within the Fusilier Brigade to be recognized. Subsequently Sergeant David Scott of the 1/23rd was awarded an ensign's commission in the 11th Foot, as was a sergeant from each battalion of the 7th Foot. At the immediate conclusion of the battle Captain Stainforth's company was commanded by Corporal Thomas Robinson, a former weaver from Lancashire, who was promoted to sergeant.

26. Casualties sustained in this battalion were 2 officers killed and 14 wounded from 28 present at the battle, 1 sergeant killed, 17 wounded and 46 rank and file killed with 269 wounded. Present at the commencement of the battle were 568 all ranks and the total casualty numbers were 349, 61 per cent of the total.

27. 4,159 British and German troops were reported as being killed and wounded, across the Allied force. Within the Fusilier Brigade, 2,015 officers and men had commenced the battle; 1,045 were killed and wounded. The two 1/23rd officers killed were Captain Montagu and Lieutenant Hall, who were stripped of their possessions and clothes by Spanish peasants before they died. The number of officers wounded was substantial the list being: Lieutenant Colonel Ellis, Captains Hurford, McDonald and Stainforth, Lieutenants Booker (lost his forefinger and thumb of the right hand to a sabre cut but in his usual good spirits, christened himself, 'Obi or three fingered Jack'), Castle, Harris, Harrison (who sustained a musket shot through the left thigh, three inches above the knee, grazing but not fracturing the bone), Ledwith, McLellan, J. MacDonald, Thorpe and Treeve (grape shot entered near his right instep and extricated near his ankle). Captain McDonald and Lieutenant Castle were the officers who subsequently died of their wounds.

Captain Colin McDonald was a great friend of Harrison's and maintained his faculties and presence of mind to the very last, passing away with 'great resignation and fortitude at Valverde from whence he was never able to be removed'. RWFM, Acc. 1335, Harrison to father 22 June 1811. Lieutenant Castle's wound was not thought to be of a serious nature but, 'it took such an effect on his spirits that the poor fellow died almost in a fit of despondency'. Ibid.

Harrison was fortunate in the wound he suffered, 'I had a close shave when we first went into action, a ball passed through the centre of my cap, taking the point of my pocket handkerchief which was in my cap. I cut open my coveralls, as no mark was through, I was afraid the ball had lodged in. It entered about three inches above the knee and luckily had passed through on the under side and lodged in the overalls just under the knee, where I found the gentleman myself, and mean to keep it for a memento of the day.' Ibid. The cap and handkerchief, complete with bullet holes, survived as a relic within the Harrison family until the 1920s, when they then unfortunately disappeared.

28. The aftermath of the battle of Albuera was distinguished by much discussion on how command of the Anglo-Portuguese troops could possibly have been better executed. Harrison commented that, 'I believe every soldier did his duty, but there is not much doubt a great want of Generalship was evinced throughout the whole affair, otherwise our success must have been more complete.' RWFM, Acc. 1335, Harrison to mother 18 May 1811.

   Marshal Beresford's account of the battle written in the aftermath gave most of the credit to the 2nd Division, with little mention of the 4th Division and the Fusilier Brigade, which greatly upset Lowry Cole. The perception of unfair distribution of accolades also contributed to grievances within the battalions. In a letter written six weeks after the battle, Harrison said, 'Everybody has been excessively indignant at the indifferent way that Marshall Beresford passes over the Fusilier Brigade in orders, in consequence of which General Stuart, who was an eyewitness to our conduct, wrote him a letter which of course must be published and which you will see. The circumstances perhaps will do us more credit and make our merits more conspicuous than if the Marshall had done us justice at first, and known how to appreciate the merits of good soldiers when they were unfortunately placed under his command. Had not this want of talent been supplied by the most determined bravery of the Fusiliers, he would no doubt have met with defeat, and no retreat left for him.' RWFM, Acc. 1335, Harrison to father 22 June 1811. Wellington had previously recognized some of Beresford's limitations but also acknowledged that there was no one better overall: 'the ablest man I have yet seen with the army, and the one having the largest views, is Beresford', A. J. Griffiths, *The Wellington Memorial*, London, 1987, p. 308.

29. Harrison commented: 'I cannot tell you which was victorious only that we gained the ground we fought on. I believe never was British bravery more conspicuous on this occasion and the French fought with more than their usual intrepidity.' RWFM, Acc. 1335, Harrison to mother, 18 May 1811.

   Similarly, Captain Hill wrote, 'The carnage was without exception far more terrible than any I ever before have seen.' RWFM, Acc. 3777, Hill to mother, 18 May 1811.

Chapter Six

Ciudad Rodrigo and Badajoz

———•———

Following the battle of Albuera, the battalion had three months' grace to recover. The Fusilier Brigade required the temporary addition of another battalion, the 1/48th, in order to keep it at fighting strength as the 1/7th and 2/7th had amalgamated due to the number of casualties sustained. The next significant action was a further siege of Badajoz, which commenced in mid-May but was lifted after a month's duration and two unsuccessful assaults.

The battalion was then positioned on the north side of the River Guadiana and unfortunately sickness slashed numbers. Operationally, there was a near stalemate in the campaign, with factors evenly balanced between the two sides. Wellington decided that the next important objective was to capture the French-held fortress of Ciudad Rodrigo. In August the 3rd and Light Divisions screened Ciudad Rodrigo, whilst the 4th Division constructed a defensive position at Fuente Guinaldo to the south. Despite these efforts, the French re-provisioned and reinforced Ciudad Rodrigo and also forced the 3rd Division to fight a hard withdrawal from its screening positions back toward Fuente Guinaldo. Realizing the scale of the French force, Wellington ordered the Light Division to reinforce but he was still significantly outnumbered. He decided to withdraw to the west and the Fusilier Brigade was tasked with acting as the rearguard.

The chosen defensive position was the Portuguese border settlement of Aldea da Ponte. The pursuing French force consisted of a division of infantry and a brigade of cavalry, commanded by General Thiebault.

Wellington next withdrew his army from Guinaldo, leaving Bentinck's Division at the little village of Aldea de Ponte, as his rear guard. Early in the morning following, the Division were under arms. Rations were served out before the fighting began, for the first time in Bentinck's experience, and scarce had the hungry men filled their stomachs ere the French made such a heavy and ferocious assault upon them as to drive them out of the village.

Sir Lowry Cole at once reformed them and led them to retake it, which they did with severe loss. Again the French poured down with horse, foot, and artillery, sweeping them clear of the place. For the second time the British re-took it, and this time kept it in spite of overwhelming numbers. The fighting was close and deadly. Once or twice the rush of the French was so sudden and fierce that Bentinck's Regiment had not time to get into line to receive them, but fought pell-mell, in a confused heap, and not until nearly 100 brave fellows had fallen in the effort could they regain anything like a formation.

Bentinck evaded several bayonet stabs aimed at him, but got hit with a ball, which knocked off his cap and ploughed up the skin on top of his skull. The wound bled so profusely that he went to the Doctor to get it plastered up, and on his way back fitted himself with a cap from the head of a dead Frenchman who happened to possess one of his size.

Private Finch, the man in front of him, fell on his back, with a bullet through his forehead. This poor fellow had on a pair of new shoes, which Bentinck took off his feet at the request of a comrade who was almost barefoot. This man instantly put them on, under a fire that in a moment rendered them as useless to him as they now were to their late owner.

'The Captain of their company was stricken down as he gallantly gave edge and point in the wild melee. Colonel Ellis immediately called out to one from the next Company, Captain Courtland, to take his place. The Officer was greatly esteemed by the men for his kindly behaviour. He had been with the Regiment in Martinique, in Canada, and thus far through the Peninsula, and had just sent home to England his wife and three children, who usually accompanied him.'[1]

Scarcely had he taken his place at the head of the Company, when a cannon shot hummed past, sweeping the legs off three men who stood in file and carrying away the front of the Captain's stomach. With a convulsive motion the latter dropped his sword and placing both hands to his bowels to keep them in, staggered back against Bentinck who was next behind him. Bentinck caught him and supported him towards the rear, but the Captain, faint with his awful wound, sank on the bloody ground ere they had got thirty yards on their way. Just then the Colonel rode past. 'Who have you got there Bentinck,' he asked. 'Captain Courtland, sir,' replied Bentinck, whose tears, accustomed as he was to such sights, fell fast at the loss of his favourite officer.

'Ah, well,' said the Colonel pompously, looking down upon him, 'Never mind, Captain Courtland, you die on the bed of honour.' 'Ah,' gasped the dying man, with an expression that Bentinck never forgot, 'Poor honour for my dear wife and children.' The Colonel, whose words Bentinck subsequently recalled when he saw him at his death agony at Waterloo, replied not to this dying lament except by bidding Bentinck stay by him and see him decently buried. This Bentinck did within half an hour after. He tore his blanket in two, keeping one half himself and wrapping his late Captain in the other, burying him beside a huge stone, with the help of a couple of Spaniards. He took from his shoulder one of his gold lace epaulettes, in the hope of bringing it home to the late Captain's widow, but he was never able to find out her address.[2]

The French were successfully forced out of the village. At dusk they mounted a determined second attack but the Fusilier Brigade held on and subsequently mounted a counter-attack.[3]

When night came on and both sides had got busily to work at their cooking fires, not far from each other, Major Pearson, the Officer Commanding the Light Companies of Bentinck's Division, bethought himself to make a dash at the French bivouacs, and win distinction by giving them a bloody surprise. He was a daring, able Officer, but very bad with his men, flogging them terribly at the least excuse, so that he was hated by them all, though they liked well enough to follow his lead.[4] They crept up to the French firelight unseen and with deadly volley and sharp steel the sortie, for a brief space, bore all before it, aided by surprise and panic.

Then the French, yielding to command, got together and drove them back almost as suddenly as they had come, but not before the sharp little affair had cost on both sides between 200 and 300 men. Major Pearson, the leader of the assailants, enjoyed it immensely until his horse fell beneath a shot, as they were retiring. He was partly under it, and could not release himself. He shouted out for some of his men to help him, but they were too glad at the prospect of seeing him killed or at least taken prisoner, to do so. They went on their way rejoicing, the last they heard of him being a shout that he would 'tan their hides for them' if ever he got to them again.

Wellington decided to abandon the village and ordered his army to withdraw deeper into Portugal. He asked Pakenham, the commander of the Fusilier Brigade, to 'provide a "stop-gap regiment" as rearguard and Pakenham replied that he had already assigned the Royal Welch Fusiliers that task. "Ah", responded Wellington, "that is the very thing".'[5]

This was the final engagement of 1811 as the French did not pursue the retreating Allies. The allies moved into winter quarters, with the battalion occupying cantonments near Gallegos on the banks of the River Coa. Throughout the winter the army prepared equipment for forthcoming siege operations. At the turn of the year Wellington learnt that the French had redeployed a significant number of troops to reinforce other French forces in Catalonia in north-eastern Spain, and seized the opportunity to go on the offensive.

The investment of Ciudad Rodrigo commenced on 8 January 1812. The construction of trenches and batteries was undertaken by the 3rd, 4th and Light Divisions. However, for the battalion, the conduct of the siege was peculiarly unpleasant, due to the lack of supplies, the appalling weather, an uncomfortable battalion bivouac in nearby woods, lack of rations, and finally the attentions of the French artillery and sharpshooters whilst they constructed the trenches and batteries.

The men called this Starvation Camp. Their provisions not having come up, they were reduced to live upon acorns, with which the ground in the woods was thickly strewn. Six men were sent out of each company every day to gather them. The droves of pigs which lived on these acorns were also laid under by way of stealthy contribution. The men used to conceal their bayonets under their coats when they went out, and to bayonet the grunters without mercy when neither Officer nor owner was in sight, and fat pork boiled with the acorns helped them down nicely, or fried in wine, which was the one commodity that could be had almost anywhere at two pence a quart.

Nor were the Officers any better off. They would look steadfastly another way if they came upon a soldier staggering under a side of pork, and a piece of it quietly dropped into their tent would seal their lips to silence. Before we moved again there were several men who deserted and went to the French on account of there being no provisions. Then the working parties, 1,000 or so at a time, were sent near the town to begin the earthworks, and to put up our batteries ready for the siege. We worked night and day until we had got them completed. Then we mounted the guns, ready to open on the enemy. A part of the army of the Portuguese came up to assist us to take it.

Fusilier, 23rd Regiment of Foot, in marching order, 1812, with the regimental mascot. The first records of a goat as regimental mascot date from 1777 as the regiment passed, 'in review preceded by a goat with gilded horns, and adorned with ringlets of flowers'. Bentinck's comments about the mascot illustrate his pride in being part of the 23rd Foot. The tradition of this regimental mascot continues and the goat is given the rank of corporal and attended to by the goat major. (*Courtesy RWF Museum Trustees*)

The bombardment of Copenhagen by the British forces, 2nd to 5th September, 1807 (Martens, 1845). The ruthless and destructive bombardment achieved the surrender of the Danish forces and the capture of the Danish fleet. (*Courtesy Anne S. K. Brown Military Collection, Brown University Library*)

Martinique 1809. British troops assault a French position. The parapet and ditch are believed to be representative of positions forward of Fort Desaix. (*Print after painting. Courtesy D. E. Graves*)

Badajos taken by storm on the 6th of April 1812 by the Allied Army under Lord Wellington (Atkinson, 1813) The 23rd Foot formed part of the 4th Division's ferocious assault through the breach in the Trinidad bastion.
(Courtesy Anne S. K. Brown Military Collection, Brown University Library)

The Battle of Toulouse, April 10th 1814 (Jenkins, 1815). This was the last significant event of the Peninsular War for the 1/23rd Foot before it returned home after over six years abroad. *(Courtesy Anne S. K. Brown Military Collection, Brown University Library)*

Lt Col Henry Walton Ellis (1782–1815). (*Courtesy RWF Museum Trustees*)

Major Thomas Pearson (1781–1847). (*Courtesy RWF Museum Trustees*)

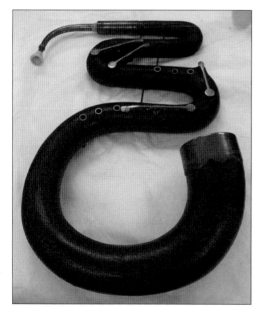

Bentinck was a bandsman after 1815 and marked his instrument, a serpent, to commemorate his service at Waterloo. It is now kept in the Bate Collection of Musical Instruments, Faculty of Music, University of Oxford. (*Courtesy A. Lamb, Bate Collection of Musical Instruments*)

RIGHT: Fusilier, 23rd Regiment of Foot, 1815. An artist's impression of a Welch Fusilier in full dress uniform, *c.* 1815. *(Painting by G. K. Tipping, courtesy RWF Museum Trustees)*

BELOW: St David's Day in the officers' mess of the 23rd Foot. The drum-major marches round the table carrying a plate of leeks, accompanied by the regimental goat. Each officer or guest who has never eaten one before, mounts a chair and eats a leek while a drummer beats a roll. *(Courtesy RWF Museum Trustees)*

HIS MAJESTY'S

_____ _Twenty Third_ Reg___ of _First Royal Welsh Fusiliers_

Whereof _Major General Sir James Willoughby Gordon Bt KCB_ is Colonel.

THESE ARE TO CERTIFY,

I.
Age and Enlistment.
THAT _Pte Richd Bentinck_ born in the Parish of _Baxton_ in or near the Town of _Baxton_ in the County of _Suffolk_ was enlisted for the aforesaid Regiment at _Bury St Edmunds_ in the County of _Suffolk_ on the _10th_ Day of _Jany 1807_ at the Age of _Eighteen_ for _Unlimited Service_.

II.
Service.
THAT he hath served in the Army for the space of _Eighteen_ Years and _292_ Days, after the Age of Eighteen, according to the subjoined

Statement of Service.

IN WHAT CORPS.	PERIOD OF SERVICE. From.	To.	Serjeant Major. Yrs. Days	Qr. Mast. Serjeant. Yrs. Days	Serjeant. Yrs. Days	Corporal. Yrs. Days	Trumpetr. or Drummer. Yrs. Days	Private. Yrs. Days	Service prior to the Age of Eighteen to the Yrs. Days	Total Service. Yrs. Days
23rd Regt W.F.	10 Jany 1807	28 __ 1823						16 292		16 292
Waterloo								2		2
Total of Service								18 292		18 292
In East or W. Indies	29 Decr 1808	15 April 1809								

III.
Authority and Cause of Discharge.
THAT by Authority of _Genl__ _____ _ dated _Dublin 28 Octr 1823_ HE IS HEREBY DISCHARGED in consequence of _being consumptive_

IV.
Not disqualified for Pension.
THAT he is not to my knowledge incapacitated by the Sentence of a General Court Martial from receiving Pension

V.
Character, &c. &c. &c.
THAT his general Conduct as a Soldier has been _good and a worthy___ _____

VI.
Settlement of all Demands.
THAT he has received all just Demands of Pay, Clothing, &c. from his Entry into the Service to the date of this Discharge, as appears by his Receipt underneath.

VII
I _Pte Richard Bentinck_ do hereby acknowledge that I have received all my Clothing, ___ Demands whatsoever, from the time of my Entry into the Service the ___

Certified by _J. W. Harris Lieut 23. Foot_
Commanding the Troop or Company.

Signature of the Soldier } _his mark X Bentinck_

VIII.
Description &c. &c. &c.
TO prevent any improper use being made of this Discharge, by its falling into other Hand the following is a Description of the said _Private Richard Bentinck_
He is about _Thirty four_ Years of Age, is _Five_ Feet, _Seven_ Inches in height, _Brown_ Hair _Dark_ Eyes _Fresh_ Complexion, and by Trade or Occupation a _Labourer_

Given under my Hand, and the Seal of the Regiment, at _Dublin_ this _28th_ Day of _October_ 1823.

Signature of the Commanding Officer _____

Adjutant General's Office. _29 October_ 1823, confirmed _JJ Gordon D.A.G._

Front page of the discharge certificate of Richard Bentinck. It confirms his participation in the Martinique campaign and notes the two years of pensionable service for being present at Waterloo. Although the certificate records his age as eighteen on joining the army, this is debatable. (*Author's collection*)

Back page of the discharge certificate of Richard Bentinck.
Across the middle, Dr Smith, the 23rd's medical officer has
written, 'I certify that Richard Bentinck has suffered from
pulmonary complaints for the last three years.'
(Author's collection)

Rochdale and Heywood Waterloo Veterans at the Rochdale Parish Church Gardens, 18 June 1856. It is believed that Richard Bentinck is the fifth from the left. He would later drum the veterans into dinner. (*Courtesy Local Studies, Rochdale Arts and Heritage Service*)

ABOVE: Bentinck's gravestone. Note the record of his service at Waterloo and unfortunately the incorrect regiment inscribed. (*Author's collection*)

LEFT: Richard and Mary Bentinck. (*Author's collection*)

The substantial manpower allowed the investment to be conducted rapidly.

Bentinck's Division, the 4th, lost many men by the heavy cannonade showered upon them by the French, who fired shells and grape. On the fourth day of the siege, the great convent of Santa Cruz was carried by storm and the attackers had three batteries of eleven guns each replying to the French fire and smaller ones were established within 600 yards, in the hope of effecting a breach before Marshal Marmont could arrive with the numerous French army he was collecting for that purpose.[6] The French Garrison sallied out nearly every night in the attempt to destroy our works, but every time were driven back, though not without severe loss. In a week the British had nearly 30 pieces of cannon ready to open against the ramparts.

On the 14th the assault on Ciudad Rodrigo commenced amongst the bellowing of large cannon on both sides as shells hissed through the air in both directions.[7] The 40th Foot[8] on the left of the attack successfully assaulted and captured the convent of San Francisco. The next day the breach was extended through sustained bombardment and a sharp musketry kept up against the French gunners. Over the following couple of days the bombardment on both sides continued and although the Allies sustained losses to their artillery, by the evening of 18th a wide enough breach had been constructed for an assault to be ordered.[9]

When the batteries were open, nearly the first shot that was fired took the arm off one of the Portuguese close by my side.[10] We began firing the guns for us to make a breach so we could storm the town. We remained making the breach until we had sufficient room to enter. We got orders two or three hours before that it was to be taken that night by storm. There were three Divisions engaged in the battle, 3rd, 4th and Light Divisions.

The assault was to be conducted by Major General Picton's[11] 3rd Division and Major General Craufurd's[12] Light Division, with the 4th Division in a supporting role. The Light Division was tasked to assault the smaller breach headed by a storming party of 300 men.[13] The Portuguese brigade received orders to execute a false attack on the outworks of Saint Iago, and the convent of La Caridada, with instructions to turn it into a real one, should circumstances permit.[14] Concurrently an Anglo-Portuguese force was tasked with a further supporting attack across the Agueda River to attempt to break into the castle outworks.

The French sentries were alert to an attempted attack and as the Anglo-Portuguese intentions became clear, a withering fire of grape and musket was launched upon the attacking troops gathered in a ditch under the ramparts. The raking fire from a few yards away soon created many dead and wounded but the 'forlorn hope' in the main breach carried the objective by vigour with the bayonet and entrance was gained.

The fighting at the main breach was especially intense but the first elements of the Light Division were able to push against the defenders' right flank which wilted under the pressure. Within a few minutes three wall magazines exploded which gave the 3rd Division the opportunity to break through the entrenchments. The French garrison fought desperately whilst withdrawing to the castle but then the other supporting attacks were successful and resistance was useless, with surrender the only option.

> Throwing off the restraints of discipline, the troops committed frightful excesses.[15] The town was fired in three or four places, the soldiers menaced their Officers and shot each other; many were killed in the market-place. Intoxication soon increased the tumult; disorder everywhere prevailed and at last, the fury rising to an absolute madness, a fire was wilfully lighted in the middle of the great magazine, when the town and all in it, would have been blown to atoms, but for the energetic courage of a some Officers and a few soldiers who still preserved their senses.

The French suffered about 600 casualties from a garrison of 1,900 men; the survivors were taken into captivity and a number of artillery pieces seized. British casualties were some 1,100 killed and wounded in the siege as a whole. During the actual assault, some 100 rank and file were killed and around 400 wounded. Officer casualties were high with 59 being killed or wounded, but not an unusual number.[16]

> General Craufurd and General McKinnon, the former a man of great ability, were killed (and it was sad that with them died many gallant men). General Vandaleur, Colonel Colborne, and a crowd of inferior rank, were wounded.

The battalion as part of the 4th Division consolidated with the 3rd and Light Divisions in Ciudad Rodrigo and what he and his comrades saw shocked Bentinck:

> 'When we entered the town by the breach to my surprise I saw one of my own comrades lying dead, dressed in French uniform who had been

fighting against us, one of the men that had deserted us at the starvation camp. Two others who also deserted from the 'Starvation Camp' were captured alive, dressed as Spaniards. One belonged to the 7th and the other to the 23rd Regiment.'

They were sentenced to be shot and Bentinck was on the assigned duty for the Provost guard but was not one that was picked out to fire on them. The following morning they were marched out on the plain in the presence of the whole army and killed. One of them was a very big man, belonging to Bentinck's company.[17] He did not like to be shot in Spanish dress, so bought a forage jacket of Bentinck for three shillings, for that purpose. He begged for a pint of rum, but the quartermaster would not allow it, though he gave him as much food as he would eat. All the Army had orders to parade on a Plain out of the town to see them executed. He was for standing in the grave to be shot, but was made to get out, and he then knelt by its side. The Clergyman was reading a portion of the scripture to him. Two soldiers fired at him, and failing to kill him he was finished by a ball through his head by the Provost Marshal's pistol. The other, a little weakly man, almost dead before, was slain by a single bullet.[18]

Unhappily the slaughter did not end with the battle. The next day as the prisoners and their escort were marching out by the breach, an accidental explosion took place and numbers of both were blown into the air, the explosion attributed to the actions of plunderers in a French magazine.

Once Ciudad Rodrigo had fallen, Wellington's focus switched to Badajoz, the second great fortress in western Spain. A great deal of effort was expended to conduct preparations for the siege in utmost secrecy. Despite the lack of the necessary siege train equipment, which was slow moving up to Badajoz, the Allies continued with their plan of investing the fortress city, with work commencing on 17 March 1812.

There then came an order for us to return to Badajoz and we took the same route back again and we saw heaps of dead men buried for two or three miles round like manure in a field. The works we had put up were all pulled down during our absence and we had to begin again.

When we all got there we mustered about ten thousand men and our sufferings were almost past bearing. We had to work very hard and the weather was so much against us as it was continually wet and the winds very stiff. On the clay ground our shoes were worn off our feet and all our clothes turned to rags with the work and the weather. Some of the men had to whip their blankets that they had to lap them in to make trousers of. I myself was not as bad as a great many of them. I was not without shoes to my feet and my trousers were not so bad. I went many a time and waited until the butchers had killed the cattle and brought the hides for the men to make shoes of as we had no supply from England.

We had to make shift as we could and there were about three hundred men and Officers who came from England to us.[19] All their clothing was clean and good, they were quite surprised to see us in such a poor state. But it was not long before they was nearly as bad. When they came up at first our Officers made fire with them and took them in their camps and helped them to eat and drink what they had. We remained in that position until the works was finished.

The French commander of the fortress, Brigadier General Philippon, had some 5,000 troops to defend Badajoz and experience of twice repelling Allied siege attempts in May and June 1811. He had improved the defences by creating a marsh to the east and by digging counter-mines under the most likely approaches.

Wellington's plan was to attack the south-eastern part of the fortress and this approach required the taking of an outwork, Fort Picarina, which in turn demanded substantial work to create a zigzag trench running parallel to it. The French made strenuous efforts to block the progress of this trench, deploying up to 140 guns to harass the Allied working parties.[20] Fort Picarina was taken by assault on 25 March 1812. It was subsequently used as a battery for heavy guns which fired against the Trinidad and Santa Maria bastions, the intended breaching sites.

We then went out in turns by Regiment to keep the enemy away for while we were working they came out very often to try to destroy our works. Sometimes we had a great deal of men killed and wounded but we got them finished at last and we got the guns all prepared in the batteries ready for the siege. Wellington was determined to take the town whatever might be the loss.

Over the period of the construction of the trenches, 17 March–5 April 1812, the battalion suffered 1 officer, Brevet Major William Potter, and 13 men killed, and 50 wounded. Lieutenant Colonel Ellis was among the wounded, being hit in the forehead by a musket ball. The breaching batteries started firing at the walls on 30 March and by 6 April, three breaches had been achieved which were deemed practical to undertake an assault. Wellington had accordingly drawn up plans for five separate attacks.

The 4th and Light Divisions were the main effort, assaulting the breaches in the Trinidad and Santa Maria bastions. The 3rd Division was to launch a feint attack at the north-east of the fortress, whilst the 5th Division would also conduct a feint attack, but at the south-west of the fortress. A small detachment from the 4th Division was given the task of taking the lunette of San Roque, an outwork to the north-east of the main breaches. The original orders stated that the attacks were to begin at 7.00 in the evening, but the time taken to assemble the forces brought a delay of three hours.

This delay afforded a huge advantage to the French, who worked feverishly to improve the ruptured defences. The gaps in the breaches were filled with prepared explosive charges, whilst at the top temporary breastworks were constructed with sword blades attached to wooden beams and nail studded planks interspersed. The French also ensured that they stocked up on defensive equipment from loaded muskets to a large number of items such as grenades, explosive charges, large rocks and baulk timber to throw at the advancing Allied troops. Additional implements were nail-studded planks placed amongst the routes to be used by the attackers.

The assault began at 10.00 on the night of 6 April. The 4th Division, of which the battalion was part, was given the task of taking the formidable Trinidad bastion. During their advance, the attackers were discovered by the French defenders, who immediately unleashed a withering storm of artillery and musketry from the ramparts above, assisted by the firing of illumination rockets which burst above the attacking troops. The lead men of the 4th Division moved as quickly as possible to get across the protecting glacis and then jumped into the ditch, which was partially filled with water. Some of the attackers came prepared with bags of grass in a very crude attempt to fill the ditch.

The French defenders fought hard, firing down continuously on the attackers, whilst concentrating on preventing the use of scaling ladders. In the main breaches, it was said that some 2,000 troops fell in the space of a thousand yards. The 4th Division was resolute in its determination to gain entry into the city and the breach was assaulted time and time again over the period of an hour, but the defences provided too formidable, the weight of French fire too great and the casualties so many.

The guns were firing on the walls until April making a gap for us to enter. When we got up to the walls there was all sorts of sharp instruments to prevent us going forward. When we got through the first wall there was a trench of water about twelve feet deep and we had to get scaling ladders to get across. We had men going out everyday to get bags full of ferns or anything to fill up the river. The night we entered the town the big guns fired and cut down the sharp instruments that was in our way and then we rushed in, my Regiment was first into the breach of the town.[21]

Whilst the 4th and Light Divisions were having a torrid time against formidable defences, the diversionary attacks of the 3rd and 5th Divisions on the other side of the city were more successful. They managed to force their way over the walls and into the bastion of San Vincente and the castle. This disruption of the French defence allowed the 4th and Light Divisions to push their way ferociously into the city until at last organized French resistance collapsed in the face of the critical mass of Allied forces.

While we were getting in at the breach another Division got in on the other side at the castle. Our men took possession of it and when we got ourselves in through the breach the enemy all made an attempt to get to the Castle. To their disappointment they saw that we had possession of it and then they threw down their arms and surrendered. There were a number of guns fixed at the gates of the Castle for the intention to blow us all to pieces but we were on them too soon. The Portuguese was much tardy and should of come forward but they turned cowards and kept all behind them back and it caused a great many lives to be lost. All our Officers was killed and wounded. All but two.

The success of the attack on Badajoz was then undermined by the near-complete breakdown in discipline of the British troops, who had experienced ferocious fighting and desperate circumstances.[22] What followed was even worse than the excesses of Ciudad Rodrigo.

This was the only town Bentinck ever knew Wellington allow his men to plunder, and it was because the inhabitants had mounted the walls and cheered at his defeat on the occasion of his former unsuccessful assault. Wellington said then he would make them smart for it when he did get in, and he now redeemed his threat by giving his excited and victorious troops 24 hours' leave to plunder the town.

'We had orders from Wellington to put all the inhabitants both young and old to death by the bayonet but I never saw one wilfully murdered. We was all too busy plundering as he gave us twenty-four hours to plunder and some of the men got a great deal of valuable things and money.'[23]

'Every dwelling of importance was entered. Each and every shop emptied, and for several days the British camp was set out like a fair with every kind of spoil, and thronged with the townspeople buying back their goods. The Officers got their share. They did not themselves carry off the articles, but if they saw a watch, a jewel case, or any other thing they fancied, they would tell one of their men to get it for them.'[24] Bentinck was too young a campaigner to find much of value. His chief prize was a very large and splendid velvet mantle which he stripped from an image of the Virgin Mary in the Principal church,[25] and this was so heavy and cumbersome that after carrying it about for a few days he sold it for a trifle to one of the Officers.

'The next day the inhabitants came to bury their dead. In the morning we went out and found all the Officers we could and we brought them back to the camp and buried them. Some of them was knocked down in the trench with the men and the trench was completely filled up with dead bodies so that we could walk over the trench without difficulty. We was supposed to have lost seven hundred men from four of our Regiments in about two or three hours fighting in the morning. In our tent we mustered six out of eighteen and two of the six was wounded. I was wounded in the leg by the explosion of a shell and the Sergeant was wounded by a ball in his head. It then became very quiet and we stopped in our camps several days till they were selling us the goods they had got. We had plenty of wine and some of my comrades were burdened with gold and silver pieces, which lasted them to toss and gamble for days.'

The battalion was under fire from 9.00 at night until 7.00 in the morning and sustained very heavy casualties: 163 officers and men, over a quarter of the battalion were killed and wounded.[26] The siege decimated the battalion which was not long rebuilt following the bloody battle of Albuera. The most seriously injured were evacuated to the military hospital near Lisbon. The lucky ones were sent back to England for recuperation and posted to the 2nd Battalion. Across the Allied force the losses were equally substantial: 1,035 killed, 3,789 wounded and about a hundred missing during the siege, most of these losses being sustained during the assault.

The Army stayed nearly a week before Badajos after its capture, looking to the 3,500 killed and wounded it had cost them. The former were not burnt as at Albuera, but decently buried. Bentinck's Regiment, the 23rd, or Welch Fusiliers we find again lost 700 men, as at Albuera, after which battle their numbers had been made up. Not many of them were found amongst the wounded, most of them being stricken dead in the breaches. Two of his comrades, Marsh[27] and Quinn[28] were wounded by his side. A cannon ball came just between their shoulders, taking off an arm from each, Quinn's close to the socket, Marsh's close to the elbow. He recognised Marsh, who was a Lancashire man, some years ago in the market place at Halifax, whither he had gone to draw his pension. Observing that he was without an arm Bentinck asked him where he lost the limb. The old warrior replied 'at the taking of Badajos.' 'Then I helped you to the rear,' replied Bentinck, and his old comrade joyfully conducted him to his home and set before him the best refreshment it afforded.

The experience of the desperate assault on Badajoz and the slaughter of so many troops in attempts to gain the breach became notorious within the Army. Wellington subsequently wrote in a dispatch to London, 'The capture of Badajoz affords as strong an instance of the gallantry of our troops as has ever been displayed, but I anxiously hope that I shall never again be the instrument of putting them to such a test as to that which they were put last night.'[29]

In the regiment the legend of Badajoz spread. Fusilier Thomas Jeremiah, who joined the 2nd Battalion in 1812 and subsequently moved across to the 1st Battalion, composed a poem about Badajoz:

I was at Badajoz one evening one evening in May.
That we had turned to rest ourselves after a bloody day.
For the cannon had ceased roaring and the battle cry was still.
And though beneath a Spanish sky the air was keen and chill.
That day there had been meeting fierce meeting on the plain.
That day full many an eye had closed to open not again.
But now the mighty shock had passed the trumpet had rung out.
And the British banner flapped above each fortified redoubt.
And we sat ourselves that evening that evening by the board.
And unto God we gave our thanks to our protecting Lord.

And we called our muster over one answered not our call.

Twas the youngest, and the bravest, and the noblest of us all.

He had gone forth at morning with the bugle's first shrill sound.

He had gone forth at morning with a smile and with a bound.

As he took his sabre from the wall and waved it in the air.

But at night his place was empty and untenanted his chair.

By torch light then we sought him we sought him on the plain.

God grant that we may never look upon such a sight again.

Mid the moaning and the tortured and the dying and the dead.

Who were lying heaped together on their green and grassy bed.

And at last we stumbled o'er him for the stars were waxing pale.

And our torches flared and flickered in the breathing of the gale.

Ten paces from his comrades he was lying all alone.

Half shrouded in the colours with his head upon a stone.

There was little blood upon him and yet his cheek was white.

And his hair was twined and matted by the moisture of the night.

He was breathing when we found him but his breath was spent and weak.

And though he strove to thank us he could neither sigh nor speak.

We lifted him and carried him it was a weary track.

And we laid him down tenderly within our bivouac.

He was dead ere long we laid him ere long we laid him on the ground.

But perhaps he had not suffered for he died without a sound.

Then we turned again in sadness we turned unto the board.

And each man put off his mantle, his helmet and his sword.

And with the dead before us with the blazing of the red pine.

We strove to pass the wine cup and to drain the ruby wine.

But our revel was a sad one so awhile in prayers we kneeled.

And then slumbered till the morning called us forth into the field.

Then we called our muster over and one answered not our call.

Twas the youngest, and the bravest and the noblest of us all.[30]

———•———

1. Jacob Ogden Van Courtland was the second son of Phillip Van Courtland (or Cortlandt), a Dutch pioneer, of Manor Cortlandt, New York, a staunch Loyalist, who fought against the rebel army in the American War of Independence and thereby lost his property and possessions. Jacob Van Courtland was commissioned

on 28 October 1795 having been on the half pay of the Provincials. He received promotion to lieutenant on 1 June 1796 and captain on 25 June 1803. He served in the West Indies and the Peninsula. Regimental Records noted that he was killed by a cannonball at the defence of Aldea da Ponte on 27 September 1811.

2. Van Courtland had married Anne Warrington in 1805. She did not re-marry and died at the age of ninety-six in 1870.

3. The engagement cost the battalion Captain Van Courtland killed. Major Pearson, Captain Cane and thirteen rank and file were wounded with one reported missing.

4. Thomas Pearson joined the battalion as a mere seventeen-year-old in 1796 and was promoted rapidly, reaching major by 1804. He also gained a considerable amount of experience in this time. He served in the 1798 Ostend expedition, at the Helder in 1799 and Ferrol in 1800. Pearson was wounded in the thigh during the storming of the heights of Aboukir in the Egyptian Campaign of 1801. Subsequently he was present at the siege and capture of Copenhagen in 1807. He commanded the Light Company during the capture of Martinique and was wounded in the leg by a grape shot during the taking of Fort Desaix.

Pearson served in the Peninsula during the defence of Torres Vedras and the first siege of Badajoz. He was present at Albuera and succeeded to the command of the Fusilier Brigade after the battle. he was in action at Fuente Guinaldo and was then severely wounded in the thigh when repelling the attack on Aldea da Ponte.

After a period of recuperation he was appointed to the staff in Canada in 1811. He was present at the Battle of Crysler's Farm on 11 November 1813. While on passage to Niagara he volunteered to join the 2nd Battalion, The Royal Marines, at the storming of Fort Oswego and was noticed in despatches. After the fall of Fort Erie, he was in the thick of the fighting during the withdrawal from Chippewa. He fought in the actions at Lundy's Lane, Niagara and Fort Erie and on 27 September 1814 was dangerously wounded in the head. He returned to Britain in 1815 and was appointed to command the 43rd (Monmouthshire) Light Infantry, but this regiment was soon afterwards reduced and he returned to command the 1/23rd Foot on 24 July 1817, achieving the rank of lieutenant colonel at the same time.

He retained this command until his promotion to major general on 22 July 1830. He was nominated CB on 4 June 1815 and KCB in 1835 and promoted lieutenant general in November 1841. He was appointed Colonel of the 85th Light Infantry on 21 November 1843 and nominated KCH. He received the Army Gold Medal for his services at Albuera and Crysler's Farm and also the Sultan's Gold Medal for the 1801 Egyptian campaign. Lieutenant General Sir Thomas Pearson, KCB, KCH, died at Bath on 20 May 1847. For a definitive biography refer to Graves, *Fix Bayonets*.

5. Graves, *Dragon Rampant*, p. 149. Wellington's remark is commented upon in Broughton-Mainwaring, *Historical Record of the Royal Welch Fusiliers*, p. 128.

6. Marshal Auguste Frédéric Louis Viesse de Marmont, Duke of Ragusa (1774–1852). In 1811 he became Commander-in-Chief of the French army in Portugal, in place

of Masséna. Wounded in 1812 at Salamanca, he returned to France to fight in the campaigns of 1813 in Prussia. In 1814 he switched sides to serve with Louis XVIII.

7. The Allies had thirty-four 24-pounder cannon and four 18-pounder cannon at the siege; the French had a total of 153 cannon.

8. 40th (2nd Somersetshire) Regiment of Foot. It was raised by General Philipps in 1717 from independent companies stationed in the West Indies and North America. In 1751 it received the numbering 40th of Foot and in 1782 took on its county title. The 40th was one of only three regiments to serve throughout the Peninsular campaign, including Rolica, Vimiero, Busaco, the sieges of Ciudad Rodrigo and Badajoz, Vitoria, Pyrenees, Nivelle, Orthez and Toulouse.

9. 'For five days they battered the wall, firing 9,515 rounds and using 834 barrels of powder (each barrel holding 90lb of powder).' M. Glover, *The Peninsular War 1807–1814*, p. 180. The main breach achieved was some thirty-five yards wide and the lesser breach about fifteen yards.

10. Roberts also provided a graphic account of an experience of French artillery fire. 'One night, I was on a working party, and always kept a sharp look-out for their shells. At last a very large one came whistling in our direction, as if to explode over our heads. I called to the men to lie down, and we all threw ourselves on the ground in a heap. Many were above me. The moment it touched the ground, the shell burst. The groans of my wounded comrades still ring in my ears! One poor fellow had the crown of his head taken clean off; another was literally disembowelled; and others had their limbs shattered and lopped off. On extricating myself from this mutilated group, I was surprised to find that my limbs were still serviceable; and after making proper arrangements for the dead and wounded, I returned to my night duty.' Roberts, 'Incidents in the Life of an Old Fusilier', p. 21.

11. Lieutenant General Sir Thomas Picton (1758–1815). 1771 commissioned ensign in 12th Foot, transferring to 75th Foot only for the regiment to be disbanded in 1783, forcing him into early retirement. 1794 gained captaincy in 17th Foot, then became a major in 58th Foot. Present at the capture of St Lucia and St Vincent, becoming lieuteant colonel in 56th Foot. For five years he was governor of Trinidad, with a harsh reputation, resulting in his resignation in 1803 and a trial for use of torture. Promoted to major general, and in 1809 was governor of Flushing during the Walcheren expedition. In 1810 he was appointed as a divisional commander in the Peninsula, being present at the battles of Fuentes d'Onoro, El Bodón, Ciudad Rodrigo and Badajoz (where he was badly wonded), Vitoria, the Pyrenees, Orthez and Toulouse. He was known as a competent and determined commander. In 1815 he fought at Quatre Bras, before being killed at Waterloo by a musket ball striking his temple. He was the highest-ranking allied officer to die at the battle. Owing to the absence of his luggage, he fought at Waterloo in civilian clothing and a top hat.

12. Major General Robert Craufurd (1764–1812). 1779 ensign in the 25th Foot, captain in 1783 with the 75th Foot and served in India in the campaigns of 1790–2 against Tipu Sultan. Served on attachment with the Austrian Army in Europe against the

French. In 1797 was promoted to lieutenant colonel and in 1798 was the Deputy Quartermaster-General in Ireland, then served in the Netherlands as a staff officer during the Helder expedition. In 1802 was elected a Member of Parliament. 1805 promoted colonel and in pursuit of active service gave up his seat. In 1807 he commanded a light brigade in the South American expedition under General Whitelock, then commanded a light brigade in the Iberian Peninsula. Throughout 1808 his brigade was heavily involved in the fighting as part of Sir John Moore's army. In 1809 he returned to the Peninsula and took command of the Light Division, furthering his reputation as a skilful but very disciplinarian commander, becoming known as 'Black Bob' Craufurd. Promoted major general in June 1811, he was at the front of the Light Division at Ciudad Rodrigo when he received a serious wound to the abdomen. He lingered for four days before dying on 23 January 1812. He was buried in the breach of the wall at Ciudad Rodrigo.

13. Major George Thomas Napier from the 1/52nd Foot commanded the storming party of the Light Division, which directly followed the forlorn hope led by Lieutenant Gurwood which was tasked to assault the lesser breach. The forlorn hope was traditionally a party of volunteers led by an officer who would be promoted if he survived and was successful in his endeavours.

14. Brigadier Denis Pack commanded an independent Portuguese brigade. The outworks of St Iago were to the south of the River Agueda, across from the main fortress.

15. There was a period of about twelve hours during the night where looting, drinking and pillaging took place. By mid-morning, control over the troops had been re-established.

16. Generally officer casualties were higher than those of other ranks. 'Taking six Peninsular actions at random: at Nivelle and Fuentes de Onoro there was approximately a one in sixteen chance of an officer becoming a casualty, against a chance of 1:17 for other ranks; at Busaco, 1:30½ chance for officers: 1:40 for other ranks; at Salamanca, 1:7½ for officers, 1:10 for other ranks; at Barrosa, 1:4 for officers, 1:5 for other ranks; and only at Albuera was the chance equal, 1:2½ for both officers and men. Very roughly, officers were probably about one-fifth more likely to be hit than other ranks.' Haythornthwaite, *The Armies of Wellington*, p. 28.

17. Donald Graves has shown that this was individual was Private Thomas Jones of the 23rd Foot. See Graves, *Dragon Rampant*, p. 155.

18. On completion of the execution, the entire Fusilier Brigade was marched past the open graves in single file. Lieutenant Knowles of the 1/7th Foot later wrote that, 'it was the most awful site I ever beheld'. Knowles, *War in the Peninsula*, p. 51. The execution of deserters was not uncommon.

19. The regimental records do not tally with Bentinck's account. On 2 August 1811, 6 officers, 6 sergeants, 2 corporals and 246 rank and file arrived as reinforcements from the 2nd Battalion. On 25 December 1812, 7 officers, a surgeon, 2 sergeants and 72 rank and file arrived from the 2nd Battalion, then at Haverford West, Wales, as reinforcements.

20. 'At five o'clock one morning during the second siege, I well remember having a number of Portuguese to carry ammunition into a temporary magazine, covered over with dry deal and tarpaulin. This was an object with the French gunners; for, seeing the ends of the boards, they immediately began throwing shells, hoping to set the place on fire, and thereby insure an explosion of the magazine. Suddenly a large shell fell and burst at the very door. I was inside at the time, and dropped with my face on the powder bin. The explosion over, I stood up to see what damage was done. It had buried itself two feet in the ground. The tarpaulin was on fire in several places. The moment was critical. What could be done to prevent the sparks from dropping among the loose powder? – for the seams between the board were so open, that in another minute or two the fire might send us all into the air. With the utmost precaution, though with some trepidation, I approached the burning splinter, caught it with my cap, held it fast till it was smothered, and then threw it out at the door. It was one of my many hairbreadth "scapes!"' Roberts, 'Incidents in the Life of an Old Fusilier', No. 1, pp. 21–2.

21. The 4th Division's attack broke down into efforts by groups of determined men and no one entered via the main breach so Bentinck's claim that members of the 23rd Foot were first into the town lacks credibility.

22. Roberts provided a very vivid narration of his experiences during the taking of Badajoz: 'On several occasions a flag of truce was sent in by Lord Wellesley, summoning them to surrender; but without effect. Consequently, an order was given to take the place by storm – and to it we went! Our scaling ladders were instantly applied, and there was such a rush who to be first! On getting to the top, I was in the act of placing my foot on the wall, when a stout Frenchman made a cut at my head with his sword; but at the same moment I had twelve inches of my bayonet in him, and he fell on his face on the wall. The cut I received in my head was so severe, that, but for my brass cap-plate, my skull would have been cloven in two. I lost all recollection for the moment, and tumbled off the ladder into the ditch, about twenty-five feet; and there I lay for some time. When I came to my senses, the blood was flowing very freely, and blinding my eyes. Trying to stench it the best way I could, I again scrambled up the ladder, and joined my comrades – such of them as survived – and got into the town. There the slaughter was immense; but we overcame all opposition, and made ourselves masters of the place. It was dearly bought. When we came out of the town, all that could be mustered of my company including myself, was eight men!' Roberts, 'Incidents in the Life of an Old Fusilier', No. 1, p. 22.

23. The suggestion Wellington ordered or allowed his men to plunder is utterly incorrect. Very simply the commanders were unable to control their men. Thomas Browne of the 23rd was serving as a staff officer and subsequently wrote of the soldiers in Badajoz, 'With faces as black & dirty as powder can make them, eyes red & inflamed, & with features full of wildness & ferocity, & of the insolence of victory, after a desperately contested struggle, they break into houses, ransack every spot where wine or spirits can be supposed to lie hid, & after repeated intoxicating draughts, begin

their work of plunder. Woe to that unfortunate owner of a mansion, if any such remain, who attempts to remonstrate. Discipline being at an end, the whole world seems given up to their indiscriminate rage & plunder.' Browne, *Napoleonic War Journal*, pp. 152–3.

This experience was similar to that of Wellington who 'Remembered entering a cellar where soldiers were lying so drunk that wine was actually flowing from their mouths, and he was nearly hit by a soldier firing in the air. A General Order of 7 April 1812 announced that it was time that the looting ceased, and a gallows was erected in the square to drive the point home. An aide de camp wrote that Wellington was so angry that he could hardly bring himself to thank the troops.' Holmes, *Wellington – The Iron Duke*, p. 163.

The indiscipline of the army at Badajoz was a black mark on its record. It took forty-eight to seventy-two hours to restore discipline in the army as they engaged in an orgy of plundering and drinking. It has been supposed that the enlisted men rationalized their behaviour by the myth that Wellington wanted the town punished. The people of Badajoz have not forgotten this and recently refused a request by the Royal Regiment of Fusiliers to place a memorial plaque to their part in the action.

24. A fusilier recollected the events, 'When we got into Badajoz I saw some of our fellows coming out of a shop with clocks and copper images, so I thought, "I may as well have something too." Into the shop I went and took a small watch with jewels on the back. My Sergeant laid hold of me and said I must come out to help him to get the men together. I slipped the watch into my pocket and thought myself mighty clever not to have taken a large article.' 'My recollections of "Old Hugh General"', from Howel Thomas, *A History of the Royal Welsh Fusiliers, late the twenty-third Regiment*, p. 16.

The selfish plundering made many a soldier rich for a short period, MacDonald related that, 'some of our men were obliged to buy mules to carry off their plunder. Others have delivered to the amount of 900 Dollars to their officers to take charge of.' RWFM, Acc. 5935, MacDonald to father, 12 Jun 1812.

25. Possibly this refers to the cathedral, Catedral de San Juan.

26. Battalion casualties at Badajoz were: Captain Maw and Lieutenant Collins killed, along with 1 ensign, 4 sergeants and 29 rank and file. Lieutenant Colonel Ellis, Brevet-Major Leaky, Captains Hawtyn and Stainforth, Lieutenants G. Browne, T. Farmer, Fielding, Harrison, Tucker, Whalley and Wingate, Second Lieutenants Holmes and Llewelyn (subsequently died of wounds), 7 sergeants, 1 drummer (Bentinck) and 84 rank and file wounded; 1 sergeant and 19 rank and file were listed as missing.

MacDonald was not listed as wounded, though he received a light wound during the battle, 'a shot in the left arm has merely gone through a little flesh, the other happened to hit on the knot of my sash which was luckily tied in front and did not penetrate the skin, though it knocked me down for a few seconds'. RWFM, Acc. 5935, MacDonald to father, 26 July 1812.

Harrison's wound was more serious; he had pushed himself forward and was halfway up a siege ladder ascending the breach when a ball passed through his right arm, around an inch above the elbow. As he recoiled from the impact, another ball fired from above struck the back part of his right shoulder, ran six inches down his arm and then came to rest in his right calf. He struggled to maintain a grip on the ladder and fell back into the ditch, which was full of his dead and dying companions, and was fortunate not to receive any further wounds during the night. Like many of the attackers wounded in the breaches, Harrison lay unattended all night – it was not until late morning that anything was done for them. He considered the entire affair to be a most desperate one with both resolute defenders and attacks but 'I was attended with my usual good fortune and was able to get off this business cheap.' RWFM, Acc. 1335, Harrison to mother, 23 April 1812.

The bullet which passed through Harrison's right shoulder was cut out of his arm by a surgeon. The bullet is still in existence; embedded in it are fragments from the gold lace of Harrison's epaulette which it penetrated first. Harrison's wounds were sufficient to oblige the wearing of a sling for the remainder of his active service.

27. Possibly Private Harry Marsh, born at Wigan, Lancashire, former trade – weaver. Attested 5 May 1796 aged eighteen. Awarded bars for actions at Egypt, Corunna and Badajoz. Holme & Kirby, *Medal Rolls*, p. 196.
28. No soldier of this name is listed in the medal rolls.
29. Wellington to Earl of Liverpool in Oman, *History of the Peninsular War*, Vol. V. p. 255.
30. The original document is held by the Royal Welch Fusiliers Museum.

Chapter Seven

Salamanca and the Offensive of 1813

The capture of the two great fortresses of Badajoz and Ciudad Rodrigo gave Wellington the option of taking on the French army under Marmont in the north or Soult in the south. He decided to move north, whilst retaining an ability to keep Soult occupied. After a march north, the Fusilier Brigade was given time to re-organize and re-supply at the village of Traves. Here the 1/23rd received reinforcements from the 2nd Battalion which took total numbers up to a meagre strength of 331 all ranks.[1]

> The town of Badajoz having been cleared of the slain by its British captors, the dead before the walls having been buried, the wounded having been attended to, and the soldiers furious with the excitement of the terrible slaughter and with the drink found among the plunder, being once more reduced to order, the British Army again pressed onward in their victorious career, in pursuit of the now retreating French.
>
> Wellington's object was now to break the communication between the French Army under Soult and the one under Marmont, which was by means of a bridge of boats at Almarez, defended by strong works at both sides of the river.[2] This was accomplished by storming these works and capturing nearly 1000 prisoners and then Wellington pursued Marmont to the River Douro, where the latter was joined by another large army under General Bonnet.

Marmont and Bonnet's commands consolidated at the River Douro on 4 July, establishing a force of close to 50,000. Wellington lacked a decisive number of troops to conduct offensive operations, whilst the French, although in slightly greater numbers, faced extended lines of communication and could not sustain their dispositions. Marmont went on the offensive, forcing Wellington to retreat by conducting a flanking move. The French pursued the allies for six days, as Wellington hoped to exhaust the French and would not commit to a battle unless a suitable opportunity arose.[3] On 21 July, the opposing forces reached a point of

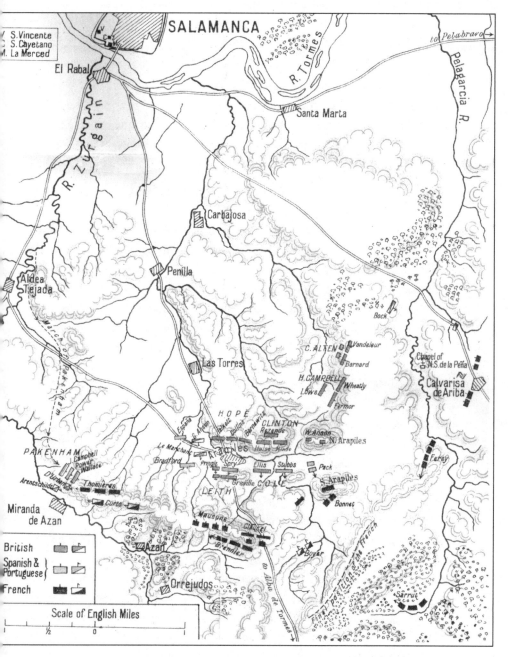

Salamanca, 22 July 1812. Dispositions in the early stages of the battle.
(*From C. W. Oman,* History of the Peninsular War)

confrontation some seven miles to the south-east of Salamanca. Thunder and lightning that evening provided an ominous suggestion of the violence that was impending but the morning of 22 July was warm and sunny.

> These combined forces obliged Wellington to halt. Then the hostile armies both marched forward side by side within a very short distance of each other, each watching a favourable moment for the onset. They had not long to wait before our friend Bentinck and his comrades were again enveloped in the smoke of battle, the battle of Salamanca.

The terrain of the battlefield was a series of rocky ridges interspersed in rolling countryside, punctuated by the hill features of the Lesser Arapile and the Greater Arapile. The dispositions could be summarized as the Allies to the north, focused around the Lesser Arapile and the French to the south, around the Greater Arapile. Wellington had disposed his forces well. The most forward defensive position was that of the 4th Division around the village of Los Arapiles with five of the other six infantry divisions within two miles of this position. The hidden Allied dispositions led Marmont to perceive that Wellington was continuing to manoeuvre and accordingly the French were set off in pursuit. That the French had a poor under-standing of Allied dispositions was to prove to be a key advantage to Wellington.

Marmont was confident and anticipated that Wellington would retreat. He ordered two divisions to seize key terrain beyond the Greater Arapile but the lead division became over-extended and its northern flank was vulnerable. Wellington was patiently observing the French dispositions when he noted this opportunity and was quick to take action. 'Lord Wellington was at dinner when he was informed of this movement; he saw at once the advantage which had been given; he rose in such haste as to overturn the table, exclaiming that "Marmont's good genius has forsaken him," and in an instant was on horseback.'[4]

The 3rd, 4th and 5th Divisions were immediately ordered by Wellington to attack. The 3rd Division moved against the lead French division and, after firing a volley, charged at the enemy, who panicked and fled in general confusion. As the 5th Division advanced on another French infantry division it was accompanied by a heavy cavalry brigade. The French, seeing this ominous threat, formed regimental squares, which unfortunately for them gave the 5th Division the best conditions to rout them. About the same time, Marmont was seriously wounded, which added to the confusion.

The 4th Division at this time had two brigades, the Fusilier Brigade and a Portuguese brigade, providing a total of seven battalions. The division was tasked to advance up a slope toward a ridge-line held by the French. The enemy artillery fired heavily upon the advancing troops but the crest of the hill was reached and five French infantry battalions were engaged in disciplined volleys by the fusiliers and the Portuguese brigade, which pushed them back. A second French brigade held in reserve moved forward decisively in good order. The Portuguese troops were attacked on their flank and crumbled, then the French resolutely continued the advance and the unthinkable happened, the Fusilier Brigade broke and, nearly as a body, turned and ran. French cavalry pursued the troops, who formed ragged squares as protection, whilst two brigades of French infantry advanced to take advantage of the situation.

The 23rd Fusiliers, was thrice beset by masses of the enemy's cavalry, but each time beat them off by forming squares and pouring forth destructive volleys. The first time they were taken completely unawares, through mistaking, in the dense smoke, the French squadrons for our own squadrons, returning as they supposed from a charge. Not a shot was fired until the big troopers began cutting down the front ranks, and their horses had well nigh trampled down our formation ere our men could recover their dismay. Several were cleft to the earth within a few yards of where Bentinck stood, and he narrowly saved his head from the sweep of a Frenchman's sabre. Captain Harrison, of his company, was smitten through the right arm, which was useless to him all his life after.[5]

Several rapid discharges of musketry, delivered within bayonet reach, hurled back the dangerous squadrons, broken and ruined. Lieutenant MacDonald then, after Captain Harrison's wound, took command of the company.[6] Sir Lowry Cole, the General of this, the 4th Division, was gallantly leading it onward when a cannon ball struck his horse and rolled both to the ground. The General struggled to his feet covered with the blood of his dead horse, and waving his plumed hat to signify that he was unhurt (for at that moment so great was the roar of battle that no voice could be heard) he instantly mounted another, but had not got many paces when it was also wounded and the General was still spurring it forward when he dropped from his saddle with a ball through his thigh.

'The Spanish troops were assisting us there but they saw but little use. For when we came into action they retreated instead of coming forward until Wellington observed it and he sent dispatches to their

Generals to rally them together again and bring forward again. We lost a great many men through their behaviour so bad.[7] The French stood until dark.'

Fortunately for the 4th Division, Wellington had sent the 6th Division to advance in support. This successfully stopped the French and then the 6th Division advanced up the slope, pushing back the French as it did so. For a period musket fire was traded until eventually the French relented and retreated. The battle concluded with the French reserve division coming forward to form squares on the flanks and use the cover of a nearby wood to pour volleys into the pursuing allies. The declining light, the cover of the woods and the efforts of the reserve division allowed the French to make a disordered withdrawal.

The French initially retreated to the south-east of Salamanca and, due to the withdrawal of a Spanish garrison, were able to cross the substantial obstacle of the River Tormes without significant hindrance. Wellington's army, although splendidly victorious, had no momentum to conduct a pursuit.

It had been a vicious battle. The figures for French casualties are notoriously difficult to assess for accuracy, but it was reported that 7,000 French were killed, wounded and missing, whilst a further 7,000 were captured along with twenty guns and two eagles.[8] The French Generals Bonnet, Thomières and Ferey were killed at Salamanca. The Allied figures were 5,214 killed, wounded and missing. The Fusilier Brigade commenced the battle with 1,357 ranks and sustained 380 casualties.[9]

After the battle had ended our hungry and ill-clad soldiers began the work, almost necessary in those days of bad supply, of overhauling the dead, both their own and the enemy's in search of any food contained in the haversacks, or a decent pair of shoes or other article of clothing which might replace their own used up outfit.[10]

After some recuperation, the battalion marched to Valladolid[11] before it became clear to Wellington that the French could not reinforce Marmont's defeated army and so he decided to advance upon Madrid.

The morning after the battle of Salamanca the main body of the Allies pressed on after the defeated French, and our cavalry overtaking them captured 900 more prisoners.[12] They were followed to Valladolid, then to Burgos,[13] in which stronghold they finally took refuge, well-knowing that it was too strong to be taken by such appliances as Lord Wellington had then with him.

Bentinck's Division being one of those that had suffered heaviest in the battle, was left to bring up the rear more leisurely and it remained at Salamanca for two or three days caring for its men before it set out on the march. It came up with Wellington's force on July 1st 1813, the whole army crossing the River Douro, so often the line of combat during those stormy campaigns.[14] Wellington with the main body pushed on over the mountain into New Castile, and thence into the capital Madrid, which they reached on the 12th August, King Joseph, Napoleon's brother, having fled from it the day before on hearing of their approach.[15] The reception of the victors by the oppressed Spaniards was enthusiastic, all business being suspended and every building decorated.[16]

The battalion records state that it was posted at the Escurial, which is an exceptionally beautiful sixteenth-century monastery, now listed as a World Heritage site. After a few weeks, Wellington took most of his army to besiege the important town of Burgos. The 4th Division (and with it the 1/23rd) was spared this task and had six weeks in the relative comfort of the Escurial to recover from the trials of campaign. There were only six fit officers in the battalion, including Major Dalmer, the temporary commanding officer, who was himself recovering from a wound sustained at Salamanca, and around 200 men.

In two or three weeks, two large armies of fresh foes, under Marmont and Clauzel,[17] began to approach the Douro. Wellington withdrew his forces from Madrid and came to meet them. The French, however, retired before this powerful reinforcement beyond Valencia. Our Fourth Division then returned with Wellington to lay siege to the great fortress of Burgos. It did not at that time approach near the place, but lay at some distance along with another Division to keep off the French. 12,000 for the Allies formed the besieging force,[18] the 5th and 6th Divisions were British[19] and the remainder Spaniards. The size of Burgos, its admirable position, strong defences, and large supply of ammunition and provisions, decided Wellington to attempt its capture, though he had but very inadequate means; only eight large guns[20] and a scanty supply of ammunition.

Burgos had a very important geographical location, lying next to the main highway running from France to Valladolid. The fortress was a substantial castle, stood on a steep hill, with supporting artillery positions on two nearby hills, able to dominate the two bridges crossing the River Arlanzón. The French, during their possession, undertook limited improvements to the defences and provided a garrison of roughly 2,000 men. In all, it was a vital location for enabling French operations in central Spain. Wellington's attempts to take Burgos were not successful. He lacked adequate equipment and ordnance. A month of effort and three attempted assaults brought nothing but 2,000 casualties.

The French took advantage of this situation to consolidate and reinforce their armies, forming one Army of Portugal, under Marshal Soult, which advanced to relieve Burgos and re-occupy Madrid. Wellington's force at Burgos was exposed by being around 150 miles away from the nearest credible supporting force, Lieutenant General Rowland Hill's joint Anglo-Portuguese and Spanish army, which was predominantly disposed for the defence of Madrid. The geographical division between Wellington's two corps and the numerical advantage of the French meant that abandoning the siege of Burgos and the occupation of Madrid was the only sensible option.

Wellington lifted the siege of Burgos. The initial withdrawal from Burgos, at night in the face of the enemy, was achieved after great preparation and planning by Wellington, including the muffling of cart wheels by straw. Although the French pursued and harassed the retreating Allies they surprisingly did not mount a serious attack. On 31 October the battalion and other allied units withdrew from Madrid and Wellington consolidated his forces. A defensive posture was established in front of Salamanca but Soult opted to conduct a flanking manoeuvre. The number and dispositions of the French caused Wellington to order a further withdrawal to Ciudad Rodrigo on 15 November.

> Bentinck's Division was ordered up from its distant post for the last assault, but was not required to take part in it,[21] for two days after, the retreat began. It was a retreat that it is said, tasked the Chief's talents as severely as any of his battles. A hostile army threatened his front and another was coming up in his rear, amounting together to 90,000, against his 50,000, most of whom were unreliable Spaniards. For protection against the latter he destroyed every bridge when his last man had crossed it, and left strong rear guards to defend the passage as long as possible.[22] The foes in front he awed by skillful positioning of his troops and threatening demonstrations.
>
> 'It became a long retreat for they drove us down into Portugal. We lost a great many men in the retreat what with taken provisions and with want a great many died.[23] It is more than I can describe the

hardships we had to get through what with hunger and fatigue and for want of shelter. One morning when I got up I found nine or ten men lying around me dead and stiff. We was forbidden to plunder if it was known but we were so put to it or we could not have lived at all. They would not allow us to fall out of the ranks and get a drink of water by the road side. There was many a score flogged for it.'[24]

The old soldier Bentinck wags his head mournfully over the memories of that painful retreat. He well remembers the torrents of rain that daily and nightly drenched them through, the muddy plains that pulled their worn shoes off their feet, the mountain roads that cut those feet till every step was imprinted with blood. The suffering soldiers tore the warm hides from the beasts as the butchers killed them, and wrapped them round their wounded feet in lieu of shoes.[25] He recalls the figures they cut with trousers ragged away upwards to above or downwards to below the knee, as the case might be, so that they had to cut up their blankets to mend them in order to preserve anything like decency.

No fires could be lighted, so heavy was the rain, no provisions could be got, save by plunder, and in spite of the presence of Wellington himself, they did plunder. So discontented did their condition become that he forbore to punish the offence as was his wont, contenting himself with generally censuring their misconduct after the retreat was over.[26] Bentinck became an adept in stealing pigs, droves of which ranged the woods through which the retreating army passed.[27] He used to go with one or two companions and slay them in the darkness, meeting many other hungry assassins on the same commission. The pork he asserts, was flabby and tough, being fed on acorns, and the bristles as stiff and thick as those of a shoe brush.

The withdrawal to Ciudad Rodrigo took four painful days in terrible conditions. The retreat cost the allies 3,000 soldiers dead, injured or captured. The battalion lost one officer and thirty-eight men. The French ceased pursuing when it became clear that the allied force would reach Ciudad Rodrigo, and both armies then retired to cantonments for the winter. The battalion took up quarters in the Portuguese border village of Soitella on 5 December.

The end of operations was welcomed by the battalion. The men tried to recuperate physically and repair clothing and other personal equipment, while the officers dealt with the wider consequences of the retreat. Unfortunately, the general health of the battalion was poor with a constantly high rate of sickness amongst the men.[28]

'They made us a present of a pair of shoes each when we got into Portugal again. We stopped there all winter in cantonments.' Our old soldier spent the Christmas with tolerable jollity. Several men of his company had served their term of enlistment,[29] and of course could either enter again or await an opportunity of going home. The large bounty then offered for enlistment – 16 guineas[30] – and the difficulty of returning home, decided them to remain. The guineas were claimed, and at the rate of two pence a pint for wine in that country, the whole company made merry for nearly a fortnight. A period of indulgence of a fortnight was granted to the whole army on reaching the end of the retreat, and the officers left them almost to themselves. During the winter some reinforcements had arrived from England,[31] and all the men had been carefully equipped for the campaign of the coming season.

The Portuguese living there did not at first know the value of the guineas and refused to let the soldiers have much for them, but on an official proclamation of the value being made they were just as eager to get hold of them, as they had been dubious before. Some of the soldiers were billeted on them, and exchanged their guineas into wine so freely, that the clay floors of the dwellings became covered in puddles of it. When the money was all spent, some ingenious fellows of Bentinck's company devised the expedient of drawing bills on the Colonel, under fictitious names. As the old farmers and cottagers could not read a word of them and the guineas had turned out so well, they were readily persuaded that these worthless scraps of paper were of equal value, notwithstanding the stipulation that they were not to present them to the Colonel till the troops were about to move.

When the order to march did come, the Colonel was surrounded by eager Portuguese, who had come for their money. Deep were their protestations when he gruffly informed them that he had no such men in his regiment as the 'Sergeant Glazecap,' 'Corporal Musket,' and so on, whose names were affixed to these little bills.

In April 1813 training in preparation for the campaign was increased, with route marches, additional drilling and a welcome issue of new personal equipment. In mid-May Wellington took the field, with an army of some 81,000 British, Spanish and Portuguese troops. The French had around 200,000 troops in the Peninsula, but the activities of Spanish guerrillas and the Royal Navy provided distractions in the north and south. The consequence was that the French could muster about 80,000 men for the forthcoming 1813 campaign.

Wellington's plan was audacious. He intended to outflank the French and cut their communications by marching north of Madrid and concurrently switching the allied supply lines to ports in northern Spain. The allies advanced in four huge columns, sufficiently far apart for the French to have great difficulty in fighting an effective rearguard action.

> The object of Marshal Jourdan[32] was to keep the allies on their side of the Douro, for which purpose he had strongly fortified every fordable part of the rapid river, rendering, his task, he thought, very easy. Sir Thomas Graham's[33] Division, however, soon forced a passage at one point, Wellington with the Second Division bore swiftly down on Salamanca, and ere the French could quit it, took 200 prisoners and some guns from their rear guard. The Third Division under Sir Rowland Hill,[34] soon after joined it and they crossed the Douro together and joined Sir Thomas Graham on the other side, thus scattering in a few days the carefully prepared plans of the French leader by a few brilliant marches from quarters that he had deemed quite impracticable.

> 'In the year 1813 we began very early to advance on the country after them again till we came to a place called Busaco.[35] There they blew the bridge up that was across the water and we had to wade it across up to our middle. The enemy retreated and went to a place called Adowall and they blew the bridge up again after them. We had to cross the river up to our breast and the current was so strong that we had very hard work to get across.[36] Some of the donkeys belonging to the women was taken off their feet and taken down with the stream.'

The next major obstacle was the River Ebro, which the 4th Division crossed on 15 June unopposed. The French were making efforts to fight an effective rearguard action but it was increasingly apparent that a decisive battle was going to be fought.

> Marshal Jourdan once more hurriedly abandoned Madrid by withdrawing an army from there, evacuated his headquarters at Valladolid, and retreated before Wellington from Valladolid to the

Carrion,[37] from the Carrion to Stornesa, from there to Burgos, and from
Burgos – whose impregnable fortifications the French blew up in such
haste as to kill many of their own men[38] – to the Ebro,[39] where they
halted in such a formidable position as to keep the Iron Duke at bay. He
therefore feigned to retire, but marched his troops by a circuitous route
down the river, crossed it, passed unopposed through a strong country,
and on June 18th suddenly came upon two French Brigades, attacked
and defeated them[40] with a loss of 300 men and drove them forward to
Vitoria[41] where King Joseph was holding his court.

Graham's Division fell upon an outnumbering force of the enemy,
defeated them and then pursued them to Espesa, and on the next day,
the 19th Wellington attacked their rear guard[42] and drove them upon
the main body. The same, day Joseph arranged his troops for battle
before Vitoria; the day after Wellington came up with him, drew all his
Divisions together, and prepared for the onset.

————•————

1. In May 1812 the battalion received a draft of seventy-four reinforcements from the
    2nd Battalion. On 25 May, the battalion was inspected and was recorded as having
    strength of 331 all ranks. At this time, Lieutenant Colonel Ellis was temporarily
    commanding the Fusilier Brigade, and at some point close to this Major Offley,
    who had completed six months' suspension from service for an incident whilst
    serving with the Portuguese, took on temporary command of the battalion.

2. Almaraz is about 100 miles south-east of Ciudad Rodrigo. The River Tagus flows
    east–west across much of Spain and flows just south of Almaraz. In order to
    enhance manoeuvre options and shorten lines of communications, the French
    constructed a 250-yard-long pontoon bridge here in the autumn of 1809. On the
    north bank a fort had 400 men, with a defended location on the south side.
    A further fort with 450 men was on high ground to the south whilst five miles to
    the south along the main road a further fort, a tower and a house had also been
    fortified. On 7 May 1812 Wellington ordered General Hill to destroy the bridge,
    which he duly did on 20 May, the French losing over 400 men, of whom two-thirds
    were taken prisoner.

3. It was recorded that Lieutenant Leonard was killed on 20 June by an errant French
    cannon ball whilst sitting on a hill watching a small cavalry engagement. The 1/23rd
    was lying in a valley between two hills, with a Portuguese regiment stationed on the
    hill opposite. 'I went to look what the French were doing, and stood on the watch for
    about two minutes, when a cannon ball from the enemy struck Lieutenant Leonard,
    who was standing beside me, and knocked off his shoulder and back bone, so that
    his head came upon my foot. The same ball, rising again, struck and killed two

Portuguese soldiers on the hill side opposite.' Roberts, 'Incidents in the Life of an Old Fusilier', No. 1, p. 23.

4. Napier, *History of the War in the Peninsula*, Vol. IV, p. 262. It has also been suggested that he commented to his Spanish liaison officer, 'Mon Cher Alava, Marmont est perdu.' M. Glover, *The Peninsular War 1807–1814*, p. 201.

5. John Christopher Harrison transferred from the 20th Foot to become a second lieutenant in the 23rd in March 1805. Possibly it was the family friendship with a dashing 22-year-old major, Henry Ellis, of the 23rd Foot and his descriptions of active service and honour which prompted Harrison's transfer. He was promoted to lieutenant on 27 May 1806 and served in this capacity with the 1st Battalion at Copenhagen, in North America and the Martinique expedition. He was promoted to captain in 1812. He was wounded at Albuera and at the storming of Badajoz, where the wound was so serious that he was required to wear his right arm in a sling for the rest of his life – it is presumed that this is the wound that Bentinck comments upon. He was not present at Waterloo, joining the 1st Battalion on 24 November 1815 with reinforcements from the 2nd Battalion. Harrison was subsequently promoted to major on 29 October 1825, during service in Gibraltar, and lieutenant colonel on 22 July 1830. He commanded the 1st Battalion July 1830–March 1837. Harrison is renowned in regimental history for formally establishing the right to wear the 'flash'. Harrison was entitled to the MGSM with claps Martinique, Ciudad Rodrigo and Badajoz.

6. John MacDonald joined the battalion as a second lieutenant on 26 October 1809 and was promoted to lieutenant on 10 October 1811. He was seriously wounded at both Albuera and Salamanca. He was with the battalion at Waterloo, as one of three subalterns in the Grenadier Company, in which Bentinck also served on the day. MacDonald was eventually promoted captain on 28 August 1827 and appointed paymaster on 16 October 1828. He retired on 15 March 1831.

7. This is most likely a comment on the Portuguese troops that formed part of the 4th Division and is slightly unjust.

8. Lieutenant Pearce of the 2/44th East Essex Regiment captured an eagle of the 62nd Line. An eagle of the 22nd Line was subsequently discovered amongst the detritus of the battlefield.

9. The battalion lost Major Offley and ten men killed. Lieutenant Colonel Ellis, Major Dalmer, Captain G. Browne, Lieutenants Clyde, Enoch, Fryer and J. MacDonald and ninety men were wounded. Between the Allies and the French, around 8,000 men were treated by surgeons.

10. The substantial numbers of wounded had an uncomfortable night as Roberts narrated, 'My next battle was that of Salamanca, where I was wounded at half-past three o'clock in the afternoon. My commanding officer, Colonel Ellis, was twice hit. But the result was as usual – another victory. A number of wounded officers and men, as well as myself, lay all night on the field of battle. A long night it was to those who were conscious of our position! In the morning they sent Spanish carts for us, and

carried us to the hospitals in Salamanca.' Roberts, 'Incidents in the Life of an Old Fusilier', No. 2, p. 22. The nocturnal activities of the camp followers ensured that many of the wounded did not see the dawn. It was rumoured that Major Offley, who fell wounded when in command of the battalion, met this fate. Francis Needham Offley was an interesting character, allegedly the illegitimate son of Major General Francis Jack Needham, an Anglo-Irish aristocrat and aide-de-camp to King George III. Offley had joined the battalion as a second lieutenant in February 1796. He was infamous for being suspended from the Army by Wellington from 1 January 1812 to 30 June 1812 as a result of a court martial following an incident when he was in Portuguese service.

11. A city in central Spain, upon the Pisuerga River, about 75 miles north-east of Salamanca.
12. The lack of Allied cavalry actually precluded a comprehensive pursuit of the French.
13. A city in northern Spain approximately 100 miles to the north-east of Valladolid.
14. The River Douro is one of the most significant rivers of the Iberian Peninsula, running 540 miles from north-central Spain to the Portuguese coast at Porto. It was a key defensive obstacle at a number of times during the Peninsula conflict.
15. Joseph Bonaparte, elder brother of the Emperor Napoleon. He was appointed by his brother as King of Spain, styled as Joseph I, ruling from 6 June 1808 to 11 December 1813.
16. Lieutenant MacDonald wrote that, 'Nothing could equal the joy of the inhabitants on seeing us enter Madrid, in fact no language that I can use can convey the least idea of it, they surrounded us in immense crowds, embracing the soldiers, pulling the officers very nearly off their horses, & every body exclaiming, "Viva los Inglezos". Any unconcerned spectator would have thought them mad, the Young and Old dancing about all parts of the City, the church Bells all ringing, the Bands of the Different Regiments playing, the houses most beautifully decorated with tapestry, & at night illuminated, in fact the whole scene exceeded any description that can be given of it.' RWFM, Acc. 5935, MacDonald to father, 25 August 1812.
17. Bertrand Clauzel, Marshal of France (1772–1842). He fought in the Peninsula and distinguished himself with the withdrawal from Salamanca and the retreat to Burgos. In 1815 he commanded an army in France, then fled to America, returning five years later. He subsequently sat in the Chamber of Deputies and led the military campaigns in Algeria in 1831 and 1835–7.
18. The size of this force is more likely to have been around 35,000 and of Anglo-Portuguese composition, rather than Anglo-Spanish.
19. An error. The British 1st and 6th Divisions conducted the siege.
20. Three 18-pounders and five 24-pounders.
21. The battalion had remained in Madrid.
22. Wellington blew up all the bridges over the River Douro.
23. Allied casualties have been estimated as around 3,000 dead or taken prisoner. In the immediate aftermath of the retreat 22,000 Allied troops were listed as sick or missing.

24. In regimental records there is no mention of such flogging and indeed a review of the behaviour of Lieutenant Colonel Ellis 1808–15 illustrates that, although he enforced high standards of discipline, he most commonly did not implement all the lashes that had been sentenced. In the six months covering the retreat and the following period Ellis had awarded a total of 8,600 lashes but had remitted 5,105 of them.

25. Numerous accounts comment on the particularly inclement conditions with substantial rain and strong winds. Thomas Browne wrote that, 'Groupes [*sic*] of women & children & drum boys lay perishing with cold – some had already died in a sort of rolled up posture – others were not yet dead, but convulsed with a sort of hysterical laugh which sometimes precedes death – there were stout soldiers too, who had breathed their last by the roadside on that bitter night, & many a gallant spirit, that would have been unmoved in the thickest fire had been bowed down by cold & hunger.' Browne, *Napoleonic War Journal*, p. 197.

26. Immediately after the completion of the retreat, John MacDonald wrote that it had been 'the first time I have been in a serious retreat & I hope it shall be the last'. RWFM, Acc. 5935, MacDonald to father, 26 November 1813.

27. The desire for pork was the downfall of some of the battalion: on 11 December 1812, Privates Batt, Edwards and Cotter were sentenced to receive 200 lashes each, actually receiving 170 each, for 'destroying a pig' and, on 8 March 1813, Private McLaughlin was sentenced to 300 lashes, actually receiving 75, 'on suspicion of killing a pig'.

28. The battalion entered winter cantonments at Soitella on 5 December 1812. A muster parade on 25 December showed 26 officers, 30 sergeants, 14 drummers and 294 rank and file present fit.

29. Under normal circumstances enlistment was for life, until the soldier's services were no longer required or until he was no longer able to perform his duties. In 1806 the concept of limited-service enlistment was introduced, intended to improve the attraction of military life. For the infantry this brought in a three-period system of service: seven years in the first period, followed by two (optional) periods, each also of seven years. These men would have been among the first 'limited service' men in the army.

30. The enlistment bounty for new recruits was at this time £23 17s 6d.

31. Captains Dalmer and Strangeways, Lieutenants Cowell, Harris and Wingate, Second Lieutenants Gledstanes and Griffiths, and Assistant Surgeon Smith, with 2 sergeants and 72 rank and file arrived from the 2nd Battalion on 25 December.

32. Marshal Jean-Baptiste Jourdan (1762–1833). In 1776 served in a French regiment in the American War of Independence. During the French Revolution he rose rapidly to become Commander-in-Chief of the Army of the North in 1793. He fell out of political favour but then returned, being victorious at Fleurus in 1794, and in 1796 led the advance toward Vienna which culminated in a decisive defeat at Amberg and a difficult retreat. This failure removed Jourdan from military command, whereupon he became a politician for a short period, drafting the famous conscription law of 1798. In 1799, again in military command, his force was defeated at Stockach.

He then returned to politics, before becoming a marshal of France in 1804 and serving as a military advisor to Joseph Bonaparte as King of Naples and then King of Spain. During the Peninsular War his position as advisor to Joseph meant he was undermined by supporters of Napoleon. After the defeat at Vitoria, Jourdan did not hold any real command until the restoration of Napoleon in 1815. After the fall of Napoleon, he was reconciled to the Bourbons and became a politician, holding a number of important appointments. At Vitoria his marshal's baton was captured by Corporal Fox of the 18th Hussars, who unscrewed the gilded caps and put them in his pocket as he perceived these to be most valuable. The baton was stolen in the night by a sergeant of the 2/87th, who got the credit for finding it, but subsequently Fox gave the caps to his commanding officer who sent them on to Wellington and hence the Prince Regent.

33. General Thomas Graham, 1st Baron Lynedoch (1748–1843). Born into a wealthy Scottish family, he concentrated on land management. Following the death of his wife in 1792 and the mistreatment of her corpse by the French, he joined the British Army as a volunteer and, after experiencing the defence of Toulon against the French revolutionary government, he returned to Scotland and raised the 90th Foot, which he commanded at Gibraltar in 1795. In 1796 as British Commissioner he participated with the Austrian Army in the defence of Mantua. In 1798 he fought at Minorca and then in the subsequent two-year siege of Malta. The 90th Foot then served in Ireland and the West Indies before participating in the 1808 Portugal campaign, including the retreat to Corunna. In 1809, as a major general, Graham commanded troops in the Walcheren expedition. Then promoted lieutenant general, he led an Anglo-Portuguese force in the defence of Cadiz, raising the French siege by defeating them at the Battle of Barossa. Graham then joined Wellington's army and fought at Ciudad Rodrigo. Subsequently he commanded the left wing of Wellington's army, participating in the success at Vitoria, the capture of San Sebastian and the eventual advance into France. Ill-health forced a return to the United Kingdom but Graham returned to command British forces in Holland in 1814. He received a peerage in 1814 and numerous other honours, reaching the rank of general in 1821.

34. General Rowland Hill, 1st Viscount of Almaraz (1772–1842). Commissioned into the 38th Foot he saw service in Egypt, Ireland, Hanover and the siege of Toulon. From 1808 he served in the Peninsula, commanding a brigade at Vimiero, Corunna and the second Battle of Porto. He then led the 2nd Division from the 1810 invasion of Badajoz, including at Busaco, the siege of Badajoz, the battles of Almaraz, Vitoria, the Pyrenees, Nive, Orthez and Toulouse. He later commanded the Second Corps at the Battle of Waterloo and in 1828 succeeded the Duke of Wellington as Commander-in-Chief.

35. It is unclear where this refers to.

36. Most likely a reference to the crossing of the River Esla where the stream was faster and deeper than anticipated, with a width of at least thirty yards.

37. Carrión de los Condes.

38. The French mined the defences but an accident occurred with two detonations happening before the fortress was evacuated, resulting in the death of around 400 French.

39. A significant river, with a source in Fontibre, Cantabria, before discharging into the Mediterranean in the province of Tarragona, running a total length of 576 miles.

40. The engagement at Osma.

41. Vitoria-Gasteiz, the capital of the province of Alava in the Basque country of north-east Spain.

42. The engagement at Subijana-Morillas. The battalion had a lieutenant and one sergeant and three rank and file wounded. Regimental records name the dead lieutenant as Sidley but it is most likely that, after being shot through the lungs and badly wounded, he went on to recover and serve in No. 6 Company at Waterloo where he was again wounded. He later participated in the Burmese War and was appointed a military knight of Windsor and was governor of the military knights in 1875, finally dying in 1876. He was the son of George Sidley who was promoted from the ranks to become the battalion quartermaster in 1808.

Chapter Eight

Vitoria, the Pyrenees and Sorauren

---•---

The town of Vitoria was not a particularly suitable defensive location but it was a hub for five key roads; most importantly these were the Madrid to France road and the Bilbao to Logroño road. Wellington was advancing quickly to force a battle before the French could concentrate additional forces. He was able to assemble some 52,000 British troops, 28,000 Portuguese and 25,000 Spanish. The French force was 66,000 strong, including 11,000 cavalry and 138 artillery pieces and from 19 June began to occupy a defensive position to the west of Vitoria, anticipating Wellington would attack from this direction.

> At Vitoria, the French had about 70,000 men and 100 pieces of artillery. The Allies were weaker in artillery, but had nearly 75,000 men, though three divisions were Spaniards, who never could be trusted to do much fighting when any crisis came.

For the advance on Vitoria, the Allied force was divided into four columns in pursuit of Wellington's ambition of surrounding and capturing the French. The right column consisted of two brigades of cavalry, the 2nd Division, a Portuguese division, a Spanish division and some artillery. The right centre column was commanded by Wellington with four brigades of cavalry, the 4th Division, the Light Division and artillery. The left centre column had the 3rd Division, the 7th Division and two artillery batteries. The left column consisted of two brigades of cavalry, the 1st Division, the 5th Division, a Spanish division, independent Portuguese brigades and two batteries of artillery. Wellington's intention was to mount rear and flanking attacks first and then, when the French were distracted, to attack with the 4th and Light Divisions the centre mass of the French position.

The French position was enclosed by heights to the south and the River Zadorra west and north. A tactical mistake was to leave a bridge over the Zadorra at Trespuentes intact, which the allies were quick to take advantage of, with the Light Division crossing. The 3rd Division also crossed the Zadorra and began to attack the French right flank, although suffering heavy casualties in one brigade that could not be adequately supported.

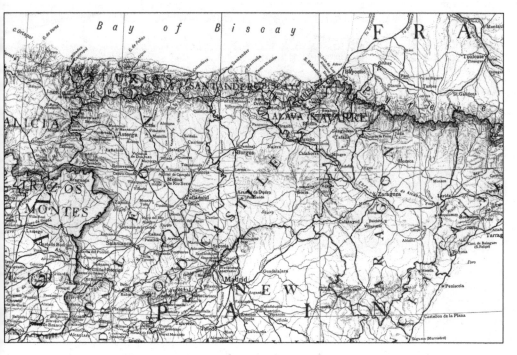

Area of Operations, 1812–13. (*From: J. W. Fortescue,* History of the British Army)

The 4th Division crossed the Zadorra by way of a bridge and a ford, then advanced in three brigade lines, with the division's light companies on the left flank. The terrain of hedges and ditches placed the cavalry at a disadvantage and the unrelenting advance of the Light and 4th Divisions very soon forced the French to flee in all directions. Concurrently villages to the north-west and north of Vitoria that were situated on the roads most likely to be used for a French withdrawal were captured.

In the late afternoon Joseph Bonaparte ordered a retreat by way of the Salvatierra road, but the majority of the French force was already engaged in this activity and, to speed their movement, a great deal of equipment and other such items was dumped. Two divisions of French troops fought a commendable rearguard action on high ground, which gave the opportunity for battered and disparate formations and regiments to flee. The mass of abandoned equipment also slowed the Allies, as collective discipline broke down, with all taking the opportunity to plunder what the French had left behind.

Allied losses were estimated to be some 5,000 men killed and wounded, with the majority being British. French losses were slightly higher at 5,200; in addition,

some 2,800 were captured. The most important loss was of artillery pieces, which
was a serious degradation to French combat power. In all 151 artillery guns were
taken, more than 400 caissons, more than 14,000 rounds of artillery ammunition,
and nearly two million musket cartridges.[1] French pride was also greatly
undermined. Joseph Bonaparte was very nearly captured and his carriages, fulsome
baggage, food supplies and equipment fell into British hands.[2] It has been
suggested that Wellington was initially content for his troops to plunder but then
grew frustrated at the breakdown of collective discipline.[3]

> Lieutenant Browne,[4] a young officer of Bentinck's company of the
> Fusiliers was sent with some of the captured trophies of the fleeing
> King, and received his promotion on arrival there. A Sergeant of the
> same company, whom Bentinck knew well, had his leg shot away and
> died from it, another a Lancashire man was also mortally hit.[5]
>
> Bentinck did not come in for much of the immense plunder, the
> older soldiers clearing all before them so quickly that those who came
> up afterwards found but little left. One of his comrades, an Irishman of
> the name of John Mclaughin,[6] was one of those who emptied the
> captured money chests. He crammed every pocket, his shoes and
> stockings, his linings and his knapsack with gold and silver pieces.
> Bentinck saw him that night sorting them out on his blanket, spread on
> the ground. In the morning he went to the Colonel and asked him if he
> would kindly take charge of some of the money for him, as he could not
> march with it. The Colonel kindly promised to do so, and calling the
> quartermaster committed it to him.[7]
>
> On reaching Pamplona, Mclaughin went and asked him for it,
> intending transmitting some home and purchasing things with the rest.
> To his dismay the Colonel roared out, 'Be off you rascal, if you had
> been minding your duty you would have got no more than any other
> man.' He at once instructed the Quartermaster to divide the money
> among the entire Regiment. This was done to the satisfaction of all but
> the foolish Irishman himself, every man receiving seven or eight dollars.

After a day of consolidation, the Allies commenced their pursuit of the French,
but were hampered by the bad weather. Toward the end of June the battalion
participated in a couple of short engagements[8] against French rearguards but the
main objective was capturing the French-held fortresses of Pamplona[9] and San
Sebastian.[10] A lack of siege equipment and the scale of the challenge meant that

Wellington chose to blockade Pamplona and besiege San Sebastian but acknowledged that the path to ultimate victory lay in subsequently entering France and inflicting a comprehensive defeat on Napoleon's forces.

After the defeat at Vitoria and the retreat back to Bayonne, Soult worked tremendously hard to re-establish a credibly sized army and he consolidated, in just two weeks, the remnants of four armies into one force of some 80,000 troops. Soult understood that his only chance of success lay in conducting a fast-moving assault on the Allied defensive line across the Pyrenees and driving on to lift the sieges of San Sebastian and Pamplona.

> Before Pamplona Bentinck was seized with the small pox, and for several days had to ride in the Bullock wagons, with many more sick, but happily the foul disease soon left him. Bentinck then continued with his Division in pursuit of the defeated French armies, who had now been driven out of every fortress in Spain except two, St. Sebastian and Pamplona. Nor was Wellington, now Field Marshal of England, the man to let these remain long undisturbed, and though Bonaparte, then in the midst of conquest in Germany[11] was collecting his vast forces against him, the Duke at once blockaded Pamplona and besieged St. Sebastian; the former, bristling with 200 cannon and the bayonets of 4,000 men.[12] This being too strong for a regular assault except prefaced by a much longer cannonading than the approach of Soult with 100,000 Frenchmen was likely to allow.

Wellington had some 62,000 troops to defend from the River Bidassoa at the Bay of Biscay along the line of the western Pyrenees, around a forty-five mile front. The 6th and 3rd Divisions, along with most of the cavalry and a number of Spanish and Portuguese units, were held to the rear of this line acting as a reserve. The 5th Division was gainfully employed in conducting the siege of San Sebastian, while a Spanish division blockaded Pamplona. The other divisions were deployed along the defensive line as follows: the 1st Division on the west of the River Bidassoa, Light Division at the town of Vera on the Bidassoa, the 7th Division at Echelar, the 2nd Division, holding the important Maya pass, a Portuguese division positioned between the Maya and Roncesvalles pass, and the 4th Division at the pass of Roncesvalles. Wellington's assumption was that Soult would prioritize an attempt to lift the siege of San Sebastian and the defensive dispositions reflected this.

> Our old veteran's Division, the 4th under Sir Lowry Cole, was one of those blockading Pamplona. They along with Picton's Division were

supporting Morillo's Spanish infantry in guarding the Pass of Roncesvalles, so famous in song and story, in the Pyrenees.[13] The other passes of these lofty mountains were kept by the 2nd, 6th and 7th Divisions, with Campbell's Portuguese Brigades and Longa's Spaniards in support, altogether covering a line of nearly 60 miles.

This region, from which they could almost look down on the fertile plains of France, was exceedingly grand and picturesque. Mountains of startling forms piled together, at one part piercing the clouds with their snowy pinnacles, at another stretching upwards to green and rounded summits. The roads were mere stony tracks, crossing sometimes stupendous depths on the frailest of bridges and again clinging along the breast of a precipice, [with] the eternal rush of the torrent, and the wild scream of the eagle alone breaking the stillness of the lofty world.

The scarlet warriors of Britain were well in keeping with the scene. Their huts clustered here and there in the savage glens, their bayonets glittered from craggy outlooks and the blast of their bugles echoed o'er ravine and cliff, as they waited day by day for the French columns to unwind themselves from the grim defiles through which they were to emerge upon the waiting British. They had not very long to wait, and once more our friends of the 4th Division had to bear the worst of the onset.

Despite their being increased reporting of French movement in their vicinity, Soult's offensive on 25 July 1813 was a surprise to the allied commanders, most of whom thought it would at most be a feint. Cole heard a rumour of increased French movement and deployed the Fusilier Brigade forward toward the pass of Roncesvalles. By 6.00 in the morning the Fusilier Brigade was just arriving at the pass when the lead elements of the enemy were engaged by the forward company. The restricted terrain meant that the opposing forces were closely engaged with a rare instance of bayonet fighting. The French had three divisions with nineteen battalions attempting to push across the narrow pass. Despite this the 4th Division was able to hold off the enemy for a period. Each brigade rotated its battalions through the front positions as ammunition stocks were depleted. The fighting was intense and at close quarters until a late afternoon mist arose and a retreat was called for the 4th Division.[14]

Soult himself burst upon Roncesvalles with 40,000 men, in the dim morning light of the 25th July. General Byng's[15] brigade stood and fell by scores before them, but not a foot of ground did they lose. Fired by example, and skilled in mountain warfare, the Spaniards, too, fought fiercely and long[16] and when joined by the 4th Division made several gallant charges. But the defenders of the pass could not hope to keep every outlet against such swarming foes and towards the evening a French Division succeeded in turning their flank. Then each rock, each glen, was gradually abandoned to the wounded and the dead, and our out-numbered men slowly and sullenly withdrew to Zerberi, a little mountain town a few miles in their rear.[17]

Concurrently Soult ordered the French III Corps, which had three divisions, to attack the British 2nd Division at Maya Pass. Despite being hugely outnumbered, the forward British troops held off the French for a couple of hours, but were slowly pushed back. The withdrawal at Roncesvalles meant that the 2nd Division also had to pull back so that Wellington could consolidate his forces somewhere where the terrain could afford the greatest advantage for a pitched battle.

The same day General Hill's Corps was attacked at Bustan Pass[18] under very disadvantageous circumstances. Two of his advanced sentries posted high up on the pass fell asleep and the French, bayoneting them as they lay, poured down upon the camp before an alarm could be given. For once Hill, the ablest and most wary General in our armies, was completely surprised. Almost frantic with fury he beheld his men, unprepared and almost unarmed, driven from a position that else would have cost his enemies thousands of lives to take.[19]

The loss of these two inlets to their position greatly imperilled our scattered forces. The defenders of Roncesvalles were driven from their place of retreat at Zerberi, and forced back to the blockading camp at Pampeluna. This so alarmed the Spanish General[20] then conducting the blockade, that he began spiking his guns and the Garrison, sallying forth captured 14 of them.[21] But now, as always when needed most, Wellington joined them, bringing with him Pakenham's veteran Division. Without wasting a single day the work of death once more began.

The 4th and 6th Divisions retreated from the pass of Roncesvalles toward Pamplona. At Sorauren, a village about six miles north of Pamplona, Cole and Picton established a defensive position on a favourable east–west ridge about 2,000 feet high. Soult and a force of around 35,000 men were poised to attack. Wellington personally intervened with an intuitive and theatrical appearance in front of his force which greatly motivated the allied troops whilst reducing the French appetite for an assault that day. This pause provided Wellington a crucial opportunity to gather reinforcements to increase his troop numbers to 24,000.

After a night of an exceptional lighting storm with accompanying heavy rain, the French attacked the position just before noon with 15,000 men. The first French attack was pushed back by a bayonet charge, as was the second. The third attack was more successful as part of the Portuguese Brigade broke, whilst the Fusilier Brigade was pushed back and the French were able to gain a foothold on the crest of the ridge at two locations. A bayonet charge by elements of Anson's British brigade was the decisive moment and, despite further fighting, the Battle of Cole's Ridge or Sorauren was an Allied victory.

> In pursuance of their late successful tactics, the French rolled forward in overwhelming masses with the view of sweeping away those red patches of men that crowned every rock in their front. But the latter were not going to be again beaten, even by numbers, for Wellington himself had posted them on every position and their withering fire swept front and rear and both flanks of the French host as it advanced, until it gave back with immense loss. Along the height held by the 4th Division the battle raged the fiercest, because that height was striven for by both sides as the key of victory. 'Every regiment of this brave Corps,' says Napier, 'charged with the bayonet, and four of them made four different charges.' Soult's most obstinate efforts could make no impression on the Allied front and after this one bloody trial he sent back his guns and heavy baggage to France, and resolved to have a try at the left, which his old foe, General Hill, commanded.[22]

Bentinck, our ancient veteran, added considerably to his experience of battle sights in these sharp engagements near Pampeluna. 'We had a sharp engagement outside the town and they stood very hard and they came to the charge of bayonet. The charge of the Welsh Fusileers was needed several times and though they killed many, they had many killed too.' The bayonet, as is well known, leaves more dead than wounded (unlike the bullet), for the breast of the combatant is the part chiefly aimed at and at arm's length is too near to miss the aim. The French rushed to meet them in one charge, with such strength and fury as to break through their line.

His Drummer's uniform once more failed to protect Bentinck from hostile weapons and having before let in upon him both bomb shell and bullet, completed the round with taste of steel. A black looking Frenchman who had skewered a Fusileer as he burst through their line, and jerked him off his bayonet dead, next lunged the weapon at Bentinck, but receiving at the moment a blow on the skull from the butt end of a musket, he fell senseless, his bayonet passing through Bentinck's thigh instead of his body.

'When we came to the prisoners there was great rejoicing and shaking of hand for they was the same number on the button as us. They were also the 23rd regiment.'[23]

Disliking much to have 4d per day taken from his pay for being in hospital,[24] Bentinck limped by the side of his comrades all day, with his shoe full of blood, and both trousers and stocking glued to his leg so fast with it that he had to soften them with water to get them off when evening came. He then went to the doctor and got some plaster and bandages on the wound, and as they rested for some days after this, it soon healed.[25]

Soult was defeated and withdrew into France, heading north up the Bidassoa valley. Some of Wellington's Spanish troops were able to slow the French retreat and this allowed additional pursuing Allied troops to inflict more casualties on the French before they reached the frontier. The casualty figures for the Battle of the Pyrenees over the period 25–30 July were around 15,000 French dead, wounded and captured. Allied figures were some 10,000 dead and wounded.[26]

The defeat of Soult's army allowed Wellington to concentrate on capturing the fortress of San Sebastian. Siege operations had begun on 28 June with the Chofre Sand Hills to the east selected as a position for some of the artillery batteries which began blasting the eastern wall of the fortress. It was not until 25 July that the first assault was made by the 5th Division and a Portuguese brigade, neither of which were able to breach the defences and were repelled by a determined garrison of about 3,000 French troops. Subsequently the French were inventive in using small boats to resupply the fortress with men, stores, shot and shell.

Heavier artillery was brought from England and by 26 August the breaching batteries were in position, with fifteen cannon firing from the south and forty-two cannon firing from the east, supported by mortars shelling the town. By 31 August a main breach had been established on the south-east corner and a further breach on the east side. The position of the breaches achieved in the eastern wall meant that any assault would involve crossing the River Urumea. At high tide the river formed an estuary and so any assault would only be possible at low tide and the attackers would have to wade over 300–400 yards of water to reach the breaches, where the strewn rubble, arranged at a high angle, presented a further obstacle.

Parts of the 1st, 2nd, 4th, 5th, and Light Divisions, formed the assailants. Each Regiment had been invited to send volunteers, and 200 responded from the 4th Division.[27] Sir James Leith commanded.[28] Just as they reached the wall it was blown up by the French, and many were crushed thereby.[29] 'The Forlorn Hope,'[30] says Napier, 'was cut off to a man, the front of the following parties were swept away as by one shot, the breach was actually covered with their bodies; many as they ascended, were thrown off their feet by those above them rolling down, and the living, the wounded, and the dead, were hurled down the ruins together. From the Mirador and Prince batteries, from the keep of the Castle, from the high curtain to the left of the breach, from some ruined houses about 40 yards in front, loop-holed and lined with musketry, a concentrated fire was kept up; a line of entrenchments carried along the nearest parallel walls swept the summit of the breach; and the hornwork flanked and commanded the ascent; almost every possible point was manned.

'All that the most determined courage could do was repeatedly tried in vain by the troops, as they were successively brought forward from the trenches. A heavy supporting artillery fire immediately above the attacking force was ordered, and a narrow breach gained.

'The assailants now effected a lodgement on the summit of the breach, and the troops impetuously pushed forward.[31] The contest was still continued from barricades in the streets and musketry from the houses. The spectacle was terrific; for as the Garrison of the Castle fired down the streets, the flames raged and the falling ruins crashed, the soldiery, mad with intoxication, were plundering the houses and the frequent explosions of firearms showed that a fearful work was going on. Several days elapsed before order was restored.[32] The bodies were thrown into the mines, and there covered over, so as to be out of sight, but so hastily and slightly that the air, far and near was tainted; fires were kindled in the breaches, to consume those that could not be otherwise disposed of. In the assault, 2,000 men and officers had fallen.[33]

'Preparations were now made for reducing the Castle, but the operations of the besiegers were retarded by the necessity of quenching the flames which had spread through the whole town. On the 5th September, 59 pieces of artillery opened on the Castle with such terrible effect, that in a few hours the white flag was hoisted on the Mirador battery;[34] and the Garrison, amounting to 1,800 effective men, and 500 sick and wounded, surrendered prisoners of war. After the fall of St. Sebastian, nearly a month elapsed before Lord Wellington could commence his movements on the frontier. Then on the 31st October the Garrison of Pamplona, 4,000 in number, surrendered after a few months' blockade.'[35]

The members of the battalion who did not participate in the siege of San Sebastian were camped on a mountain ridge for a number of weeks. Even though the location provided a fine perspective into France and down to the coast, heavy rain, low temperatures and high winds did not make it a comfortable stay.

In the autumn of this year, the British, exposed on the cold and cloudy summits of the Pyrenees, with only rude huts and tents to shelter them from the blasts, suffered many hardships; the piquet and night duties were rendered peculiarly harassing in consequence of the inclement weather. Their propinquity to France caused many desertions, which severe examples were required to check.

———•———

1. Only one French artillery piece was successfully brought away as part of the retreat. It was subsequently captured on 24 June.
2. The chaos of the scene is illustrated well by Browne, 'All the Baggages, Carriages, Mules & Equipage of King Joseph & his Court – the Military Chest which had arrived with the arrears of pay for the Army of the Centre only a few days before, & contained some Millions of [Spanish] Dollars in Silver & Doubloons – Coaches with their Coachmen on the Boxes or Postillions on the Horses, flogging & swearing to the utmost extent of their lungs – Ladies with imploring arms, or outstretched Infants thrusting themselves from the windows of these Coaches, or descending from the them to the ground – others on Horseback or on Mules, endeavouring in vain, to extricate themselves from the mass of impediments that blocked up their way, & to gallop off… all these mixed up with Cannon, Tumbrils, drunken French Servants, the wounded, the dying & the dead.' Browne, *Napoleonic War Journal*, pp. 213–14.
3. Wellington expressed a strong opinion in correspondence nine days after the battle: 'The soldiers of the army have got among them about a million sterling, with the exception of about 100,000 dollars which were got for the military chest. The night

of the battle, instead of being passed in getting rest and food for the pursuit of the following day, was passed by the soldiers in looking for plunder. The consequence was that they were incapable of marching and were totally knocked up. The new regiments are, as usual, the worst of all. The Eighteenth Hussars are a disgrace to the name of soldier, in action as well as elsewhere; and I propose to draft their horses from them and send the men to England if I cannot get the better of them in any other manner.' Wellington to Bathurst, 29 June 1813, in J. Gurwood (ed.), *The Despatches of Field Marshal the Duke of Wellington*, Vol. X, p. 473.

4. Lieutenant George Baxter Browne initially joined the 2nd Battalion in July 1806. He participated in the Battle of Corunna and the Walcheren expedition. He joined the 1st Battalion in spring 1811 and saw service at Albuera, Ciudad Rodrigo, Badajoz, Salamanca, Vitoria (there is no record of him obtaining trophies) and the Pyrenees. He was badly wounded at Badajoz, Salamanca and again at Roncesvalles in 1813. He received promotion to captain on 26 August 1813 before being placed on half pay in 1814. Despite this status he was given the rank of major unattached on 29 August 1826 and lieutenant colonel on 23 November 1841. He died in 1879, aged 91. He was the younger brother of Thomas Henry Browne.

5. At Vitoria, battalion casualties were one private killed, one sergeant and two rank and file wounded. The Fusilier Brigade only suffered twenty-four casualties in the battle.

6. Private Mclaughlin is not listed in the 23rd Foot medal rolls for the Napoleonic period, but see p. 95, n. 28 above for a further explicit reference to a soldier of that name.

7. On the morning after the battle, the Fusilier Brigade's bivouac area 'more resembled a Fair, than a regular encampment' with 'every man selling or buying some article of plunder'. RWFM, Acc. 5935, MacDonald to father, 1 July 1813.

8. On 25 June, sixty miles north-east of Vitoria, the 4th Division fought against a French rearguard. Jack Hill was commanding the light troops of the Fusilier Brigade at the very front of the advance and drove the French troops back onto hills where it was discovered that a stronger French force was posted. The Fusilier Brigade did not pursue the option of an attack and Hill commanded the light troops in falling back, 'In extended order, firing all the time'; his men 'behaved very coolly, and extricated themselves well, out of the scrape'. RWFM, Acc. 3777, Hill to mother, 26 June 1813. The next day the Fusilier Brigade engaged a further French rearguard on high ground to the front of the town of Tolosa and a skirmish of some duration took place, until flanking Allied movements caused the French to withdraw and Tolosa to be occupied.

9. The fortress, which commanded two of the three roads from France into Spain, was well prepared and strongly defended.

10. Donostia-San Sebastian, the capital city of the province of Gipuzkoa, in the Basque country, Spain. It sits on a peninsula and can only be directly approached on land from the south. During this era the fortress was designed and constructed so as to enclose the town within its walls. Within the fortress the Castle of La Motte stood on

the highest ground, Mount Urgullo. However, the defensive strength of the position was undermined by hills to the east.

11. Although Napoleon had been the victor at both the battles of Lützen and Bautzen in May, the casualties sustained had been considerable and he realized that he was too weak to pursue the defeated Prussians and Russians. The Prussians and the Russians asked for an armistice. The Armistice of Pleischwitz was signed between France, Prussia and Russia on 4 June 1813, lasting until 10 August 1813. During this period, substantial diplomacy was undertaken by Napoleon's enemies. Victory at Vitoria gave an added impetus to the belief that France could be defeated. Napoleon rejected a peace settlement which would have established France's future border on the west bank of the Rhine. On 12 August 1813 Austria declared war on France, and the size of the coalition thus formed against France meant that victory would eventually be assured.

12. Pamplona was garrisoned by three battalions of the Army of the North and a further 800 men. There were 54 field artillery pieces and 80 other guns in the fortress. The principal difficulty was food. Although 77 days of rations were brought in on 15 June for the garrison of 2,500 men, a large number of sick, injured and stray individuals added greatly to the ration requirements.

13. The pass of Roncesvalles sits at an altitude of 2,950 feet on the small River Urrobi. It is only five miles from the French border. In 778 it was the site of the defeat of Charlemange (King of the Franks) and the death of Roland, the Frankish military leader, at the hands of the Basques.

14. Lieutenant Booker recollected the efforts of the 23rd Foot: 'There was a very high mountain in the front of our position but separated from us by a deep ravine and a very thick wood which extended about halfway up the hill on which we were posted … We arrived and were ordered by companies into the wood. The enemy in vain endeavoured to pass the ravine and we remained opposed to a very superior force until we had twice expended our ammunition. We were relieved by the 7th Fusiliers and about six o'clock the right [Anson's 1st Brigade] and Portuguese [Stubbs's] brigades made their appearance.' RWFM, Acc. 2686, Booker to Collins, 27 July 1813.

Roberts provided a slightly different account of the engagement: 'Our next engagement was on the heights of Pampeluna. It was on July 25th – a Sunday morning. My company was first called out to skirmish. The officer, Lieutenant Booker, was severely wounded, when I took charge of the company at the moment, and then left it on a hill in charge of another sergeant. The French were in fields within 200 yards of the wood, when a private soldier and myself went down to it, and picked out a large tree for shelter. One of the company brought ammunition: and there, to the best of our knowledge, we fired 300 rounds, every one of which took effect among the enemy, either killing or wounding them. The bugle then sounded "fire and retreat!" which accordingly we did, and joined our company.' Roberts, 'Incidents in the Life of an Old Fusilier', p. 22.

The retreat was undertaken by tired and hungry men, in increasing darkness and over very awkward terrain. Lieutenant Colonel Ellis 'made the men hold by each [other's coat tails] otherwise we should have lost half the Brigade'. RWFM, Acc. 2686, Booker to Collins, 11 August 1813. Across the 4th Division some 450 men had been killed and wounded.

15. Major General John Byng commanded the 2nd Brigade (1/3rd, 1/57th Foot, 1st Provisional Battalion [2/31st & 2/66th], Coy 5/60th Foot) as part of Lieutenant General Sir William Stewart's 2nd Division. It was attached to Cole's 4th Division for the defence of the pass of Roncesvalles.

16. The Spanish division under Morillo was also attached to Cole's 4th Division.

17. The town of Zubiri is some twenty miles to the south-west of the pass of Roncesvalles.

18. Baztan pass is around twenty miles to the north of Pamplona.

19. Hill authorized a retreat toward Elizonda, a small town to the rear of Maya pass.

20. General Henry O'Donnell (1769–1834), who was commanding the 'Andalusian Reserve'.

21. Most accounts state that the French attempted numerous and spirited sorties against the encircling troops but there is no record of the capture of guns. The closest the garrison came to being relieved was the period 26–28 July when a French force reached no further than five miles from Pamplona.

22. The 23rd Foot's contribution to the battle was summarized by Lieutenant Colonel Ellis, 'The battle of the 28th of July was a beautiful display of military manoeuvres: the enemy formed his columns in the most perfect order, and advanced to the attack with a rapidity and impetus apparently irresistible. I was in immediate support of the seventh Cacadores (Portuguese), who were the advanced piquet, and consequently received the first shock of the enemy's columns. My people only thought of fighting, and at once checked their progress. Our supports on both sides were brought up, and the contest continued with varying success till four o'clock, when the enemy withdrew, only leaving his voltigeurs in our front. We had three divisions upon us, – the fourth, fifth and seventh: the two former were chiefly opposed to the fortieth [also the 27th and 48th], who made two unheard of charges: indeed, the whole day was a succession of charges.' Ellis to Harrison, July 1813, in *Regimental Records*, Vol. 1, pp. 261–2. The battle resulted in some 4,000 French and 3,500 Allied casualties. Amongst the 23rd Foot, Captains Stainforth and Walker, Volunteer Basset, 1 sergeant, 1 corporal, 1 drummer and 13 rank and file were killed; Lieutenant Colonel Ellis, Lieutenants Neville, Harris and McLellan were wounded.

23. The French 23rd Line Infantry did serve in the Peninsula over the period 1810–12. However, in 1813 they were part of Marshal Ney's III Corps and on 2 May 1813 fought at the Battle of Lützen. The meeting of correspondingly numbered regiments was not unique. On 28 October 1811, at Arroyo dos Molinos, the 34th Foot fought the French 34th Line, which they called 'le parlez-vous'. The 34th Foot routed their French counterparts, capturing many men and the baggage train, which included the

drums and the drum major's mace. The successors of the 34th Foot celebrate the anniversary of this battle by an elaborate parade on 'Arroyo Day'.

24. When a soldier was wounded, his pay was reduced by this amount in order to account for the food he received in hospital.

25. Roberts was also wounded in this engagement, an experience which he described thus: '[In] the general action on the 28th ... I received a shot through my left knee, which crippled me. I lay eight days in hedges and ditches before I was brought down to the Vitoria Hospital. There the surgeons were desirous to remove my leg; but I declined the operation, and consequently lost the pension.' Roberts, 'Incidents in the Life of an Old Fusilier', No. 2, p. 22.

26. The Fusilier Brigade lost 627 casualties and the 23rd Foot lost 24 killed and 99 wounded. Lieutenant Colonel Ellis wrote after these engagements that the battalion was 'only the semblance of one' as with the losses in action, sick, 'and attendants on the wounded I am reduced to one hundred and sixty bayonets'. Ellis to Harrison, July 1813, in *Regimental Records*, Volume 1, pp. 261–2.

27. The 4th Division was not formally committed to the assault but a detachment of 200 volunteers from across all regiments was raised, commanded by Major Alexander Rose of the 20th Foot.

28. Major General Sir James Leith (1763–1845) commanded the 5th Division during the siege. Leith had considerable experience in the Peninsula: in 1808–9 he commanded a brigade, including at the battles of Lugo and Corunna. In August 1810 Wellington appointed him to command the newly established 5th Division. The 5th Division performed well at Busaco, the defence of the Lines of Torres Vedras and the assault on Badajoz. Leith was subsequently badly wounded at Salamanca, but returned for the siege of San Sebastian, again being wounded. He later became Commander in Chief in the West Indies.

29. The French initiated a prepared explosive charge under the sea wall opposite the north end of the hornwork. In contrast to this account, most of the forlorn hope were not affected by the detonation of this charge, but a party of British engineers sent to find and render safe this known charge were killed.

30. The forlorn hope at San Sebastian was commanded by Lieutenant Francis Maguire of the 4th Foot, who was killed during the first part of the assault at the base of the breach. Maguire had served with distinction in the Peninsula, being mentioned for bravery at Albuera, Vitoria and Salamanca. He had also twice volunteered to lead a forlorn hope. In 1912 past and present officers of the King's Own (4th Foot) commissioned for 100 guineas an oil painting illustrating the 'Forlorn Hope at San Sebastian'. This fine work by James Prinsep Beadle is now in the possession of the Duke of Lancaster's Regiment.

31. On gaining the breach, a drop of about 30 feet was discovered behind it, causing a temporary delay to the assault.

32. In the aftermath of the successful assault the Allied troops again plundered and destroyed for over four days, with numerous historical reports compiled of shocking

behaviour from rape to murder. In addition, a significant fire got hold in the town and swept through, destroying all but a handful of buildings. It has been suggested that this was a deliberate act to punish the inhabitants of San Sebastian for their favouritism for, and strong trading relations with, the French. The tragedy of the siege of San Sebastian is remembered every year with a candlelit ceremony on 31 August.

33. Only a handful of men from the 23rd Foot were among the 200 volunteers from the 4th Division and this explains why battalion casualties were comparatively light with only four rank and file killed, and Lieutenant Griffiths and four rank and file wounded. Across the Allied force the casualties were 856 killed and 1,520 wounded.

34. The defenders of the Castle of La Motte, around 1,000 men, began negotiating terms of surrender on 5 September and formally surrendered on 8 September.

35. The garrison was effectively starved into submission.

Chapter Nine

Battles on the Road to Toulouse

———•———

The capture of Pamplona and San Sebastian, the last two fortresses of the French in Spain, left Wellington free to carry out his long-cherished object of pursuing them into their own country. He had an Anglo-Portuguese force of about 64,000 troops to conduct the invasion. Some 25,000 Spanish troops were also available, but fear of them wreaking revenge on the French resulted in the majority of them being put into defensive positions on the Spanish border. The French under Marshal Soult had roughly 61,000 infantry and artillery to man the defensive line, with most forces massed to receive an Allied attack over the Maya pass, down the Nivelle valley and toward St-Jean-de-Luz.[1] On 7 October the Allies conducted a feint attack at the Maya pass, whilst simultaneously launching the main attack across the wide Bidassoa estuary, where reconnaissance had identified fordable locations at low tide. The French town of Hendaye was captured whilst a supporting attack to seize Mount Larroun, five miles to the south-east, was eventually successful.

After the successful Allied assault in October, a period was spent by both sides consolidating their positions and preparing for the next engagement. The vulnerability of the seaward sector following the crossing of the Bidassoa forced Soult to focus on this area, but the twenty-mile length of the defensive line, the very difficult terrain and his limited number of troops afforded various opportunities to the Allies.

At the beginning of November 1813, Bentinck found himself, along with the rest of the 4th Division, descending the Pyrenees into France. The object was to break through the strong line of defence 12 miles in length, which Soult had formed from the sea to the heights of Ainhoa, in front of the town of St Jean de Luz. Thus protected and reinforced by 30,000 men, the French Marshal felt himself secure.

The French position was dominated by a 3,000-foot-high mountain called the Greater Rhune. After the Battle of Bidassoa, the French had constructed three strong defensive positions on the Lower Rhune, a crest below the Greater Rhune.

Wellington planned an attack all along the French line but concentrated his forces in the centre on the Lower Rhune defences. These fell to a vigorous Allied attack, as did an important fort on the Mouiz plateau. The French were generally too surprised to mount a serious defence. The battalion played a limited role as it was positioned with the rear brigade of the division.

> On the 10th of November, the British Army debouched from the mountains they had crossed and creeping forward with remarkable silence lay down until morning, so near to the enemy's outposts that their voices could be heard. On daybreak, discovering their array, they were saluted with a tremendous cannonade, which owing to the uneven nature of the ground did them but little damage.
>
> Bentinck's Division was ordered to take a redoubt on the edge of the ravine just above them. Scrambling quietly up, they entered it unawares, bayoneted the gunners before they could fire and took all the rest prisoners, the whole affair not lasting ten minutes.

The French troops holding the 4th Division's objective of Sarre retreated initially but then consolidated and put up a creditable defence, before sheer numbers of Allied troops forced them back.

> His Division then pushed forwards to the little village of Sarre, on the right of St Jean de Luz and after a severe struggle and several bloody repulses succeeded in taking it.[2] The French advanced again and again to drive them out, but by dint of obstinate fighting and heavy loss they were each time forced to retire.
>
> Again, at the close of the day Bentinck found himself unscratched, though several of his immediate comrades slept with the dead. One man from his own district, Sergeant Walker, had both his legs cut off by a cannon shot. He lived, notwithstanding his injuries, and in after years used to draw his pension along with Bentinck, at Stowmarket, in their native Suffolk.[3]

The other divisions were similarly successful and for a period Soult's forces were cut into two halves, which forced a general retreat by the French.

> Sir Rowland Hill stormed the heights of Ainhoa[4] and carried the defences of the French right. The Second Division forced back their centre and compelled the whole line to retire, lest their retreat should be cut off. Again the French formed on the heights of Ascain[5] and

St Pe;[6] again they were driven onward before the victorious British, leaving their boasted defences and their entire winter camp in possession of their foe. The French lost 50 guns, nearly all their stores and ammunition, 1,500 prisoners and above 4,000 killed and wounded. The British losses were about 3,000 killed, wounded and missing.[7] Soult subsequently retreated to Bayonne.

After his defeat Soult formed a new defensive line along the natural obstacles of the Nive and Adour rivers and the fortified city of Bayonne. The geography favoured the defenders and Soult anticipated that Wellington at some stage would have to split his forces, which would provide an opportunity for the French reserves to counter-attack. On 9 December 1813 the crossing of the Nive by Wellington's forces commenced. The French fought hard to try to prevent the establishment of a credible bridgehead.

The wet weather halted the intentions of Sir Rowland Hill to immediately pursue Soult. When he eventually crossed the river Nive, the French put up a fierce resistance but could not stop the British storming the heights of Adour,[8] the town of Villa Franca[9] and with resistless vigour bore the enemy still onward. The following morning, Soult, seeing that nothing but equal activity could save him, boldly turned on the left of his foe, Sir John Hope,[10] massed with his entire Army.

Napier relates: 'The British fought with the utmost bravery under Hope's skilful directions, who himself was in the thickest of the fight. He had his hat and clothes shot through in many places, had two horses killed under him and was wounded in the shoulder and the leg.' The French were again defeated, but not dismayed. Drawing off his forces, Soult next hurled them swiftly against the right flank, the very next day. Sir Rowland Hill had only 13,000 men while Soult massed 30,000, with the odds very much in the favour of the French.[11]

The 4th Division and hence the battalion were only employed in a supporting role for these contests. They were frequently on the move responding to French attacks but never committed. On 13 December Soult attacked an isolated Allied force of 14,000 men on the east bank of the River Nive with six divisions. It was a bitter fight but then reinforcements sent by Wellington assisted in achieving an unlikely Allied victory.

Bentinck passed through these dangerous scenes with his usual good fortune, escaping sound in wind and limb. At the capture of St Jean de Luz, the troops were as usual very short of provisions and as the French had been driven from their camp so suddenly, they left behind some very welcome pickings. On many fires their camp kettles were left boiling, filled with the savoury messes that the Monsieurs are so adept at concocting. Bentinck made a good supper of the contents of one huge kettle, mutton broth made with wine instead of water. He then looked about for a sleeping place. Every hut and building was filled with cavalry horses, which were generally housed with much greater care than the men. So at last he lay down on the manure in front of a stable and slept soundly till morning. The heat rising from the manure kept him warm on one side and the night wind having chilled him on the other, he found himself very ill. For a day or two after, he struggled to drag himself along with his duties.

In mid-December the weather was so inclement, with torrential rains making rivers sweep bridges away and roads a quagmire, that the decision was taken to commit the troops to occupy winter quarters. Furthermore, Wellington realized that his troops' temperament was not conducive to sustained campaigning in these conditions. In the cantonments, housekeeping and foraging were the main interests of the soldiers.

After the sharp and rapid actions sketched above, the troops rested for the winter in the camp which their confiding enemies had prepared for themselves, nothing particular occurring to disturb their much needed repose.

The 23rd Foot was at first quartered near Saint-Pée before moving in January to Ustaritz. In February 1814 Wellington decided to push Soult's forces away from Bayonne. On 14 February hostilities recommenced with Wellington tasking General Hill with 20,000 troops to threaten the French left flank. The French withdrew, whilst Picton's 3rd Division was also successful in pushing the French in the centre back to the River Bidouze. The French forces from the left flank stood and fought at Garris but were defeated. This forced Soult to re-form his defensive line along the Gave d'Oloron with six divisions. On 23 February, the 4th and 7th Divisions attacked the French at Hartingues and Oeyregave and forced the enemy to retire toward Orthez and the Gave de Pau. Bayonne was left isolated and besieged.

Soult destroyed all bridges over the Gave de Pau between Bayonne and Pau itself, except for the medieval bridge at Orthez, which was only partially destroyed. However, his troops still failed to prevent the Gave de Pau being crossed. General Hill had been tasked only to conduct a demonstration against the bridge at Orthez with but a Portuguese brigade, before later revealing his full force of 12,000 troops, who rapidly overcame the two defending French battalions and one cavalry regiment to cross the Souars ford, a mile to the east of Orthez.

The geography of Orthez afforded the French the greatest potential for fighting a successful defensive battle. Soult massed 36,000 troops and 48 artillery pieces along a ridge rising from the western edge of Orthez and turning west towards the village of Saint-Boes. The four-mile-long ridge presented a concave arc towards any approaching enemy and at parts was only approachable via very steep inclines. Allied cavalry found a way across the Gave and a pontoon bridge was rapidly built to allow more troops over, whilst the French were disorganized. On 27 February Wellington with 43,000 troops attacked and the 4th Division was tasked to defeat the French right flank to open the battle. The 3rd and 6th Divisions were also subsequently committed to drive wedges between the French forces. Eventually the French broke and commenced a disorderly retreat.

On February 27th 1814, Bentinck marched with the British Army to attack the French positions at Orthez, crossing a river in front of it by a pontoon bridge. Here and there a dead Frenchman marked the track of the advanced skirmishers in the dim grey of the early morning.

Our friends, the 4th Division, were to attack St Boes,[12] a village protecting Soult's right wing. For two hours, wave after wave of our red coated men beat in vain against this stubborn point; then its defenders, diminished and weary, abandoned it to them. They were next sent against two lines posted on the hills beyond, so steep that they could not deploy to attack and after several attempts and the loss of many brave fellows, they drew back. Ordering up two more Divisions to their support, Wellington directed them to try what they could do with the left wing. Their onslaught here was successful and compelled Soult to order a retreat, under the direct fire of the British guns which now crowned the heights.

In the meantime, Hill had crossed the river so near their rear as to almost cut off their retreat, causing the French force to break and run, with hardly a vestige of order. Hill's men ran too, catching them when they could, shooting them when they could not, until 1,200 prisoners were taken and the ditches along the road were filled with the dead and wounded. The French admitted to a loss of 15,000 men themselves. The Allies had not more than 3,000 slain and disabled.[13] Lord Wellington was hit on the hilt of his sword by a musket ball, the blow bruising him so severely that he had to be lifted from his horse.

In this affair, the 23rd of Foot lost three or four Officers.[14] Bentinck himself narrowly escaped having his head shaved with a French sabre. The French Dragoons made such a dashing charge on the 23rd of Foot that several of them managed to break through. One of these, wheeling his horse round and galloping back encountered a Corporal, standing a few paces from Bentinck. Evading the bullet that greeted him and by a tremendous blow hurling the bayonet from the Corporal's grasp, the trooper made a slashing cut at his head. The Corporal threw up his hand to protect it, only for the blow to take off his arm. Passing onwards like a meteor, the Dragoon was swooping down on Bentinck when another soldier fired and brought him from the saddle.[15]

On the conclusion of the battle most of the army bivouacked on the heights of Sallespisse, away from any habitations. Wellington understood that hardening the resolve of the local population toward the allies would be extremely detrimental – this was indeed one of the reasons why he limited the number of Spanish troops that crossed the border into France. The experience of substantial looting at Vitoria had cost Wellington tactical opportunities and, on this occasion, although opportunities were limited, discipline was also more strictly enforced.

The Allies remained at Orthez a day or two after the battle, resting and collecting their men. Then they followed on after the enemy, in the direction of Toulouse. The first morning, as they marched out of town, Bentinck saw a man, one of the 5th Regiment, hung up on a tree by the road side, with his coat turned inside out as a mark of disgrace, quite dead. He had been caught in the act of stealing, his haversack full of flour from a shop. This was the punishment by which the Iron Duke protected the people of the country through which his soldiers passed.[16] All this severity did not make the men more honest – only more wary in thieving quietly, so as to keep from the Duke's hearing. Their own Officers they never feared in matters of that kind, because they knew that hardships and want often forced them to plunder and the officers were indeed glad to receive snacks of it. An instance of this occurred on the very night that the poor fellow had been hung as an example.

After his defeat at Orthez, Soult retreated to Saint-Sever[17] pursued by Wellington and then made an unexpected decision to concentrate further resistance on Toulouse, rather than Bordeaux. At the same time, the French retreat eastwards provided the opportunity for Wellington to send some troops to Bordeaux, where the mayor had indicated that he was likely to support a restoration of the French monarchy, and the city was taken with the minimum of fuss. On 18 March, Wellington then ordered his troops to march on Toulouse and, in just over a week, the battalion was in sight of the city.

The British then marched long and far, covering fully 25 miles ere they halted for the night. The last few miles of their march was over a wide moor, dotted with flocks of sheep and covered with furze bushes, which necessitated the shepherds to watch their flocks mounted on long stilts, much to the amusement of our soldiers. Bentinck, among others, noted the plump appearance of the unsuspecting sheep, as they waddled out of the way and he made a silent contract with his stomach to obtain a taste of one that very night.

The halt was called soon afterwards and whilst others munched their dry biscuits, Bentinck saved his for better enjoyments on offer. As darkness fell he stole away across the moor. Creeping along behind the furze bushes he got close up to the bleating flock, made a sudden dash into it and caught a sheep with each hand. They were big ones; they dragged him off his feet and over the rough ground until he was obliged to let go of one in order to stick to the other. Then Bentinck managed by the persevering use of an old blunt pocket knife to execute his deed in darkness. He slew, skinned and cut up the poor bleater and bore it in triumph to his mess. He deposited a leg at the Captain's tent door, another at the Lieutenant's and giving a comrade a shoulder he got help to cook the rest.

Eight or ten men of their Regiment came in that night similarly laden, only they brought their sheep in whole, flaying and dissecting them in camp. When the Colonel turned out in the morning he saw sheep's heads, hides and entrails littered about in all directions. He was far too old a soldier to ask disagreeable questions and remembered that he had himself found juicy mutton chops on his breakfast table that morning. 'What's all this?' he cried with profound astonishment. 'Are you turning the camp into a slaughterhouse? Clear away this nuisance as quickly as possible, I expect the General here every minute.' All was promptly cleared away, as much as would fit into the knapsacks of his faithful followers. Bentinck, with his usual forethought for number one, contrived to make a canteen full of rich broth ere they set out.

The geographical position of Toulouse, in particular the courses of the nearby rivers, afforded many defensive advantages to the French. The Calvinet ridge to the north-east was the preferable point to launch an assault from but this required the River Garonne to be crossed.[18] Furthermore, Soult had fortified this position with redoubts. Heavy rains and the size of the rivers meant that only pontoon bridges constructed by the engineers were a viable option. This took time and gave the battalion the chance for a short rest, which they took advantage of.

The Allies then pressed on, driving Soult before them from Dax,[19] from St Severe [sic], after sharp engagements to Toulouse before which town they arrived on March 27th. They remained on the opposite side of the Garonne River about a fortnight, owing to the flooding of the river and the destruction of all the bridges by the French.

Bentinck's Company was billeted in a large farm house, which held them all without inconveniencing the residents. There was an immense brick oven in the large kitchen set apart for them. The first night one of the soldiers noticed that the mouth of this place was newly bricked up. With shrewd curiosity, they soon picked out the bricks with their bayonets and found a large store of wines, preserves, pickles and other delicacies, which were speedily engulfed in their ever ready stomachs. Wine was so plentiful that the men cooked potatoes and meat in it. In a village close by, deserted by the inhabitants, were found manufactories of it, containing hundreds of casks. The men used to fetch it in buckets. They had to take a Corporal with them in consequence of some mischievous fellows having run off with a number of casks, until even the horses in the adjacent stables were fetlock deep in wine.

One of Bentinck's companions was flogged with four dozen lashes for stealing apples from a farmer's garden. Plenty of his comrades had filled their knapsacks from the same trees, but had been more skilful about it. This poor fellow had been seen by the farmer who followed him into camp and made a formal complaint. The farmers hereabouts had carefully cut the tops off their growing potatoes, so that the soldiers might take them for ploughed fields, but the latter, keen of scent by long and hard practice, found out the dodge and had their fill of stolen potatoes as regularly as could be.

While lying before Toulouse, Bentinck's Regiment, the 23rd of Foot, captured a French vessel, coming unscrupulously up the river. She was laden with cloth. This was a God send to the ragged soldiers, the best clad of whom had tattered trousers made out of old blankets; the worst clad had nothing much in the way of clothing to describe. The Colonel at once portioned out the cloth to each Company, gave orders that every man who could cut or sew must be put to work and in a day or two had every man rigged out in new trousers. As the cloth embraced every colour of the rainbow, blue, green, red and even yellow, the effect was laughable in the extreme, but the poor fellows had so long been near to breechless that they wore them with pure joy.[20]

On 4 April the allies established a pontoon bridge across the Garonne north of Toulouse and 19,000 troops crossed. The bridge was swept away but the French failed to defeat the force and the bridge was rapidly rebuilt. Wellington's plan for the taking of Toulouse was for the 4th and 6th Divisions, under command of Marshal Beresford, to attack the Calvinet ridge. After a long approach march, the assault commenced with the 4th Division on the left and the 6th Division on the right. The Fusilier Brigade advanced in the second line, behind another brigade. The allies deterred a French infantry and cavalry attack, whilst under near-constant fire from forty enemy artillery pieces.

We crossed early on the morning of 9th April 1814. There was but little opposition and the pickets went and gave an alarm at the town that we had crossed the river. We marched up to a little village near the city. Old Napoleon was just returning from Russia with what few men he had. He sent a telegram to General Soult to give up the town but we took the messenger before he had delivered his message. It fell in our hands and was given to Wellington. He sent a flag of truce unto Soult with the message to surrender the town as peace was made. But Soult would not believe it as he thought Wellington was playing a trick on him.[21]

On the 10th April it being Easter Monday that year, we advanced on the town to take it by force. Our Army was divided according to the work they had to do as we had a strong force to take command of the town. Our Division was not appropriate to storm the fort but our Colonel wanted very bad to go and storm the fort. He sent a message to Wellington to ask him to let him do it. But Wellington himself came back and said, 'Colonel Ellis, I wish you would obey my orders for your Regiment.' Ellis had announced that our Regiment had lost very few men but the Regiments that stormed the fort got almost cut to pieces.

When the other Divisions was going onto the hill, we had to send two hundred men from each Regiment to reinforce them. The French sent out a flag of truce for about three or four hours while they buried their dead and it was granted them. We buried ours. When the time was up there came a lot of cavalry out and we thought they were coming to cut up our squares. We sent a rocket or two amongst them and they're horses fell from under them. They fled back to the town. Night was coming on and we were taking up a fresh position when a shot came from the town and took four of the men's legs off.[22]

Soult realized that his defence of the Calvinet Ridge was fruitless and he withdrew his forces behind the city's fortifications. Soult then retreated with his troops along a road to the south-east on the evening of 11 April. The battle cost the Allies 4,558 killed, wounded and missing. French casualties were 3,236; few if any prisoners were reported. The battalion lost only one man killed and eight wounded, most likely due to the favourable positioning of the Fusilier Brigade during the battle.

The French Army, about 30,000 men, were now within the city and Soult declared that they should be buried beneath its walls rather than surrender. On the following night, however, he abandoned the place, and the Allies took possession of it, greatly to the joy of the inhabitants, who longed for peace and had been terrified at the thoughts of a siege. Previous to this, Paris had capitulated. Bonaparte, so long the terror of the civilised world, had relinquished the French throne. It was said that Soult had before the battle received orders from Bonaparte to surrender, but he refused.

On the morning of 12 April a delegation of city officials welcomed the allies into the city and on that afternoon of 12 April official couriers from Paris conveyed news of Napoleon's abdication.

'There was but a little done after that night and early the next morning they blew the bridge and made their retreat. We followed them onto the other side of the river. We followed the French for two or three days and then we saw some of the men returning to Toulouse. They were discharged after Soult knew that peace was made.'

One morning, they were surprised to see numbers of Frenchmen, both soldiers and civilians, coming to meet them, with white cockades and white flags. They proclaimed peace at last, dancing and chatting wildly in their glee. The British therefore went into quarters at Bordeaux, their mighty task at last being over.

Great were the rejoicings and hearty the hospitality with which they were everywhere received, though in an enemy's country, for the inhabitants had long groaned under the iron yoke of Bonaparte. The many coloured trousers of the Fusileers were here replaced by new trousers and for the first time in years they looked like civilised soldiers.

The battalion spent nearly two months in cantonments in the Bordeaux area. A move back to the United Kingdom was far from a certainty. War was raging in North America and British troops were desperately needed there, particularly experienced, battle-hardened ones. Fortunately for the battalion, years of campaigning on the Peninsula had thinned its ranks sufficiently for it not to be chosen and in June orders were finally received to embark for England.

There were ten thousand men chosen to go [to North America] in 1814 but my Regiment came back to England as we had not sufficient number of men to go to America.

———•———

1. Saint-Jean-de-Luz is a coastal town, astride the River Nivelle, six miles to the north-east of Hendaye.
2. The village of Sarre was covered by two redoubts, the Sainte-Barbe and the Grenade. The French were encircled by a Spanish division and the 7th Division, whilst the 4th Division conducted a frontal attack.
3. It has not been possible to find any biographical information on this man. Furthermore, the battalion did not suffer any casualties in the attack on Sarre. The 4th Division drove the French 'from their entrenched positions with the greatest ease, indeed so much so that the rear Brigades of each Division even at the principal point of attack were never engaged. The enemy as usual rather abandoning the few tents they had, with all their heavy artillery, than wait for the arrival of half the troops that were brought against them, consequently the losses fell on a few particular regiments

that led the different columns.' RWFM, Acc. 5935, MacDonald to father, 26 November 1813.

4. The village of Ainhoa is less than a mile over the French border and fifteen miles to the south-east of Saint-Jean-de-Luz.

5. High ground around what was a large village of 800 people, split by a tributary of the River Nivelle and five miles to the south of Saint-Jean-de-Luz.

6. The village of Saint-Pée-sur-Nivelle was a grouping of a number of settlements, four miles north of Sarre and five miles north-west of Ainhoa.

7. Allied losses were 2,526 killed and wounded whilst the French lost 4,321.

8. The River Adour is over 200 miles long, rising in the French Pyrenees and discharging at Bayonne. It presumed that there is a slight inaccuracy in this account. General Hill crossed the River Nive between Cambo and Ustaritz on 9 December, with difficult contests in some areas, to occupy the high ground to the south of the River Adour.

9. The large village of Villefranque, on the northern bank of the River Nive and five miles south of Bayonne.

10. General Sir John Hope, 4th Earl of Hopetoun (1765–1823). Before the Peninsular campaign, he had served in the West Indies and Egypt. He commanded a division in Sir John Moore's expedition, was at the Battle of Corunna and commanded the embarkation. For a period he was Commander-in-Chief Ireland before returning to Spain under Wellington, becoming second-in-command of the allied army. During the invasion of France he commanded a corps, with a strong tendency to be involved at the tactical level. Hope was wounded and captured by the French at Bayonne. Subsequently he was a governor of the Royal Bank of Scotland.

11. A temporary pontoon bridge over the Nive at Villefranque was washed away leaving Hill with about 14,000 men and ten guns to the east of the river.

12. Saint-Boes, in this period, was a small village, with a church. It is positioned on high ground two miles to the north-west of Orthez, with the road to Dax from Orthez running through it. The initial part of the battle was a bitter contest for possession of the village.

13. Allied losses at the battle were 2,164 all ranks, which included 80 men listed as missing. The 4th Division was significantly engaged in the battle. French losses were officially 3,985, including 1,366 prisoners. However, the French characteristically understated their casualties, and desertions in the aftermath of the battle further eroded their combat power as they retreated toward Toulouse.

14. The 23rd Foot suffered 1 sergeant and 15 rank and file killed, whilst Captains Wynne and Joliffe, Lieutenant Harris, 6 sergeants and 69 rank and file were wounded. The Fusilier Brigade commander, Major General Robert Ross, was wounded and Lieutenant Colonel Ellis took over command as the French artillery extracted a terrible price. Saint-Boes was fought hard over by the brigade 'which never exceeded a thousand men, kept their ground with the greatest obstinacy & even drove the enemy for a considerable distance and before any other troops had arrived to their assistance'. RWFM, Acc. 5935, MacDonald to father, 5 March 1814.

15. There were no French dragoons at Orthez, only light regiments. This French unit may have been the 21st Chasseurs à Cheval.

16. The 5th Foot was part of the 3rd Division, which was principally engaged to the north-west of Orthez during the battle. Wellington's wound on the thigh may have made him bad-tempered in the immediate aftermath of the battle.

17. The town of Saint-Sever, seventy miles north-east of Bayonne and twenty miles north of Orthez.

18. The River Garonne rises in the Spanish Pyrenees and flows north into France, through Toulouse and Agen before discharging into the Gironde estuary before Bordeaux. During this period, the very high rainfall caused the river to swell so much as to make fording in many places impossible.

19. Dax was a large town thirty miles to the north-east of Bayonne. During the campaign it was an important logistics location for the French. It was defended by low-quality local troops who deserted on the first appearance of allied forces. Many stores were captured by the allies.

20. New clothing had been provided to the allied army in the winter of 1813, the different corps or regiments being allowed to come down from the lines to St-Jean-de-Luz, where they arrived successively. 'The day they marched into St. Jean de Luz, they halted, the day after they clothed from head to foot, & the day after that, they began their march to the Army. This operation lasted, until nearly all the Army were newly clothed. The scene of this operation was not a little amusing, & the wit of the Soldiers, at thus changing as it were their skins, was exerted to the utmost. Caps, Jackets, Trowsers, everything old, was thrown away, & the Army soon appeared as gay as it had ever done. The men became comfortable & warm, & the quantity & quality of the vermin, they thus got rid of, was sufficient, as they themselves owned, to cause their becoming fat & plump in a very short time.' Browne, *Napoleonic War Journal*, p. 255.

21. This paragraph is inaccurate. On 7 April, a British and a French envoy were sent from Paris to convey news of Napoleon's unconditional abdication and the restoration of the monarchy. At 8.00 on the evening of 12 April they arrived in Toulouse with their dispatches. Napoleon had of course been back from the Russian campaign for nearly two years. Nor were telegrams available in 1814.

22. MacDonald provides a first-hand account of the culmination of the battle, as the Fusilier Brigade 'advanced against some very strong redoubts which the French evacuated in the most cowardly manner. The sight was the finest I ever saw, & every part of the army that saw it were delighted. We completely succeeded in our part & must have taken an immense amount of prisoners if our cavalry who had moved on the right bank of the large river, had been able to cross, but finding all the bridges destroyed they were obliged to make a great detour & were consequently late in coming up.' RWFM, Acc. 5935, MacDonald to father, 13 April 1814.

A further account of the battle is also provided by Roberts. 'On Sunday morning the battle began in right earnest. We swept all the batteries before us. Our brigade formed against cavalry. I was placed outside the square to keep the men from falling out; and here the wind of a cannon ball that came close by knocked me down, and blew the cap from my head. The cap rolled away some yards, when I heard Lieutenant Henry, 7th Fusiliers, swear that "Sergeant Roberts' head was knocked off." On recovering my breath I started after my cap, when the Lieutenant shouted, "All's right; his head's still on his shoulders." This was a terrible battle. I never saw so much slaughter in the whole campaign – that is, in any single engagement. But victory declared for us; and when all was over, I thanked God heartily that I had done my duty to my King and my country.' Roberts, 'Incidents in the Life of an Old Fusilier', No. 2, p. 23.

Chapter Ten

Peace and Waterloo

———•———

O n 14 June 1814, the battalion embarked at Pauillac in the Gironde estuary on HMS *Egmont* for the return voyage. The strength of the battalion on the conclusion of the campaign was 788 all ranks, accompanied by a handful of wives and children. Of this number a few were veterans not only of this campaign but also the North American garrison duty and the Martinique expedition. This meant that some had been away from home for over six years. Bentinck was one of these and his account does display a hint of what must have been considerable emotional relief and general fatigue after such an experience.

They landed at Plymouth. Enthusiastic rejoicings were taking place there, they found, at the establishment of peace once more, after the long reign of war. Every Regiment that landed was cheered, fed and regaled as though each man of it were some illustrious hero, until it seemed like dreamland to the poor fellows after having had years of fighting and starving and marching in inhospitable climes.

Orders for the battalion were to progress along the route Ivybridge, Bridport, Dorchester and Southampton to Gosport, where they were garrisoned in a newly built location called simply the 'The new military barracks'. The battalion arrived at Gosport on 16 July 1814 and moved into the barracks assisted by the 2nd Battalion, 23rd Foot, which was also stationed there. Unusually, it was the first time that the two battalions had been in the same location.[1]

Traders' processions filled the streets, fireworks lit up the nights and free feasts were bountifully spread throughout the ancient borough. The Royal Fusileers rested and fed there for about a week and then set out on their march to Gosport, their Headquarters. In almost every town they passed through they were treated to as much meat and drink as they could use by their fellow countrymen, who were not only joyful at peace, but delighted to have amongst them the gallant soldiers who had won it for them.

The deeds of the Fusileers the people had read in every notable engagement – the veterans who first rushed to the storming of Badajoz;

and left 700 of their number smitten and slain in its awful breach; who with the rest of the 4th Division, did at Albuera what the rest of our whole army had failed to do. They stopped the French advance, when the enemy had all but won the battle, then defeated and overthrew them, but alas, at a cost of 4,500 gallant souls out of only 6,000. The Welsh Fusileers who they had heard much of in connection with the bloody capture of Ciudad Rodrigo, the battle of Salamanca, of Vitoria, of Talavera, of Fuente Guinaldo, of the Pyrenees, of Orthez and of Toulouse. No wonder that the enthusiasm of their stay at home countrymen was aroused at the sight of the Regiment, whose name was so often inscribed on history's page.

At length, however, these hospitable potations interfered so much with the men's marching that the Officers began to put a stop to them when they could, for drunkenness was an offence that the Colonel most disliked to see. Still the men got plenty of grog given to them when their day's duties were over. The townspeople would make bonfires, get the soldiers to fire volleys of blank cartridges and then roll out barrels of beer for the general delectation.

When they came to Southampton, the Militias were assembled there. The Fusileer Colonel[2] took up his quarters at the head hotel and the faithful Regimental Colours were as usual displayed from his windows. These colours the Regiment had had all through the Danish campaign, their Canadian sojourn, the Martinique invasion and the Peninsular War; and shot, shell, sword cuts, weather and battle smoke had reduced the once gay banners to what seemed like a few discoloured rags fluttering from a pole. A number of jealous Militiamen hooted and made fun of these war torn symbols saying they were not worth putting up.

There upon a gentleman in the crowd gathered around indignantly to denounce their conduct. In the course of an inspiring speech, he pointed out that the tattered aspect of the flags was their greatest honour and amid the cheers of the crowd, wound up by making a collection for the Fusileers. Upwards of fifty pounds was soon contributed in response. On taking it to the Colonel, he received much thanks for their good will, but much to the disappointment of the men, the Colonel declined to accept it, on the grounds that the men, if they got any drink would end up fighting with the Militiamen.

Not long after settling into the new barracks and the routine of peacetime soldiering substantial change followed. The successful conclusion of the war brought a perceived need to reduce the size of the army and consequently significantly reduce financial costs. To achieve this reduction rapidly a far-reaching decision was taken. Assessments were required across all battalions to identify men who could be deemed to be physically unsuitable, such as being below the minimum height of 5 feet 5 inches, or who could be perceived as to be unfit after the rigours of foreign service and hence could be discharged. Furthermore, there was no longer a need for second battalions of regiments and, on 24 October 1814, the 2nd Battalion was disbanded and merged into the 1st Battalion.[3]

The result was that the Welch Fusiliers were now but a single battalion regiment but with the considerable strength of 1,197 men. Despite the organizational changes, the commanding officer of the 1st Battalion, Colonel Ellis, demonstrated his sense of fair play to all and it was he who ensured that all soldiers who had sailed to North America in 1808 with the battalion and were still serving on return from the Peninsula received a considerable period of leave, and he also made certain that all the men's pay was up to date.

> On reaching Gosport, their destination, a number of the Fusileers were discharged, on account of being too short in stature for the peace standard, though some of them had proven to be the best soldiers in the Regiment. The Colonel went on leave of absence,[4] leaving orders for Colonel Dalmer,[5] his temporary successor, to allow a furlough to every man who had been in Canada. Bentinck was one of these. Several others tried to get leave instead of him, but Colonel Dalmer said, 'No, the boy shall go; he has been with us thus far and behaved himself as well as any of you.'
>
> Bentinck was offered three months leave but only accepted two, as he did not know whether he should find any relatives living to stay with. Owing to the busy life of the Regiment, its incessant movements and the very expensive postage of those days, especially for foreign letters, he had never written home since he had left it – eight years before, though had often intended to do so. He did not even know whether his Mother was living or dead.

Bentinck made the decision to head home by foot to Stowmarket, which was a considerable undertaking from Gosport.

Drawing back pay to the amount of £9 and smartly arrayed in new Regimentals, our friend set out, in the autumn of 1814 to look up his long-lost home. He had about 150 miles to march. This he got over in four or five days, sometimes obtaining a lift in a countryman's wagon for a few miles. On the last evening as usual, owing to his uniform indicating a Regiment known to have just come from the wars, he had partaken, contrary to his custom, so freely that when he set off on his way he found himself marching somewhat unsteadily, so he turned into a field, lay down on the ground, as he had done scores of times on foreign soil and slept. When he awoke he had quite lost all idea of the way he had come or the way he had to go. So he sat until a wagon came by. The driver could not tell Bentinck anything about his Mother, saying he knew no-one of that name about there.

Bentinck took a lift and as they were passing a cottage, a woman came out to empty the leaves of a tea pot. At a glance, Bentinck recognised his Mother, looking much older and thinner than when he saw her last, but to him he felt she was the same kind old Mother still. Of course, the change eight years had made in his appearance, from the 14 years of age to two and twenty was so great that she did not recognise him at first. She asked, 'Soldier, do you know of any boy of the name of Bentinck in your Regiment?' The young man, being too overcome for a moment to speak, stood still. She gazed at him and then cried, 'Richard, Richard, is it yourself?' and Bentinck replied, 'It is what there is left of me.' There was then quite a tearful meeting between the long bereaved Mother and her long lost son.

She hurried him into the cottage and set before him the best it could afford. She told him that his Father had died long ago and she was married again, to a decent labouring man. When the Stepfather saw him, he was very proud of him and bade him a hearty welcome.

The stepfather was a farm labourer and suggested to Bentinck that he might find employment for a few weeks at the same farm. Bentinck followed his advice and made himself known to the farmer.

'The farmer asked me would I help him in the harvest field. I said that I didn't know because I had not come home for work. The farmer said to come over as I would enjoy it. I went and helped him until the corn was all got in. He was a jovial sort of figure and we always had plenty of beer. He used to call out, "Come soldier and have your beer." Every day he would have me go to dinner with him and he was never tired hearing about the war.'

Bentinck helped the good farmer with his harvest, collecting all the corn and wheat until it was in, receiving several welcome sovereigns for so doing. He joined in the harvest home festival and thoroughly enjoyed himself until his two months leave was up.

It did not appear to be Bentinck's intention to gain employment during his leave, but he was clever enough to reach an agreement with the farmer on starting work.

I made an agreement with him at the beginning and one day when we had finished he said, 'Come soldier, what must I give you?' I said, 'Well, I don't know if three pounds would be too much?'[6] He said that would do and we had a supper for the ending of the harvest.[7] We had plenty of beer and we began to drink to his health and wife and family. But some of his friends could not finish drinking his health because they were quite drunk. I sat there to the last and we were invited to go the next day and finish what was left. When I had bid farewell to all that I had a longing for that life. My time was up and I had to join my regiment again at Gosport.

The interlude of peaceful garrison soldiering was not to last long for the battalion. In the aftermath of Napoleon's abdication, the European powers struggled to find a way to make the peace sustainable. Austria, Britain, France, Prussia and Russia were unable to reach a consensus at the Congress of Vienna in 1814. The weakness of Louis XVIII as head of state in France and discontent amongst the military prompted Napoleon to plan to reclaim power.

After spending only nine months and twenty-one days in exile on the Mediterranean island of Elba, he took advantage of poor security to escape to Antibes on 1 March 1815. Within ten days he was in Lyon and the nations assembled at Vienna decreed him an outlaw, mobilizing forces to oust him. Napoleon entered Paris on 19 March 1815. He wasted no time in re-establishing the military capability of France and by the end of May he had managed to assemble nearly 200,000 troops. Despite his limited education Bentinck had a fair understanding of the circumstances regarding the re-emergence of Napoleon.

I had not been there long when the rumours came that Napoleon had got out of Elba. They had just crowned old Louis XVIII who was at the time heir to the throne of France. All the Generals and the Army had sworn to be his loyal subjects. Marshall Ney requested 30 thousand men to go out and meet Napoleon. He would bring him either dead or alive and the King granted his request but before he had got two or three days march he stopped his men and he told them he was going to meet their friend Napoleon and they all rejoiced. When Marshall Ney met Napoleon he delivered all the Army to him. Then he proceeded up to Paris and he forced every young and able man to join it as he went to Paris and when Louis heard that he was coming up to Paris with all his force he fled to Belgium for protection under the English. He had but a very short reign when he had to run away and he came over to England while all got settled again.

The Allies were not slow to react to the re-emergence of Napoleon. The British government ordered the despatch of all available forces to the continent in an effort to mass troops under the allied banner. The battalion received its orders for deployment on 22 March[8] and the next day at Gosport, with bands playing, the uncased colours flying and all the people cheering, the battalion loaded onto three transports: *Ariel, Percival* and *Poniana*. The transports sailed on the 25th and arrived off Deal on the 26th. The uncased colours referred to were actually from the 2nd Battalion, Colonel Ellis making the decision that the 1st Battalion Colours were too battle-worn for this latest adventure. The battalion was organized into ten companies, with overall command again residing with Lieutenant Colonel (Brevet Colonel) Sir Henry W. Ellis, KCB. The muster state for the deployment was 42 officers, 31 sergeants, 24 drummers, 36 corporals and 611 privates.[9]

The nations of Europe were smitten with alarm; British soldiers who had been able to humble him before, were eagerly looked to and the Welsh Fusileers were among the first to receive orders and the first to embark for this new and unexpected war. The order was received at the end of February 1815 and on the 5th March [sic], with bands playing, colours waving and people cheering they set out from Gosport to the seat of war. Now the last great act in Bentinck's tumultuous military experiences can be narrated, the battle of Waterloo.

The crossing of the Channel was not without event. Shortly after leaving Gosport harbour, the transport *Ariel* grounded on a sandbank and once freed, experienced a tremendous gale.[10] On the 29th the battalion cross-loaded into small craft, landed at Ostend on 30 March and moved to link up with other British troops. The battalion was brigaded with the inexperienced 3/14th, which had over 300 new recruits, and the experienced 1/51st in the 4th British Brigade,[11] part of the 4th Division (British and Hanoverians) under the command of Lieutenant General Sir Charles Colville. After a few days of marching across Belgium the battalion then spent a couple of fairly pleasurable weeks in Ghent, the most taxing of duties being the occasional provision of a guard for Louis XVIII's residence.[12]

> They landed at Ostend, the first Regiment at the rendezvous. After one day's delay they proceeded by canal to the ancient city of Bruges, remained there for about a week and then, making room for the troops that by this time were rapidly coming up, they pushed on to Ghent. They were then overtaken by the 51st Regiment,[13] whom they then kept company with for a fortnight, before marching rapidly on up the country. They found the inhabitants were kindly disposed and were well treated by them.

Subsequently the battalion moved to Grammont, a small town to the south-west of Ghent and on 24 April 1815 was ordered into cantonments. The period up to 16 June was one of comparative tranquillity. The 51st and 23rd were both cantoned in this town and, under the direction of Colonel Mitchell, conducted some training every morning. The inhabitants were kindly disposed and billeted the officers and men, who in kind assisted in the harvest. Aside from this, there was little to do until Napoleon made his first move and the officers occupied themselves with field days and sightseeing. The men were quite content, 'Never did I spend such pleasant days and these kind hearted fellows were never easy unless they were contributing something toward the happiness of the British soldier.'[14] However, Wellington was not happy. A number of veteran British units were yet to return from service in North America and he could only draw on a core of around 24,000 British and King's German Legion infantry, with the remainder of his force, many of whom were raw recruits, coming from Belgian, Brunswick, Dutch and Hanoverian units. Recognizing the varying quality of each unit, Wellington mixed what he perceived to be reliable units with unreliable or untested units.

A substantial review of the army was undertaken at Grammont, which Bentinck commented upon:

> We were put into Brigades and the cavalry had review on a plain. They put in Brigades so that they would know what Regiments had to go together. It was rumoured that Napoleon was present at the review in disguise but I cannot entertain that to being true.[15]

Napoleon knew that the Allies were preparing to invade France and also that
Austria and Russia were still mobilizing. He thus drew up a plan to attack the
Prussians and the Anglo-Dutch force and take Brussels. Napoleon realized that
his chances of achieving this would be reduced if the Prussian and Anglo-Dutch
armies could affect a link-up. So on 15 June 1815 he ordered his forces to cross the
River Sambre at Charleroi and manoeuvre to achieve a position between the two
allied armies. Napoleon sent Marshal Ney, with two corps under command, to
Quatre Bras to seize the vital crossroads, whilst he himself took the remaining
three corps to launch an attack on the Prussian army.

> Advancing as a lumbering tide toward the same centre came host upon
> host of the Allies, who had under arms nearly a million of armed men,
> viz; English 50,000, Prussians 200,000, Austrians 300,000, Germans
> 150,000, The Netherlands 50,000. Napoleon Bonaparte under all of his
> pressure of time and many disadvantages, contrived to assemble nearly
> 900,000.[16] The great mass of the Allies was assembling towards
> Brussels, for the purpose of guarding that capital. On the 14th June,[17]
> Bonaparte commenced his march at the head of 25,000 Cavalry, 25,000
> of the Imperial Guard, about 80,000 Infantry and 350 pieces of
> Artillery; in all about 130,000 men. The numbers of the Allies in the
> immediate vicinity were Prussians 100,000, English 35,000, Germans
> 8,000, Hanoverians 15,000, Brunswickers 5,000, Dutch and Belgians
> 17,000; total around 175,000.

> 'On the 15th June all the Allied powers had a great ball[18] where they
> made themselves very comfortable. At the commencement of the ball,
> to their surprise the French broke out on the Russians [*sic*] and
> Prussians about two o'clock in the morning of the 16th. They were all
> greatly alarmed when they heard that the French had begun and the
> Duke of Brunswick went out of the ball soon and commanded his Army.
> Most of the British Officers and Wellington were present; until
> summoned away in hot haste to the impending battle.'

The return of key commanders to the fold resulted in some decisions being
made for the deployment of Allied forces.

Soon a mounted messenger galloped up with the news of the Prussian
defeat at Ligny. We were told that we must be off as quick as possible
and we had not above an hour to get ready.

On 16 June the battalion was initially ordered to march toward Enghien and subsequently to Braine-le-Comte. Here the men rested overnight. having heard the sounds of fighting from the battle of Quatre Bras. The march continued the next day to Nivelles and finally to Braine-l'Alleud, an area some two miles to the south-west of the town of Waterloo. The weather was poor and the distance fatiguing, but it was essential for the Allies to manoeuvre into a position to force Napoleon to engage in battle.

> On the morning of 16th June, the Brigade with which the old friend's Regiment was incorporated, were ordered to take three day's provisions for each man and march towards Waterloo, the little town that was so soon to become famous in the world's history.
>
> The day was so hot that the men were allowed to wear their white linen forage jackets. Placing their trust to the continued kindness of the inhabitants, and little dreaming of the coming needs, many of the soldiers would not load themselves with extra provisions. They marched all that day. At night they were halted, but as they were preparing for rest they heard the faint sound of cannonading in the distance.

The next day the battalion woke early to continue on the march to Nivelles, which it reached by midday. Casualties and confusion from the Battle of Quatre Bras were very much in evidence. The battalion then headed north toward Waterloo and halted in a hamlet called Merbe Braine about three miles south of Waterloo.[19]

> It was about eleven o'clock at night when we got up to Quatre Bras where there had been a sharp action that day. Before we could get there to reinforce the Prussians they retreated. After that we lay down to have a few hours rest. We had marched all that day in our white jackets but on the morning of the 17th we were ordered to put on our red ones and then we marched by the side of the road for a few miles.

Napoleon's plan of defeating the Prussians and the Anglo-Dutch force separately and preventing a link-up was being executed. On 16 June 1815, at the village of Ligny, some fifteen miles south-east of Waterloo, Napoleon's Army of the North defeated Blücher's Prussian army. An inconclusive bloody battle at Quatre Bras, a crossroads of the Namur–Nivelles and the Brussels–Charleroi road, and news of the Prussian defeat, prompted the withdrawal of Anglo-Dutch forces to a position close to Waterloo and the forest of Soignes that Wellington had pre-selected. Napoleon took too much time to re-organize his army after the fierce battle, which allowed the consolidation of Wellington's forces, whilst Marshal Grouchy with 33,000 men was tasked to pursue the defeated Prussians.

It was well known that Wellington had an eye for ground and favoured fighting from a carefully selected defensive position. In this case he had selected an east–west ridge of three miles' length with a relatively steep forward slope and gentle reverse slope providing a very convenient position. In front of the ridge there was a low valley which then rose to a second and higher ridge some 1,200 yards away. Along the length of the ridge ran a country road which afforded a degree of protection from both view and fire. This lateral road was cut by two principal north–south routes, the Brussels–Genappe road at the centre of the ridge and the Nivelles highway. On the left flank of the position there were a number of small villages and farms. In the centre, the Brussels–Genappe road dominated, with a large farm compound, La Haye Sainte, situated next to the road on the forward slope. On the right flank the Château de Hougoumont, with a collection of farm buildings and an enclosed orchard, was the most important feature.

Napoleon had managed to mass 77,000 men, nearly all of whom were veterans, and 266 artillery pieces. In comparison, Wellington had 73,000 troops and 192 guns for this battle but the quality and experience levels were variable. Key units were placed at important positions along the three miles of the Allied front on the battlefield, such as Hougoumont and La Haye Sainte. The artillery was afforded fields of fire from the frontal slope, whilst the infantry were able to use the reverse slope of the ridge for protection. From fear of Napoleon attempting an outflanking manoeuvre, 17,000 troops were positioned eight miles to the west.

The 1/23rd was marching hard, along with other units in order to reach the nominated positions:

> On the 17th, the evening before the battle, the Battalion was bivouacked in a rye-field near the village of Merbe-Braine. The night closed and it was very dark and we could scarcely tell Brunswick troops from the French until our Colonel cautioned us not to fire. There was no food to be issued to the men so they were instead issued with a half liquor ration. It was a very dismal night with thunder and lightning and rain which poured down very heavy.[20] It continued until about four o'clock on the morning of the 18th when the sun came out.[21] We had orders on the previous night not to put out our blankets but one or two or three others pulled them out against orders and put them over to

keep the rain off. In the morning when the rain gave over we rung them out as well as we could. We put them in our Knapsacks again before any of the Officers saw us.

The unfavourable weather conditions and the lack of rations meant that a number of the battalion, Bentinck included, used their initiative to find food.

Then we began to look out for something to eat as we were all very hungry. We had not had anything for two days. Some of our men chewed the green ears of the young corn. There was a potato field close by and some of the men dug into the field with their fingers and their bayonets. I went to some house close by that the inhabitants had left but I could only find one barrel of thick beer.[22] I drank about a quart of that and it filled my belly for a while for it was both a meal and a drink. As I was coming back to the regiment I happened to look behind me and I saw old Wellington coming behind me with two of his staff. They were coming to the Regiment but I got in as soon as I could and he said nothing to me nor I to him. I had not been back long when we had to fall in and form our lines. The Colonel was to make a speech and encourage the men. He said, 'Now the 23rd we are going to have a hot day of it and mind you don't lose your character that you have gained before.'

Recognizing the value of the hard-won experience of the 23rd and 51st Foot, Wellington took Colonel Mitchell's brigade and placed it on the right flank of the ridge position:

Five companies of the 51st and the light company of the 14th were placed to the west of the Nivelles road along a continuation of the sunken lane or 'covered way,' as it is referred to in most accounts of the battle, that ran behind Hougoumont. The remaining five companies of the 51st Foot were positioned about 200 yards behind in support while the 14th Foot was placed farther to the rear just south of Merbe Braine. The Welch Fusiliers were placed in the second line of the main position on the reverse slope of the ridge, immediately behind Major General Sir John Byng's Guards brigade, whose light companies formed part of the garrison of Hougoumont. Lieutenant Fensham's light company of the 23rd was stationed forward in the covered way behind the château with its right flank on the Nivelles highway, parallel to a company of the 51st,

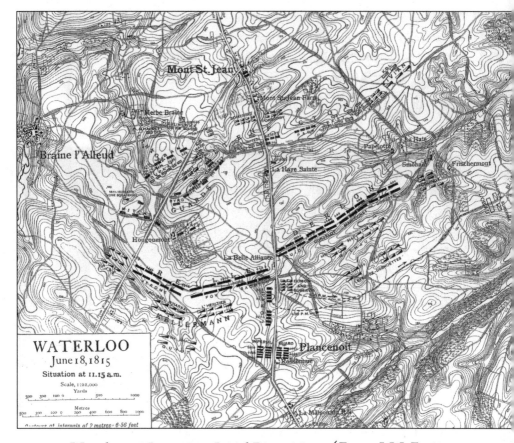

Waterloo, 18 June 1815: Initial Dispositions. (*From: J. W. Fortescue, History of the British Army*)

whose left flank rested on it. Immediately upon coming into position, both companies constructed an abattis or barrier of tangled small trees and branches across the highway to discourage its use by French cavalry plainly visible not 500 yards to the south.[23]

As the brigade marched toward the chosen battlefield, a chance French force seized the opportunity, while the army was extended, to attack the poorly defended baggage train, which included the 1/23rd's.

All of our baggage was behind us and a party of the French was laid in a little wood. About an hour after we heard that the French party had taken all our provisions. They thought they were not strong enough to attack us so they stopped and laid in wait for the baggage.

The battalion took up its positions immediately behind Hougoumont around 10.00 in the morning. Colonel Ellis kept the battalion in a formation known as column of companies, affording flexibility for movement and deployment. The men sat in a trampled rye field, which had a gentle reverse-slope gradient, and waited, watching the rest of the allied army form up for the coming battle. It has been suggested that Napoleon held back on launching his attack in order to allow the wet ground in the valley to dry and provide more suitable conditions for the cavalry.

The first element of the battle was sustained artillery fire from both sides. After some fifteen minutes of this the first French cavalry charge was launched.

Bentinck was his Colonel's orderly, so had to keep close to him during the day. Then the signal gun fired and it was soon announced all along the line that the French Cavalry were about to show themselves. When the first cannon fired, the Colonel took out his watch and said, 'We begin at twenty minutes past eleven.'[24] In a few minutes the uproar was tremendous; the roar of the cannons and rattle of the musketry making the ground shake and tremble like a bog.

The Fusileers sent out their Light Company into the wood[25] held by the French in such masses as to shoot down two thirds of the Company before they could ascertain the enemy's strength. Mr Finch,[26] a young Officer whom Bentinck liked much, was one of the few wounded who the survivors managed to bring away and he unfortunately died a few minutes after. The French had just taken the wood from the Belgians. It was a most important point, for from it they could debouch upon the vital road to Brussels, held by the Fusileers and other chosen Regiments. When it was a matter of concern, Wellington himself galloped up and ensured it was retaken, no matter at what loss.

There were up to twenty-three French artillery pieces ranged on the area of Hougoumont but the protection of the trees meant that no concerted direct bombardment could take place. Instead the artillery concentrated on engaging the troops surrounding the château and those visible on the ridge behind. Allied troops positioned in support of Hougoumont were protected by the reverse slope, though an occasional shot would come bouncing over the crest, killing and wounding men. Colonel Ellis comprehended this threat and redeployed the battalion into a two-rank line, parallel to the ridge. The nearest British battalion was the 14th Foot, which was positioned further forward in support of Hougoumont and, whilst formed in square to counter the French cavalry, received the attentions of two artillery pieces but escaped with very light casualties, with the most notorious incident being the commanding officer's horse being hit by a shell.

At around 4.00 the battalion received the order to move forward of the ridge and support the Guards Brigade in defence of Hougoumont. Ellis redeployed the battalion into column of companies. The main French attack on the ridge had commenced around 3.00. On the French right flank, it became increasingly apparent that Prussian troops were coming into position to reinforce the Allied army and the French surged their cavalry into the attack in pursuit of a decisive effect. Some 4,000 horsemen advanced on the allied line between La Haye Sainte and Hougoumont. The battalion was ordered into a four-rank-deep square to meet this threat.

They were the renowned French Life Guards, great tall men in braid and with brass jackets fitting up to the neck and reaching down to the thighs, even the mightiest swordsman could not cut into it and bullets glanced of from a distance of fifty paces.

'They came surging out of the wood at full gallop. Colonel Ellis cried out, "Form Square," and as quick as the French were, our men were quicker and in a moment they placed themselves into that formation which of the day was proved by British soldiers to be dependable. The Cuirassiers[27] came on within only the last few feet off and then drew up looking for a gap in the line of bayonets bristling before them. At every shoulder hunched a comrade and each soldier stood like a rock.'

The French wheeled round and paused, not till then did the Colonel order, 'Fire.' Very few of the horsemen were killed though some were knocked down off their mounts by the force of the bullets which were unable to penetrate chain mail of brass.[28] In about half an hour they came twice, but with no better success on either side. Bentinck's brigade was supported by the Inniskillings, the 10th, the 15th and the 18th Hussars.[29] Next time the Curassiers came up the troopers of the 10th cried out to the Fusileers, 'Boys lather 'em and we'll shave 'em, fire lower, at the horses and we will look after the men.' This advice was taken. When the Frenchmen wheeled off, a low volley was poured into them. Bentinck counted upwards of 40 poor horses left lying on the plain, besides many that could not limp away.[30] In a moment, the Hussars dashed forwards and took prisoners of the dismounted riders, who were brought into the square. We took a number of men prisoner but not that many French were killed.

Bentinck gratified his curiosity by closely examining the brass jackets to see how it fastened with clasps on one side and hinges on the other. He unclasped one from a big, black whiskered fellow above six feet high and tried it on, the jacket reaching about him as to be down to the knees. The jackets were so heavy that the prisoners were very much glad to take them off and sit down on them which they did with as much unconcern as though the bloody war raging around them were only but a play.

'I opened one of the prisoners' knapsacks to see what I could get and I found two loaves of bread. I took them and gave one to my comrades and ate the other myself. We were all very desperate for food as it was the third day of not having anything.

'One of the prisoners was nearly drunk and all of a sudden he jumped up, breaking from the square and tried very hard to run back to his own lines. One of our Dragoons rode after him and grabbed him by the jacket and told him to come back, but he was too headstrong and would not come along. The Dragoon could do nothing but raise his sword and cleave his head open.'

The battalion remained as a formed square, four ranks deep, front two kneeling, from around 4.00 until close to the conclusion of the battle, due to the threat from the French cavalry. It is estimated that the French cavalry were committed to between fifteen and twenty attacks, ceasing close to 6.00. The battalion also received one French infantry attack in column. The square was very efficiently commanded by Colonel Ellis, who ensured that at least half the muskets on any one face of the square were kept loaded, whilst bayonets provided additional discouragement. The formation was, however, particularly vulnerable to the effects of artillery roundshot and shell.

As they came thundering up, apparently determined to sweep the squares from before them, their defeat, as they recoiled from the deadly volleys, resembled a heavy sea pouring itself upon a chain of immovable rocks and then driven back. And amid all the tumult of this desperate action – the discharge of the artillery – the clash of arms – the shouts of the infuriated combatants – the groans and the shrieks of the wounded and the dying – the men behaved as on parade. In vain did desperate heroes among the French cavalry discharge their carbines and pistols at the squares to induce them to break the ranks.

Later in the day, the Hussars met the Cuirassiers but only once or twice. Their swords could do little to the brass covered troopers. They soon learnt that the only penetrable place was the throat and the side of the head. Bentinck saw these long straight swords[31] of the Hussars dart between the helmet chain and the neck and give a rasp, which in an instant put the poor fellow's head on one side and dropped him from his horse. The Inniskillings[32] were particularly dexterous at this. In returning from a charge, they came close to Bentinck and he saw several of them drawing their blades between their fingers to strip off the flesh and blood then cleaning them on their horses' mane.

Our heavy Cavalry, The Life Guards, Blues and Scotch Greys, who were from this point to the end of the day, a worthy adversary for the mail clad Frenchmen. This meeting, said one historian was stern, a combat at the sword's length and worthy of the best days of chivalry. It was kept to the most desperate blows and punches being exchanged. Officers were fighting hand to hand, like their men, notwithstanding the weight and armour of the foe, the power of the horses or the bravery of their riders they could not stand the shock but were literally ridden down in great numbers.

It is recorded that Shaw, the famous Lifeguardsman, who is reputed to have killed in one day more Frenchmen than any other man in the Allied armies, delivered in this fray a blow which cleft through the thick brass helmet, the skull, the brass jacket, down to the Frenchman's saddle, before he himself succumbed to terrible injuries.[33]

Not one British square was broken into, but they were all so fearfully thinned as to draw from the Duke the wish for, 'Night or Blucher.' And sure enough, soon after, about half past five o'clock, the guns of the advancing Prussian army were heard thundering on the enemy flank. Joyfully did Wellington cry, 'There goes old Blucher at last!'

'The Prussians came up shortly after on our left and they opened a very heavy fire on the French as soon as they got in reach of them. We were all greatly alarmed as we thought it was the French that was coming round us until the Colonel told us to steady. The Prussians came to our assistance and then we were in better spirits.'

By the late afternoon, the French had seized the farmhouse of La Haye Sainte and determined attacks on Hougoumont were still taking place but were being defeated. The impending arrival of a critical mass of Prussian troops forced Napoleon to take a great risk in pursuit of a victory. He called up his reserve, 15,000 of the famous Imperial Guard, and told them that the allied army was almost destroyed.

> Pointing to the road held by our friends the Fusileers and their compatriot Regiments, he shouted, 'There gentlemen, is the road to Brussels; forward!'

Napoleon gambled on committing the Imperial Guard, which, as his best troops, had been held in reserve, to a final frontal attack. The French artillery increased its rate of fire and then about 7.30 some eight battalions formed in columns advanced down into the valley, drums beating out the *pas de charge*. Five of the battalions advanced up the forward slope, taking terrible casualties from the Allied artillery.

> With deafening cheers, preceded by the thunder of hundreds of cannon and a perfect hail of musketry, they bore down upon that vital road. All the fighting that day had seen was nothing compared to the last, desperate struggle. Horse and foot, men and Officers went down by scores. Within a few minutes Bentinck's Regiment alone lost five Captains, seven Lieutenants and nearly 200 men.[34] Brave old Colonel Ellis, who had so long commanded them and so often led them to victory, was among them. As the French column neared the Regiment, formed up in square, he called out to his men, 'Remember the old times boys, this is their last try.' A moment after, Bentinck, who stood close to him, saw him fling his arm up. A grape shot had struck him in the breast. Quietly turning his horse round and leaning in his saddle, he rode slowly toward the rear, supported by a man on each side, but ere they had got many yards they had to lift him to the ground.[35]

Wellington had prepared for this moment and some of his best infantry battalions were well positioned to meet and defeat this attack. The French battalions met Wellington's resolute troops, who stood firm to the advancing columns and turned them through weight of musket fire. The failure of this attack, together with the arrival of the Prussians in the village of Plancenoit, broke the will of the French, who began to retreat southwards towards Genappe. The arriving Prussians began harassing the retreating French and Napoleon fled on horseback to Paris.

Across the spread of the Waterloo battlefield, it has been estimated that 50,000 men lay wounded and dying on that evening. Around 15,000 of Wellington's troops were casualties, 7,000 Prussians and 25,000 of Napoleon's men, with a further 8,000 taken prisoner. As night fell, soldiers, camp followers and civilians moved amongst the dead and wounded looting. On seeing the French retreat mark the end of the battle, the battalion advanced in line and then moved a short distance in column to establish a bivouac about 300 yards from the farmhouse of La Belle Alliance.[36]

Bentinck was one of the few who survived that bloody day without sustaining a scratch. After the last charge of the French began to break up in disorder, Bentinck followed with our army in pursuit until nearly eleven o'clock at night. The roads were so blocked up by the detritus of war, the dead and wounded, abandoned cannon and weapons that the pursuers had to keep stopping to remove them. The horses Bentinck saw alive received the hardest flogging in an attempt to make them move off the road but they chose to rather lie down in the road from exhaustion. The retreating French fought hard, for their survival depended on stopping the Allies from coming onto them so quickly. Eventually the Regiment halted, the numbers of dead and wounded were checked and the weary soldiers lay down to take rest. With his old soldier's nose he was quick to make a supper of a crush ash cake,[37] unbaked, that he discovered in a dead Frenchman's knapsack.

Reflecting on the day's events, Bentinck and his compatriots were:

Very glad when the Allied powers came up as we had been very weak for we had been greatly outnumbered all the day. And we should have had to retreat either that night or the next morning. We had a reinforcement coming from America but only one regiment got to our assistance, the 4th King's Own, as the others had not landed.

Colonel Ellis was taken to a hut to the rear of the battlefield and was cared for by Assistant Surgeon Monroe. Unfortunately the building subsequently caught fire and, although he was rescued by the surgeon, Ellis succumbed to his wounds on 20 June.

He lived but long enough to hear that the enemy were beaten and that the Prussians were ahead.[38] When the great battle was over they buried him in the little cemetery of Waterloo church and every Officer and man in the Regiment contributed a day's pay to erect to him a sculptured tomb and a monument in his church at home, in his native Worcester.[39]

<hr />

1. The 2nd Battalion was then under the command of Brevet Lieutenant Colonel Thomas Dalmer.
2. Colonel Ellis.
3. The disbandment of the 2nd Battalion occurred on 24 October 1814; 26 sergeants, 21 corporals, 23 drummers and 377 privates were moved across into the 1st Battalion. The officers were placed on half-pay.
4. Ellis had been promoted a brevet colonel in June and made a Knight Commander of the Bath so it was as Colonel Sir Henry Ellis that he travelled to his family's estate at Kempsey, four miles from Worcester, for his leave. Ellis was well known to the gentry of the area, who decided to honour him with a piece of engraved silverware 'as a Tribute of Respect due to him for his gallant Conduct during a period of upwards of fifteen years arduous Service in the Defence of his Country'. On 26 December Ellis received a silver-gilt cup (now on display in the regimental museum in Caernarfon) and the freedom of the city of Worcester. Before departing on leave, Ellis arranged for the 'manufacture and presentation of medals to soldiers who had displayed meritorious and distinguished conduct in Egypt, Denmark, Martinique and the Peninsula. These medals were cast in silver and engraved on one side with the coronet, feathers and motto of the Prince of Wales and on the other, with the names of the battles in which the man had served, surrounded by a laurel wreath. They were designed to be worn with a ribbon which was probably scarlet with blue edging.' Graves, *Dragon Rampant*, pp. 228–9.
5. Dalmer joined the Regiment in 1797 as a sixteen-year-old and within a year participated in the Ostend expedition. Subsequent expeditions to Ferrol and Cadiz, the Aboukir landing and the actions at Alexandria provided further experience. After garrison service in Gibraltar, Dalmer served in Hanover in 1805 and the 1807 Copenhagen expedition. As part of the 2nd Battalion, he was at Corunna before rejoining the 1st Battalion in 1812 in the Iberian Peninsula. At Salamanca he commanded the Light Companies of the Left Brigade of the 4th Division but was severely wounded. Dalmer received brevet rank of lieutenant colonel whilst recovering from his wounds and then re-joined the 1st Battalion near Madrid. In 1813 he was again in command of the Light Companies of the Left Brigade of the 4th Division, seeing action at Vitoria and in the advance to the Pyrenees. Dalmer then returned to the 2nd Battalion to command it. He accompanied the 1st Battalion to the Netherlands in 1815 and was present at Waterloo, succeeding Colonel Ellis and commanding at the assault and capture of Cambria on 26 July 1815. He served with the army of occupation in France until being placed on half pay on 24 July 1817.

He received the Turkish Medal of the Crescent for the Egypt campaign of 1801, a medal for services in the General Action at Salamanca in Spain, a gold clasp for the General Action at Vitoria and a medal for the Battle of Waterloo. Dalmer was appointed a Companion of the Military Order of the Bath on 4 June 1815. From 1817 he was on the half-pay list of the 43rd Foot. Dalmer was promoted major general on 28 June 1838 and lieutenant general on 11 November 1851. He was appointed Colonel of the 47th Foot on 16 April 1847. In 1848 received the MGSM 1793–1814 with clasps Corunna and Egypt. Dalmer died in 1854.

6. This is roughly equivalent to £2,600 in 2011.

7. The battalion moved into barracks in Gosport in mid-July and we can presume that the timing of Bentinck's two months of leave was around the period of August through to October.

8. Orders arrived on the morning of 22 March and the battalion was, 'In the highest spirits. Quite delighted for we received our orders for embarkation. Destination of course not mentioned but must be either France or Holland. We embark tomorrow morning at nine o'clock about seven hundred as fine men as ever fixed bayonets.' RWFM, Acc. 5935, MacDonald to father, 23 March 1815.

   Private Thomas Jeremiah noted that 'the new recruits from the 2nd Battalion were excited by the issuing of sixty rounds each of ball cartridge', and he also commented that the young soldiers who had never seen action acquired 'cannon fever' but the 'cheerful and undaunted advice' of the veterans 'dispelled their tremendous fears'. G. Glover, *A Short Account of the Life and Adventures of Private Thomas Jeremiah*, p. 13.

9. Of the officers, Colonel Ellis had served in the army for close to eighteen years and participated in every campaign from the Helder in 1799 to the culmination of the Peninsula in 1814. 'Of the ten company commanders or senior lieutenants commanding companies in the absence of the actual commanders, all had an average of nine years of service and George Dalmer and Joseph Hawtyn were brevet majors. Four had been with the regiment in Martinique and nine with it in the Peninsula, including six who had fought at Albuera. The fourteen first lieutenants had an average of five and a half years of service, with ten having served in the Peninsula and five of those having fought at Albuera. As might be expected, the four second lieutenants were less experienced, all having been commissioned in 1813 and none apparently having fought in the Peninsula.' In terms of experience, the key staff NCOs – the regimental sergeant major, quartermaster sergeant, paymaster sergeant, armourer sergeant and the two drum majors – were an average of 34½ years old and had about 11½ years' service. The sergeants in the battalion were, on average, 33 years old and had 10½ years' service while the corporals averaged just over 28, with a little over 8 years' service. The private soldiers were younger, an average of just under 25 years of age, with about 4½ years' service. Only 8.6 per cent of the private soldiers had enlisted before 1804, 26 per cent had enlisted between 1805 and 1809, while the remaining two thirds had enlisted between 1809 and 1814. The average height of a soldier was between 5 feet 6 inches and 5 feet 8 inches. Graves, *Dragon Rampant*, pp. 233–4.

It has been shown that roughly 425 of the 700 rank and file were English, 225 Welsh, and 50 Irish. In addition there were six Scotsmen and three men who were born overseas – in Canada, Italy and Holland. In 1804, the 23rd had been allocated various counties in Wales for recruiting and representation was: Denbighshire 40, Caernarvonshire 6, Anglesey 2, Montgomery 28, Cardigan 23, Pembrokeshire 18. Most English counties were represented. The best recruiting areas were Lancashire 78, Norfolk 58, Cheshire 31, Somerset 28 and Cambridgeshire 26. The occupations given by the soldiers of the battalion were as follows: around half were labourers, with others being: shoemakers 39, tailors 26, miners and colliers 16, blacksmiths 14. Also vice-makers, silk-twisters, jockeys and sailors. The regimental sergeant major gave his previous occupation as optician.

10. The unhappy experience was related, 'we had twenty Officers packed together in one little cabin, the greatest part of course quite sick, and not able to go on deck, much less ashore, from the violence of the wind and the rain.' RWFM, Acc. 5935, MacDonald to father, 3 April 1815.

11. Commanded by Lieutenant Colonel (Brevet Colonel) Mitchell of the 51st Foot.

12. Captain MacDonald accepted the invitation of Louis XVIII to dine with him, being but one guest among a number of British officers, French aristocrats and ladies.

13. The regiment was originally raised in Leeds as the 53rd Foot but renumbered as the 51st in 1757. In 1782 county titles were allotted to regiments of foot, although they retained their numbers to indicate precedence. Theoretically the geographical affiliation was meant to reflect where the regimental depots were located and recruiting occurred. The tempo of operations and constant manpower requirements meant that this rarely happened. In 1782 the regiment was named 51st (2nd Yorkshire, West Riding) Regiment of Foot. It served in the Peninsula from 1807 and following the death of Sir John Moore, who received his initial commission in the 51st, it became known as the 51st (or 2nd Yorkshire, West Riding) Light Infantry Regiment.

14. G. Glover, *A Short Account … Private Thomas Jeremiah*, p. 13. p. 15.

15. Whilst here, the 23rd Foot was inspected by the Duke of Wellington. Wellington is supposed to have said, 'It was the most complete and handsome military body I ever looked at.' Wellington to Cole, 2 June 1815, in *Regimental Records*, Volume 1. p 289.

Private Thomas Jeremiah was another individual drawn to the rumour that Napoleon was at the review, 'This grand display if report says truth did not fail to attract the notice of Napoleon himself who it was sayed [sic] that he was in disguise in the apparel of a fruit monger, it was inserted in the news of the day that he had the satisfaction to inspect the British cavalry, for whom he expressed the greatest admiration for their martial and soldier like appearance and at the same time expressing his deep regret that such a fine body of men should be brought from their happy homes to be marched against him.' G. Glover, *A Short Account … Private Thomas Jeremiah*, p. 15.

16. These figures are inaccurate. Wellington's Anglo-allied army, in cantonments around Brussels, numbered some 93,000 British, Dutch and Hanoverian troops. Blücher's army, with headquarters at Namur, was composed of 116,000 men. Napoleon had no more than 200,000 troops, of whom some 128,000 formed the Army of the North, occupying positions along the Belgian frontier.

17. Napoleon crossed the frontier with Belgium near Charleroi on 15 June 1815.

18. The Duchess of Richmond's infamous ball in Brussels on the night of 15/16 June. Her husband, Charles Lennox, 4th Duke of Richmond, although next senior after Wellington, held no command and was present in a purely private capacity. He stayed with the army through the first part of the battle but was then prevailed upon to return to Brussels as the danger was so great.

19. The battalion marched through the 16th and the 17th. 'By the evening of the 17th, we were greatly fatigued from the extreme inclemency of the day's weather and from marching nearly eight French leagues since six o'clock in the morning. Even I saw that the heavens seemed to have opened their sluices and the celestial floodgates twisted open. I need not mention that all about us were completely soaked by the rain. Our blankets which were on the back of our knapsacks were completely drenched, but that was not the greatest of our thoughts, for hunger bites harder than a wet shirt.' G. Glover, *A Short Account ... of Private Thomas Jeremiah*, p. 20.

20. An account written by Private Wheeler of the 51st comments that he and his comrades spent the night sitting on their knapsacks while 'water ran in streams from the cuffs of our Jackets', being, as one remarked, both 'wet and comfortable'. Wheeler, *The Letters of Private Wheeler, 1809–1828*, p. 170.

21. Sunrise was just before 5.30.

22. Many of the other men of the battalion were in pursuit of common aims. 'Thus happily supplied with money and good provision we lost no time to proceed to our camp where we saw our remaining 4 messmates half starved. They began to open to their eyes at the sight of such a fine cargo of flour, brandy and here we commenced to mix our flour not with water but wine and brandy, when we had mixed our flour we made cakes of it and laid it on the cinders and before they were scarcely browned, when the old saying was verified that hunger breaks through stone walls, for there was no less than half the regiment looking as if they would rob me of what I had so much trouble in getting.' G. Glover, *A Short Account ... of Private Thomas Jeremiah*, p. 23.

23. Graves, *Dragon Rampant*, p. 246.

24. It is generally accepted that the battle began at 11.30. The French opened with a sustained artillery bombardment to set the conditions for a straightforward assault on the centre of the ridge, together with a supporting assault on Hougoumont.

25. This is most likely a reference to vegetation and strips of trees to the west and north-west of the Hougoumont complex.

26. Lieutenant George Fensham. He joined the 1st Battalion as a second lieutenant on 20 April 1808, served throughout the Peninsular Campaign and was killed at Waterloo.

27. Most likely from either the 8th or 11th Cuirassier Regiments of the 2nd Brigade of the 11th Cavalry Division or the 1st or 2nd Regiments of the 1st Brigade of the 12th Cavalry Division.

28. The description of the cuirassiers having 'brass jackets' and 'chain mail of brass' is inaccurate. French cuirasses were iron but cuirasses worn by the two carabinier regiments were faced with brass/copper panels.

29. The 15th (The King's) Regiment of (Light) Dragoons (Hussars) was in Grant's Brigade and on the right wing, so would indeed have been seen by Bentinck. The 18th (King's) Light Dragoons (Hussars) and the 10th (Prince of Wales' Own) Light Dragoons (Hussars) were not in the vicinity of Bentinck's position.

30. The Allied artillery also pursued the withdrawing French cavalry and a large group of cuirassiers tried to escape by riding south along the Nivelles road. The light companies of the brigade had constructed an abattis and this canalized the French, allowing a heavy fire to be applied. Lieutenant Alexander Brice, who had assumed command of the 23rd Foot's Light Company after Lieutenant Fensham had been killed, believed that 'scarcely a man succeeded in making his escape'. Siborne, *Waterloo Letters*, Holmes to Siborne, 29 April 1835, p. 312.

31. The Hussars carried curved sabres of the 1796 light cavalry pattern.

32. The 6th (Inniskilling) Dragoons. Raised originally in 1689, at Waterloo they fought within the Union Brigade, which also included the 1st (Royal) Regiment of Dragoons and the 2nd (Royal North British) Regiment of Dragoons (Scots Greys). Bentinck probably mistook the 15th Light Dragoons for the Inniskillings.

33. Corporal John Shaw was renowned in the British Army prior to Waterloo for being a prize fighter, possibly the most competent in the British Isles. He took part in the charges of the Union and Household Brigades against the French but ultimately fell after being surrounded by a group of cuirassiers and felled by a number of sword wounds. Shaw crawled a distance toward La Haye Sainte before dying from his wounds and exhaustion. The blow stated to have been delivered by him was impossible.

34. This is incorrect. The battalion's casualties at Waterloo were comparatively light. The strength of the battalion on the morning of the battle was: 3 field officers, 10 captains, 25 subalterns, 6 staff, 35 sergeants, 23 drummers and 639 rank and file. Battalion casualties were: Brevet Major Hawtyn, Captains Joliffe and Farmer, Lieutenant Fensham, 2 sergeants and 9 rank and file killed. Colonel Ellis died of wounds on 20 June as did Lieutenant Clyde on 3 July. The other wounded were Brevet Lieutenant Colonel Hill, Captain Johnson, Lieutenants Fielding, Griffiths and Sidley, 7 sergeants and 71 rank and file. These were relatively light casualties in comparison to a number of other battalions.

35. Colonel Ellis was hit whilst in the saddle. He remained within the square for a time and then, becoming faint from the loss of blood, 'he calmly desired an opening might be made in the square, and rode to the rear but a short distance from the field he was thrown from his horse while in the act of leaping a ditch'. *Regimental Records*, Vol 1,

pp. 283–4. However, the battalion was not directly involved in the repulse of the Imperial Guard and it is more likely, contrary to Bentinck's account, that Ellis received his wound earlier in the battle.

36. Lieutenant R. P. Holmes wrote that, 'After this charge, finding that we were suffering both from the French guns and the fire from the garden of Hougoumont, we again retired to our former position, where we remained until the attack on the centre by the French Guards, when we again advanced some short distance in square, then deployed and advanced in line; but finding nothing to oppose us, we wheeled by companies to the right and moved in column on the right of the Charleroi road to [about 300 yards short of La Belle Alliance] where we bivouacked for the night.' Glover & Riley, *That Astonishing Infantry*, p. 66.

37. A mix of flour, salt and water.

38. His last words were reportedly, 'I am happy – I am content – I have done my duty.' *Regimental Records*, Vol. 1, p. 285. He was mourned by every officer and man in the 23rd Foot, as exampled by the reaction of one private: 'Among several of the soldiers of his regiment, who were in the farmhouse with him, mortally wounded, and inquiring anxiously after their Colonel, there was one who supported a very bad character, and he had been frequently punished. To this man I said, to learn his attachment, – "He is just dead; but why should you care? You cannot forget how oft he caused your back to be bared?" "Sir," replied he, his eyes assuming a momentary flash and his cheek a passing glow, "I deserved the punishment, else he would never have punished me." With these words, he turned his head a little from me, and burst into tears.' Ibid, p. 285.

39. 'Every officer, NCO and private soldier in the regiment voluntarily gave up one day's pay toward the £1,200 cost of a magnificent monument to their beloved commanding officer, which was placed in Worcester Cathedral. The work of John Bacon the younger, who had completed similar projects in St Paul's Cathedral, it portrays Ellis in the act of falling, mortally wounded, from his horse while an angel stands behind holding a laurel wreath over his head and a fusilier kneels alongside. It was the Welch Fusiliers' tribute of their "respect and affection to the memory of a leader, not more distinguished for valour and conduct, in the field, than beloved for every generous and social virtue".' Graves, *Dragon Rampant*, pp. 262–3.

Chapter Eleven

Final Combats and Peacetime in France

———•◦•———

O vernight the battalion lay in an ordered formation amongst thousands of casualties of both sides, with military and civilian scavengers moving amongst them in pursuit of loot and plunder. Despite these terrible distractions, the exertions of the past few days and the experience of battle would have ensured that some slept well.

Our last chapter left Bentinck, our old veteran, on the crimsoned field of Waterloo, sleeping the death-like sleep of exhaustion after the great battle. Dawn was but faintly appearing in the Eastern sky when the bugles of the 4th Division broke painfully in on the slumbers of the worn soldiers, arousing them to one more day of heavy labour. The wounded had now to be looked to more carefully than weariness and darkness before would admit, though the groups of the prostate would, alas, have told but too painfully where they lay. The dead and wounded of the British alone were upwards of 15,000 men. The French were estimated at 25,000 at least, the loss of the other Allied armies was heavy too.

Never in his worst dreams had Bentinck beheld such a sight as that on which his eyes fell that morning, as the darkness was slowly lifted like a mourning veil from before it. The plain was strewn thick with soldiers stricken down with every variety of wound. Here they were scattered unevenly by the pattering hail of musketry; there they lay in lines, bowled down by the cannon shot darting from head to rear of a dense column; again were short rows of dead and struggling horses, showing where French cavalry had been shot down by whole ranks as they charged madly up to the very muzzles of the British; close at hand a sprinkling of corpses slashed with fearful sabre cuts, plainly indicated the avenging pursuit of British troopers, whose big horses and heavy blades had so often that day scattered before them the boasted chivalry of France.

The track of the Prussians, whose fresher troops were first in pursuit of the broken army, was marked by fearful slaughter. Marshal Blucher,[1] their grim old chief, had ordered every man and horse in his army capable of action to press on in the rear of the French, without allowing them a moment to rally.

The night was clear and bright, and the Prussian cavalry rode after the fliers and cut them down without mercy; taking a dreadful revenge for the cold-blooded cruelty of which the French had been guilty throughout the campaign, and especially during that day. The Prussians suffered none to escape with whom they came up; the death of General Duhesme[2] was an instance of their revenge. One of the Black Brunswickers at seeing him a little distance off rode up. The general begged for quarter: the soldier looked briefly and sternly at him and only said, 'The Duke of Brunswick[3] died yesterday, and thou also shalt bite the dust.' One swoop of the uplifted sabre, and the plumed horseman rolled to the earth a corpse. The French had behaved most savagely throughout the day, their spearmen as they rode over the field thrust their lances into the wounded and many of their prisoners, after being stripped were massacred.

The suggestions of the killing of prisoners and wounded are greatly exaggerated in Bentinck's description, although there are more reliable accounts of one or two isolated incidents. The vanquished French had more to fear from the Prussians than the British or Dutch and so the coming of dawn was a welcome opportunity for surviving Frenchmen to find a British regiment to surrender to.

Bentinck's Division took many prisoners who had escaped the terrible Prussians in the darkness, and crept out from bushes and holes to give themselves up to the more merciful British. They held their hands up and cried, 'Prisoners, bon Anglais; pauvre prisoners,' and seemed right glad to be taken under protection. The 23rd came into a village and found a great many of our men who had been taken prisoner by the French but now abandoned in their general retreat.

A day after the battle, Mitchell's Brigade was tasked to march on the road to Nivelles. Over the next few days Wellington's army moved by way of Mons, Valenciennes and Le Cateau. Movement was slow as the whole army was moving on one road, which was also interspersed with the detritus of the French defeat and subsequent retreat.

Our friends of the 4th Division marched the first day to Genappe, where the French had been posted, and where a body of their cavalry were so severely cut up by our First Life Guards[4] under Lord Uxbridge.[5] The French had kept some of their prisoners there, some of whom it is said Bonaparte shot, and vowed he would keep the remainder and hang them round his Palace when he got back to Paris.[6]

The battalion's parent division was tasked with capturing the frontier fortress of Cambrai. Rather than conduct a siege, the order was given to conduct an immediate assault. Mitchell's Brigade was sent to conduct a feint while the main assault was mounted by the other brigades in the division. Resistance was minimal; the battalion moved quickly and was in the main square before the main assault began.

The 4th Division, along with the 5th, continued their way from Genappe to Paris. On the fourth day's march they reached the fortified town of Cambray. The French Garrison, though the war was now looked on as over, fastened the gates against them. An order was at once given to storm, the walls were scaled but our men found them deserted and no resistance was made.[7]

A few of the Fusiliers, Bentinck among them, after climbing the walls, went to unfasten one of the gates to admit the rest of our troops. They found it guarded by only one sentry. 'Big Will,' one of the Fusiliers, ordered him to unbolt the port, but the sentry either did not understand him or would not betray his duty. With an oath, 'Big Will,' one of the worst fellows in the Regiment, told a young man named Ellis[8] to shoot the Frenchman, and on the latter refusing to kill an unresisting man, he pointed his musket at him and made him, under the threat of driving a bullet through his head if he did not – so the faithful Frenchman was wantonly slain.

As the battalion was the first into the town it was given the task of guarding it. Unfortunately this gave an opportunity for plundering and looting as it was a day before the fortress within the town surrendered.

The force stopped in this town one day, in order to receive the submission of the Garrison, who had retired to the Castle with the intention of defending it but an old English gentleman, an esteemed resident of the town, persuaded them to yield, which they did the second night.

'A good deal of plundering was done in this town, because it had been almost deserted by the inhabitants. Some of the men happened to break into the house of a priest. He resisted their entrance and was shot in the arm. Next morning he came to the Colonel, with very good reason, to complain showing his wounded limb and describing the valuables he had lost.'

The Colonel was of course bound to investigate the matter. He had the men called out. They were each asked if they knew anything about the deed and of course answered to a man in the negative. Then their haversacks were just shaken or peeped into – not too inquisitively, for as said before the Officers were not too eager in those matters – and where a fellow was found too careless to make any effort to conceal his plunder it was lugged forth. Had the hats been taken off, many of them would have been found used as watch pockets. Even though only their haversacks and blankets were subjected to a make believe search, there was nearly a full haversack of money that could not be overlooked. This was handed over to the Priest, who was much mollified by it. One of Bentinck's comrades had managed to find his hat nearly full of gold and silver pieces in one house and hid it in a hole. In the morning he could not find the place, so had his trouble for nothing.

At the same time, Napoleon abdicated and made his way to western France, seeking passage to the United States. The effectiveness of the British blockade was such that he was left with little option but to surrender and he formally demanded political asylum from the captain of a British ship, HMS *Bellerophon*.

There was a very strict look out for him in the land and on water. Then there was a rumour come across that they had taken Napoleon prisoner on board a ship. They thought he was bound for America to his brother Joseph. He was made prisoner by the Captain of the Gelepuffin [*sic*] one of our own man of wars that was out in search of him. He was brought to Plymouth where he was exhibited in his full uniforms. [People] had to pay so much and they was rowed out in a boat to see round where the ship was at anchor. He laid there until there was a place appointed to send him to. He was sent over to Saint Helena where he spent the rest of his days.

Napoleon's capture did not stop the relentless move of the allies toward Paris and a general competition ensued as fortresses were bypassed for the sake of reaching the capital first. After the surrender of Cambrai, the battalion continued on its move toward Paris.

> The Allied Powers reached two days before us and they had been very busy preparing their batteries for the siege. The Russians were red hot against the French for Moscow and they would have blown Paris down but for Wellington. We camped round about until Wellington sent in a flag of truce to see what they intended to do. We wondered if they would surrender or if they would have it destroyed. The corporations promenaded the Governor to give it up as they would not have their property destroyed. It was given over peacefully and Wellington marched with part of the troops and took possession of Paris.

Bentinck's comments are only partially accurate. The battalion reached the Bois de Boulogne, on the western outskirts of Paris, on 4 July 1815, the day that the capital surrendered, and found the other allied armies encamped round the city. The relentless pace of the advance had taken its toll on the men who were exhausted.[9] The chance to cease marching and take a respite was greatly welcomed.

> The 4th Division took up their quarters at Neuilly.[10] When the city surrendered the Horse and Foot Guards went into it, but the rest remained outside. The men were, however, given leave to visit it, ten out of a company at once, between the hours of forenoon parade and sunset.[11] Bentinck went several times to gaze on its Palaces, its lovely gardens, the noble streets and fine buildings. He found the Parisians very civil and did not entirely escape the gay dissipation for which they have always been so notorious. The encampment of the Fusiliers was beautifully situated in groves of trees by the side of the Seine.

On 24 July 1815, the allied Army of Occupation was reviewed by the Emperor of Russia, which like any grand parade was not particularly enjoyable for the ordinary soldier, as Bentinck reflected:

> 'We had to march through the city to go to the place set for it. We got off very early as we had a long distance to go. It was late when we returned.'
>
> Afterward, the allied armies departed for their own countries, leaving the British to occupy the country for three years. This was soon after Bonaparte had surrendered himself to the British, which event was celebrated by his successor the Bourbon, by a grand illumination of Paris.

Following the grand review of 24 July, the battalion was placed on garrison duties, remaining in the suburbs of Paris, first in Neuilly and then in Montmarte.

In November 1815 reinforcements and new recruits were received from what was styled as 'The Depot Company', which had remained in Britain recruiting.[12] The reinforcements also brought over a set of new Colours for the 1st Battalion.

> While lying there they received a draft a men from their depot in the Isle of Wight and a set of new Colours, which they badly needed.[13] Indeed at Waterloo, there was so little of their Colours left on the poles that the First Battalion did not take them into the field, but fought under those of the Second Battalion, causing some grumbling among the men of the first. They said they would rather fight under their own old rags than under the finest flags in the Army. The new ones were beautifully embroidered by the daughter of the old General, Sir Lowry Cole,[14] and the first night of receiving them they were 'wetted' so freely with grog that some of the men did not stand exactly in line on the morning's parade.[15]

Despite the absence of hostilities and casualties, maintaining the necessary manning level remained important to the battalion and recruiting parties back in Britain were crucial. Bentinck was fortunate to be chosen in the beginning of 1816 to form part of a recruiting party sent home for six months. The recruiting party was successful but circumstances contrived against the battalion.

> In 1816 there was nine or ten of us picked out to come over to England for recruiting to beat up the strength of the Regiment to its regulation numbers, which it had never been able to keep up for long years. Two sergeants, two Corporals, two drummers and four men were chosen. We marched from Valenciennes to Calais and set sail to Dover and then we marched to Dale [Deal] where our Duke was lying. Before we went on to Winchester I asked for a furlough. I found I got one or two months and I went home to see my friends and relations. I returned when my pass was up.
>
> We lay there about six months and were not long in enticing 80 strapping bumpkins to, 'go and be sojers in furrin' parts.' The Regiments in France could not wait for catching and drilling recruits so had made their numbers up by drafts from the home Regiments and bad fellows these mostly were. The Colonels would of course not part with their good men when they had chance of getting rid of the bad

ones. So the 80 recruits that our party had inveigled were in their turn drafted into other Regiments than those they had entered for and the recruiting party had to rejoin their Regiment in France.[16]

In February 1816 the battalion was moved 100 miles north of Paris to a small town called Hamelincourt, close to Arras, before moving in April 1817 to the nearby town of Valenciennes where it remained for eighteen months.[17]

While at Valenciennes, an incident occurred which cast a shade over the Regiment from which it did not soon recover. Some of the men broke into a house one night and stole from it a quantity of rum. There was an official in the Garrison called the Sergeant of the town, whose duty it was to see to the behaviour of the men towards the inhabitants. On this burglary coming to his ears, instead of reporting it to the Colonel of the Regiment,[18] as he ought to have done, and the Colonel would then have meted out what he considered sufficient punishment, he reported it to the French Commandant or Mayor. This dignitary, embittered by national hatred of the British, at once wrote a flaming account of the offence to Wellington.

The Duke as promptly ordered an investigation, which resulted in the discovery of the offenders, five of the Fusiliers, named Leach, Pringle, McPhitridge,[19] Hewitt[20] and Jones.[21] Wellington ordered his usual punishment for such offences – hanging. The troops were formed up in the square in the morning, the gallows rose in the middle and the five unfortunates were marched out, accompanied by a chaplain, following their coffins. As the ropes were being put round their necks and they were about to be swung off, a Dragoon galloped up with an order to spare Hewitt, Jones and McPhitridge. The other two, both of whom were within a few months of their seven years term of services being up were 'hanged by the neck until they were dead.' Hewitt, one of the saved, was a native of Ashton-under-Lyne and Leach also of this neighbourhood. When lying in Limerick barracks, a few years after, Hewitt eloped with the wife of a Sergeant, of the name of Carlon[22] and came home, his time of service expired. Carlon took it so badly that he became a drunkard, was reduced to a Private, and finally deserted, which was the last Bentinck knew of him.

Smith,[23] the town's Sergeant, who was the means of the two men being hung, was not long after reduced by the Colonel, who took a lasting dislike to him for his blunder. Indeed it was understood that it was in consequence of this disgrace to his Regiment of having two men hung for stealing in time of peace that Colonel Dalmer soon afterwards retired from it.[24]

His retirement was an evil day for the Regiment, for he sold his commission to Colonel Pearson, their old Major, who it may be remembered was so hated for his severity that they refused to release him from his fallen horse but left him to be taken by the French. He swore he would, 'tan their hides for them if ever he got back.' He lived to keep his promise, escaping after all from the enemy, and then being sent to take part in the war with the American colonies. He was made Colonel on his return, and exchanged into his old Regiment, the Welsh Fusiliers, as their Colonel.[25]

Battle and disease had so thinned them that there were now very few in the Regiment who had known him as its Major. Bentinck knew him – too well, Pearson having once had him stripped and brought up for a flogging because he had lost his sword, but was persuaded to let him off by the Captain of his Company. When their good old Colonel Ellis commanded he sometimes used to inspect only one wing of the Regiment, leaving Major Pearson to inspect the other. Very seldom indeed did the Major miss [ordering] the flogging of one or two men.

When he came on this occasion to inspect them, for the first time as Colonel, two men came running in from five to ten minutes after he had ridden up. He at once called them out and ordered them 200 lashes each. When the flogging was over he addressed his new Regiment, 'Now then,' said he, 'I have only opened one eye yet; I'll warm your jackets if I have to open the other. If you behave yourselves I'll be as good as Colonel Ellis, if you don't, I will be the Devil himself.' 'You're nearly that now!' thought our friend Bentinck to himself. 'I hope you never open your other eye while I stop with you.'[26]

---

1. Gebhard Leberecht von Blücher, Furst von Wahlstatt (1742–1819). Started his
    career as a hussar in the Swedish Army, having been born in Swedish Pomerania.
    In 1760 was captured by Prussian hussars and impressed them so much that he was
    subsequently accepted into their regiment. He served as a hussar in the Seven Years

War before resigning in 1772, infamously also drawing the wrath of Frederick the Great. Blücher was then a farmer for fifteen years before returning to his old regiment, the Red Hussars, in 1787, and subsequently serving in the Netherlands expedition. In the years following his career bloomed: in 1789 he was awarded the Pour le Mérite, Prussia's highest military order, distinguished himself in actions against the French in 1793 and 1794 and in 1801 was promoted to lieutenant general. Blücher then fought against Napoleon's France in 1805–6, and in the 1813 War of Liberation he became the Commander-in-Chief of the Army of Silesia and defeated the French at Katzbach and Mockern and contributed to the great victory at Leipzig. Made a field marshal in 1813, he achieved a noted victory at Laon in 1814 and entered Paris after the victory of Montmartre. Napoleon's return from exile resulted in Blücher's appointment to command the Army of the Lower Rhine. Wounded at Ligny, he recovered sufficiently to inspire his worn army to march hard to meet up with Wellington at Waterloo.

2. Count Guillaume Philibert Duhesme (1766–1815), who commanded the Young Guard Division of the French Imperial Guard, was mortally wounded by a shot to the head. He was captured in the French retreat and, despite attention from Blücher's medical staff, he died at Genappe on 20 June. Bentinck's account of his death is a case of exaggerating an inaccurate story.

3. Frederick William, Duke of Brunswick-Wolfenbüttel (1771–1815). Nicknamed the 'Black Duke', he briefly ruled the state of Brunswick-Wolfenbüttel in 1806–7 and was killed by a single shot whilst leading his troops at the Battle of Quatre Bras on 16 June 1815.

4. The 1st Life Guards, part of the Household Brigade.

5. Lieutenant General Henry Paget (1768–1854). Styled Lord Paget 1784–1812 and Earl of Uxbridge 1812–15. He commanded the cavalry during the Corunna campaign and subsequently a division during the expedition to Walcheren in 1809. He was severely wounded by a cannon shot toward the end of the battle, when he is supposedly to have exclaimed, 'By God, sir. I've lost my leg.' Subsequently he did indeed lose the leg to amputation, performed on a sturdy table without anaesthetics. The amputated leg was buried in the garden of the house in Waterloo where the operation occurred and strangely the location became a minor tourist attraction. Paget was created Marquess of Anglesey and made a Knight Grand Cross of the Order of the Bath in the aftermath of the battle. He later served as the Master-General of the Ordnance and Lord Lieutenant of Ireland, retiring from the Army in 1852 with the rank of field marshal.

6. It is nonsense to suggest that Napoleon ordered the prisoners to be shot or considered hanging them.

7. John MacDonald recounted what happened: 'We entered this city last night at eight o'clock by Escalade & felt proud in our being the first regiment in the square, which however occasioned us to remain as guards all night, after a very handsome compliment by General Colville, to protect this town. We entered with very little

loss as nothing can stop our fellows now. We got over two parapets and a dry & wet ditch with amazing rapidity, placed the Ladder and was in the city before any of the [divisional] staff had any idea of our having arrived at the outerworks, as we were only intended to have made a feint.' RWFM, Acc. 5935, MacDonald to mother, 25 June 1815. Some of the defending French still fought with a degree of conviction. During the assault and capture of Cambrai, Second Lieutenant Leebody and one private were killed, with two rank and file wounded.

8. In the Waterloo campaign, two privates named Ellis served in the battalion. One was wounded in the leg during the battle. Hence, it is highly likely that Bentinck's account refers to Private John Ellis, born at Llanfyllyn, Montgomery, Wales. He was originally a tailor and attested on 4 April 1814, at the age of nineteen, having been in the Montgomeryshire Militia. He served in the Light Company during the campaign.

9. John MacDonald wrote, 'We have spent a miserable ten days since this campaign commenced, we have been marching so rapidly that we have never seen our baggage. Conceive an unfortunate Christian marching twelve to fourteen hours every day, sleeping without any covering in a wet field, raining regularly every night, not able to cook any provisions, should you be so fortunate to find any, which with such immense armies is not very easy, without a change of linen and beards like turks.' RWFM, Acc. 5935, MacDonald to mother, 25 June 1815.

10. To the north-west of the city centre and some eight miles from the Île de la Cité.

11. Officers were allowed to enter the capital freely but only 100 men per battalion were permitted to visit it each day and they had to be back in their lines by sunset.

12. When the 1st Battalion had embarked for foreign service on the continent, some 230 all ranks, under the command of Captain Harrison, remained in the north-west of England for recruiting purposes. In April this Depot Company moved to the Isle of Wight.

13. The new colours arrived on 24 November 1815, delivered by Captain Harrison, accompanying a group of new recruits and reinforcements.

14. General Sir Galbraith Lowry Cole, commander of the 4th Division in Spain. His daughter Florence Mary Georgina Cole was not in fact born until 1816.

15. At Waterloo, the two colours were borne by Second Lieutenants Lillie and Leebody, the most junior officers in the battalion. Lillie, as the more senior, carried the King's Colour whilst Leebody carried the Regimental Colour. The Colours were indeed from the disbanded 2nd Battalion. The 1st Battalion's Colours were in tatters after the Peninsula campaign, but this did not prevent the men from having a strong sentimental attachment to them.

16. The requirement to maintain a constant flow of troops was a challenge. Recruiting parties were again used in early 1817 and withdrawn in April due to the large number of men from other regiments drafted in. In May 1818, recruiting recommenced. Parties were stationed at Dudley, Hereford and Wrexham.

17. At Hamelincourt the battalion was cantoned in groups of 30–140 men in the villages and hamlets surrounding the small town, with roughly an officer to every 15 men.

In February 1816 the strength of the battalion was 53 officers, 53 sergeants, 22 drummers, 48 corporals and 760 privates. On the anniversary of Waterloo, the officers' mess marked the occasion with a day of horse races, champagne picnics and finally a dinner dance.

18. Colonel Dalmer.

19. No soldier called Leach, Pringle or McPhitridge is recorded as having served with the battalion at Waterloo, although they could have been posted in from the Depot Company subsequently. A potential identification for Leach is Private George Lee who served in Number 2 Company at Waterloo and deserted on 1 January 1816.

20. Private James Hewitt. Born in Manchester and a labourer before attesting on 14 October 1805 aged twenty. He served in Number 6 Company during the Battle of Waterloo.

21. Twenty-seven soldiers with the surname Jones were with the battalion at Waterloo.

22. Thomas Carline, born at Newton, County Louth. He was originally a labourer before attesting on 16 March 1810 aged eighteen. He served in Number 4 Company at the Battle of Waterloo, and was promoted to corporal on 26 September 1816 and sergeant on 20 June 1818. He was reduced to private on 14 November 1820 and ultimately deserted on 22 February 1825.

23. James Smith, born Lavington, Wiltshire. Worked as a labourer before attesting on 23 April 1805, aged twenty. He was promoted to corporal on 15 March 1809 and sergeant on 24 November 1810. He served in Number 4 Company at Waterloo. He was appointed Assistant Baggage Master to the 4th Division on 3 July 1815 and was discharged on 4 November 1819 with a pension of 6d per day.

24. Colonel Dalmer did indeed retire on 23 August 1817, but it cannot be corroborated that it was due to this incident.

25. Pearson was wounded at the siege of Fort Erie in 1814 and, after convalescence, returned to Britain in the summer of 1815. He was briefly a half pay lieutenant colonel, until being appointed commanding officer of the 2nd Battalion, 43rd (Monmouthshire Light Infantry) Regiment. The battalion was disbanded in early 1817 and Pearson returned to his half-pay status. In mid-1817, Colonel Dalmer agreed to an exchange with Pearson and so he became the commanding officer of the 23rd Foot, commanding the battalion until 1830. He was renowned for being a very exacting officer who set and achieved high standards. A comprehensive understanding of Pearson's character can be gained through the outstanding book by the Canadian historian, Donald Graves, *Fix Bayonets: A Royal Welch Fusilier at War, 1796–1815.*

26. In July 1830 Pearson was promoted by seniority to major general and given the command of a district in Ireland. He wrote a quite exceptional farewell letter to the officers of the 23rd, the final paragraph concluding: 'Human interest is ever liable to err and in no situation more so than in the exercise of command; be assured that in those instances when in the execution of public duty I may intentionally have given pain, the fault has proceeded from the head, and not from the heart, and it is now only

permitted me to hope that the sentiments of affectionate regard which I have ever entertained for every member of the Royal Welch, will enable me to cherish the idea that when remembered it will not be with other feeling than those with which I now in the full sincerity of an overflowing heart subscribe myself your ever attached and truly affectionate friend.' Graves, *Fix Bayonets*, p. 413.

Chapter Twelve

Leaving the Army and Civilian Life

———•———

A fter spending some three and a half years as part of the army of occupation in France, the battalion received orders for a new posting to Ireland, amongst the mountains, the wild coast and small towns. Although it had by no means been a tough posting, the battalion was glad to receive orders to leave France.[1]

We left Valenciennes and went to Cambrai where we lay until we left the country for England in 1818. We marched down to Calais and came to Dover. We had not been there long when we got given the order to go to Limerick in Ireland. We set sail from Deal and landed at Cork. We stopped there a short time and then we proceeded on our way to Buttlefield where we stopped about a fortnight. Then we went on our way to Limerick where we stopped about eighteen months. Then we went to Clare and from there to Dublin. It was about Christmas when we went to Dublin in 1820.[2]

While in Ireland Bentinck met the woman who became his wife:

She was but a sound Englishwoman, in religion and breeding, having relatives with dissenting ministers, though her Father and Mother had lived in Ireland since her birth. Up to the time of her death, some years before Bentinck's demise, he always had reason to congratulate himself on choosing such a true and suitable helpmate.

'In 1821 November we went to Londonderry, where we stopped for a few months. We stopped here for a few months. Then we went to Mullingham and was there only a short time when we return to Londonderry. Then we march from there to Boyle where stayed about twelve months and then we went back again to Dublin in 1823.'[3]

The change of location to the capital city was appreciated by many of the battalion. Bentinck's role in the battalion at this time was to act as officer's servant to Lieutenant Matheson.[4] Bentinck commented that the men were:

Glad of the change of locality, for the beautiful bay, the broad esplanades, and the noble parks, formed a pleasant contrast to many of the small tumble-down towns they had been so long quartered in.

On 10 May 1823, not long after their arrival, a grand review of all the troops in Dublin was held in Phoenix Park:

Bentinck's master was away on leave of absence, but should have been back by that time, as his leave had expired a few days before. He was not, however, so Bentinck, being relieved of that duty, had to take his place in the ranks at the review. Before it was over, he was called out by a message informing him that Lieutenant Matheson had returned and desired his attendance again, so he went. When he got there he found the Lieutenant had been placed under arrest, for exceeding his leave of absence. As a punishment he had to keep to his quarters for a week, except at parade time, when he was ordered to read over to the men the Articles of War.

However, over the summer of 1823, an unwelcome set of circumstances for Bentinck evolved:

When we had been there a short time one time we had to march out on parade. The doctor came to me and asked what the matter was with me as I looked very poorly. I said that there was nothing wrong with me but he said that I looked very ill and must go with him to the Hospital. But he said he would not put me on the hospital books and my wife could bring my meals.

Bentinck duly went through a medical inspection but the conclusions of the surgeon-general were startling:

The result of this inspection startled and saddened the experienced soldier Bentinck, in no small degree. Although he had been 18 years in the Army,[5] from a mere lad, and had during nearly the whole of that time since been undergoing the dreadful privations of war, he had never been laid up a week except when his leg was disabled by the explosion of a shell.[6] He had always been one of the hardiest and healthiest men in the Regiment, though but slight of frame. Complete was his surprise and dismay, then, when the Doctor solemnly informed him that he was very far gone in consumption and must be discharged.

'The general doctor came and examined all who had been put down for discharge. But the Colonel wanted to persuade him that I should be in better health [once] abroad. He asked what services I had. I told him sixteen years and six months. He said it was no use taking me as it would only be expected to send me back in about eighteen months.'

In addition, to citing 'living consumption' as the reason for discharge, the doctor also wrote that Bentinck had been suffering from 'pulmonary complaints for the last three years'. This raises the possibility that Bentinck mentioned ill health as a means to try to improve his pension on discharge or even as a way to secure discharge. However, it seems that Bentinck campaigned hard to remain in the battalion, including lobbying Colonel Pearson, with whom Bentinck had had a long acquaintance.

In vain he pleaded the hardships his health had survived, when scores of stronger-looking comrades had sunk under them, and the full pension he should lose if not allowed to serve his term of service, then nearly out. In vain his Colonel, the ferocious Pearson, requested the Doctor to pass such a quiet and orderly soldier, observing that if he did ail anything on his lungs, the mild climate they were going to was more likely to restore than to harm him.

However, the Doctor was determined to stick by his opinion, and solemnly prophesied that if Bentinck went out on a ship and lived till he reached Gibraltar he would have to be at once sent back and it was no use going to that expense, for he could not last long anywhere.

The battalion did not receive official notification of the deployment to Gibraltar until 7 November so presumably there was an element of foreknowledge.[7] It appears that Bentinck's physical discharge was not immediate. He remained with the battalion during the preparation for the deployment to Gibraltar, continuing with his duties as an officer's servant. This gave him the opportunity to say a formal farewell to his battalion and an emotional occasion it was, laden with memories of battles all over the world.

With bitter tears he watched his old Regiment, the famous Royal Welch Fusileers, 23rd of Foot, march down to Dublin Quay to embark once more for the sunny south, and for the first time leaving him behind. The crowds cheered to the gay music of the band, which strove to wean the soldiers' hearts from 'The girls they left behind them,'[8] but to Bentinck those strains seemed the parting wail of the Regiment he had been brought up in from his boyhood and he could not stop himself shedding tears after being with them for so long.

It was its uniform that had first kindled his young enthusiasm. Its colours he had sailed under over thousands of miles of ocean, had followed over foreign deserts, over mountains, over fields hallowed by the life-blood of many comrades, and by the memory of his own providential escapes. A few – there were not many left – of those breezed veterans he had stood beside when cannon and musket bails were playing deadly havoc around them; he had rushed with them through the fiery breaches of beleaguered walls, and had shared with them the scanty meals on which such fighting was done. He could have hugged the shaggy old goat with gilded horns which marched at the head of the Regiment, as faithfully there as he had seen it up the rugged passes of Spain,[9] where any soldier of the Regiment would spare it a mouthful of bread when bread was more precious than gold.

With such manifold emotions did Bentinck behold his comrades leave the shore on which he was left, doomed as it were to a speedy death, and defrauded of a portion of his poor, hard-won pension, by the ignorance and conceit of this wise Doctor.

Bentinck had to go before the Army Board immediately after, where his discharge was given him, and a reduced pension of ninepence a day, instead of a shilling or one-and-two pence a day he would have received had be been allowed to serve his full time, as a Peninsular and Waterloo man. The discharge is dated 1823, so that he had served nearly 18 years, with the two years reckoned in for Waterloo, as Parliament decreed to every British soldier present at the great battle, he would only have had between one and two years to serve to complete his full term. His discharge however, bears on it record of his good character, and several of his Officers presented him on leaving with certificates bearing high testimony to his conscientious service and character.

In addition to these soothing tokens of esteem, the sprightly warrior, (for then he was not 35 years of age) subsequently received from the War Office at various times three medals, in acknowledgement of his past martial services – two of them being of solid silver, the other the large Peninsular Medal, inscribed with the twenty six principal battles, and bearing in the centre the bust of Wellington, the immortal chief under whom they were won.[10]

Bentinck remained with the battalion's rear party concluding the process of discharge from the Army and trying to arrange his rapid transition to civilian life, with a young family in tow.

> We stopped in the barracks for about ten days and the women stopped there who could not go out with the Regiment because of instructions coming from London. Thus suddenly deprived of his old means of subsistence Bentinck applied for and received his journeying fares home, to his native county of Suffolk. He arrived with his wife and two little ones without mishap.

Bentinck felt that the surgeon-general had been too speedy in his conclusions and sought the opinion of a civilian surgeon:

> I went to one of the Doctors in the town and asked his advice. He said in no way was I considered unfit. He told me to go home and wear flannels.

The question of finding a suitable occupation was solved by family connections:

> He had several uncles and cousins who were gardeners, and they readily initiated him into their occupation. As soon as he could get into a cottage of his own he sent for his mother to share it with them, for her second husband had been dead two years. The poor woman was overjoyed to find he had let off soldiering for good, for womanlike, she always made herself miserable by imagining some horrible death that he would surely suffer in that occupation, so that she cared little for his loss of pension by his premature discharge. He had not been able to get home on furlough since eight years before, in 1816.

Bentinck decided to settle down back in his birthplace, the village of Bacton, near Stowmarket, and moved there with his wife and young daughter, Eliza, who was born in 1822 in Limerick. Here, for the next twelve years he worked as a farm labourer and undertook duties as a minor parish official.[11] During this time the Bentinck family grew with a child being born every year from 1824 to 1828, the order being Henry, Richard, William, Elizabeth, George and Mary. Finally in 1835 Ellen was born. The size of the family was a significant financial burden and Bentinck began to struggle as a farm labourer and took the decision to change his circumstances.

'I followed an Uncle and a cousin and went into gardening. I went in with them and I got a place which I kept for six years. Then my family had got so large that I had not the means to support them. That was when I got my name [to live] in the manufacturing district. And I followed gardening as long as I was able and my children got employment in the factories. They could then do something towards being able to support themselves.'

Bentinck began to feel ten shillings a week, which was all they could earn, was hardly enough for comfort; so he removed his family to Ripponden, in Yorkshire, where one or two of them began to work in the mill, while he obtained better wages for his gardening. After six or seven years spent there they again removed, to Gnat Bank, Bamford, and in about eighteen months afterwards to Heywood, Manchester, the old man's last earthly home. He worked at Harefield Hall,[12] while it was building and until the grounds were finished, and his children first obtained work in old Mr. Taylor's mill. Of the ten children he had in all, five survived for his comfort, four daughters and one son, the latter becoming a prosperous auctioneer and agent in Southport.[13]

In 1867, forty-four years after his discharge, the War Office tardily raised his pittance three-pence a day.[14] By continuing in his old age the steadiness and thrift he held to through the temptations of his boisterous youth the old veteran went on his journey down the hill in tolerable comfort and bearing the esteem of those who know him.

Bentinck was far from being the only Peninsula or Waterloo veteran in the area. An annual dinner was held by the Rochdale Waterloo veterans where Bentinck took the opportunity to play a central role:

At these annual gatherings of the Wellington heroes, one part of the important ceremony was to sound on the kettle drum the call to arms in battle. Richard Bentinck, one of the drummers of the 23rd Regiment, did this with the same pair of drum sticks with which he had performed that duty on the field of Waterloo. There would follow interesting details as to how each of the veterans had distinguished himself at the battle, and their stories usually pointed to the conclusion that every one had been a hero.[15]

In his later years, Bentinck enjoyed the company of a couple of other Waterloo veterans but like all old soldiers they faded away, whilst Bentinck appeared to defy the gloomy predictions of the battalion surgeon:

One or two ancient comrades who bore arms in the same bygone wars would meet with him now and then by the side of his ingle nook, but now one of these, Joe Mills, has started on his last march to the land from whence no traveller returns; the other, old Tom Whitworth, though stout in body is fading in mind, and our wiry old friend Bentinck, though judged so far gone in consumption fifty-years ago, is likely to be able to long outlast them all. Though rather reticent as to his own part in them, he loves to discourse on those old campaigning days, and once a year on the 18th of June, sallies-forth, the touching wreck of a once vigorous soldier, to remind a chosen few of our patriotic gentry that it is Waterloo Day. They willingly pay tribute to its memory by presents ranging from a sovereign downwards, one gentleman with a large soul (among his old friends the doctors) once disgracing the list with a fourpenny-bit, on which the feeble old soldier of four score years very judiciously struck his name from his honourable list.

The Doctor has long since mouldered to dust, while Bentinck, whom he so briefly doomed, could fifty years later be seen any day to thread a needle without a glass to his eye, in his little cot, 35, St. James's Street, in the town of Heywood, Manchester. Bentinck never had but one touch of illness, and that from his wounded leg, since the day on which Dr. Smith thus told him he was so far gone in consumption. So much for some Doctor's prophecies!

Bentinck died in 1874 and is buried in Heywood graveyard. Unfortunately the gravestone, despite noting that he was, 'A Waterloo Hero', records his regiment as being the 24th Foot, which to an exceptionally proud veteran of the 23rd Foot would be terribly irksome. Bentinck's account of his experiences make vividly clear the fortitude and resilience required of the individual soldier and more than hints that Britain's success in defeating the French was ultimately built upon the martial skill of the individual British soldier, a fact that Wellington knew all too well. This was recognized by the journalist who conducted the interviews with Bentinck in 1873:

We have now finished one hasty sketch of an old soldier's eventful life. If it has been found wearisome the fault must either have been in our telling, or in the sympathy of the reader, not in the experience itself, for it is an instance, a solitary one, of what our humblest class have to do and to suffer in order to win for England the military glory. This glory of which, we are always hearing as much, all the more solid prosperity arising out of it, which we of our day enjoy.

———•———

1. On 17 August 1818 the battalion left cantonments at Valenciennes, some hundred miles north-east of Paris, and proceeded to a camp near Cambrai. At the end of October it sailed from Calais to Dover. After a short period the battalion then marched to Deal and embarked on two transporters for Cork in Ireland. It spent the whole of 1819 centred on Limerick with detachments positioned nearby.

2. The battalion frequently moved between locations. Initially it was positioned at Limerick, with detachments at Shanagolden, Tarbet Island, Carrick Island, Scaberry Island, Newport and Kildimo. Toward the end of 1820 it split into sixteen detachments. In November 1820 orders were received to deploy to Dublin and by Christmas Day the majority of the battalion was garrisoned in Dublin.

3. In September 1821 the battalion moved to Londonderry, followed by Boyle, County Roscommon, in April 1822 before moving again in May 1823, back to Dublin.

4. Thomas Matheson joined as a second lieutenant on 17 August 1815, was promoted lieutenant on 30 October 1823, captain on 2 August 1826, lieutenant colonel unattached on 17 November 1843, and placed on half pay the same day. Matheson was given the rank of colonel on 20 June 1854 and finally achieved major general on 2 April 1859. He died in 1868.

5. Bentinck served over the period 10 January 1807–28 October 1823. However, he gained two years' service for Waterloo, taking his total time of service to 18 years and 292 days.

6. This wound was sustained during the assault on Badajoz.

7. The battalion was to serve eleven years in Gibraltar, which included a two-year period in Portugal in support of the Portuguese government.

8. This was a traditional song played when regiments left a station for the last time:

> I'm lonesome since I crossed the hill,
> And o'er the moor and valley,
> Such grievous thoughts my heart do fill,
> Since parting with my Sally,
> I seek no more the fine or gay,
> For each does but remind me,
> How swift the hours did pass away,
> With the girl I've left behind me.
>
> Oh, ne'er shall I forget the night,
> The stars were bright above me,
> And gently lent their silver light,

> When first she vowed to love me,
> But now I'm bound to Brighton Camp,
> Kind heaven, then, pray guide me,
> And send me safely back again,
> To the girl I've left behind me.

9. It is highly unlikely that this was the same goat that was with the battalion in the Peninsula. There is an absence of any correspondence concerning the goat during the Peninsula period. It is presumed that after Waterloo, when a detachment led by Harrison from the 2nd Battalion came out to France as reinforcements, the regimental goat was also brought.

10. Bentinck is recorded in the 23rd Foot medal rolls as having being present at Albuera, Badajoz, Salamanca, Vitoria, Pyrenees, Orthez and Toulouse. The medals referred to are the Waterloo Medal, the Military General Service Medal and the unofficial 23rd Foot Regimental Medal struck on return from the Peninsula by Colonel Ellis in 1814, for men who had served in the battalion since 1801, listing the actions at which they had been present. Bentinck's Waterloo Medal was sold at Spink's auction house in December 1985, named to 'Bentick'.

11. The churchwarden's account book of Bacton states Richard Bentinck was paid £1 a year for acting as a questman (a minor parish official). These payments began in the last quarter of 1824 and ran to the end of 1836.

12. Harefield Hall is a Victorian manor located behind All Souls' Church. It was constructed in 1846, by Robert Kay, a local mill owner.

13. This is debatable with it more likely that two daughters and two sons survived. Research about the Bentinck family has revealed the following details about Richard and Mary's children: Eliza Bentinck was born about 1822 in Limerick and was christened some time between 1824 and 1826 in Bacton. She died in December 1885 in Heywood. Eliza married James Cropper in 1846 (believed to have been born between 1820 and 1824), who was a shoemaker. Henry Bentinck was born in 1824 in Bacton, and was christened on 25 July 1824. It is presumed that he died at a young age. Richard Bentinck was born in 1825 in Bacton and died after 1901. Richard became an auctioneer and married Jane; they had a son, William. Elizabeth Bentinck was born in 1826 in Bacton and was christened on 26 August 1826. George Bentinck was born about 1827 in Bacton, but died aged fourteen. Mary Ann Bentinck was born in 1828 in Bacton and was christened on 15 June 1828. Ellen Bentinck was born in 1835 in Bacton, but died on 19 March 1836.

14. Bentinck on retirement received a pension of 7d per day, increased periodically to a final total of 1s 3d per day in 1874.

15. Robertson, *Old and New Rochdale*, p. 325.

1st Battalion, 23rd Foot, 1807–1823

———•———

1807	**Napoleon declares blockade of Britain in the Berlin Decrees.**
	1/23rd participates in Copenhagen expedition.
	France invades Portugal.
10 January	Bentinck joins the Army and the 1st Battalion, 23rd Foot.
2 February	257 men drafted from the 2nd Battalion.
26 March	Battalion is inspected by Major General Thomas Grosvenor at Colchester. Total strength, all ranks, 991; 2 sergeants, 2 corporals and 192 privates are Welsh.
26 July	Battalion forms part of the Copenhagen expedition with a total strength of 925 all ranks. Embarks at Harwich on the *Lord Melville* and *Louisa*.
1 August	Expedition departs Harwich.
6 August	British envoy begins diplomatic talks with Prince Regent of Denmark.
7 August	Expedition makes rendezvous off Jutland coast.
9 August	Expedition at anchor close to Helsingør.
10 August	Diplomatic talks conclude.
16 August	No opposition to landing close to village of Vedbaek, eight miles north of Copenhagen. Captain Hill accidentally wounded during landing.
17 August	Battalion advances toward city. Occupies positions in the avenues of the royal palace of Charlottenlund.
19 August	Significant amounts of stores and artillery disembarked. Advance guard of the battalion fights a number of skirmishes. Six rank and file killed. Construction of siege batteries commences.
20 August	Advance guard of the battalion fights a number of skirmishes. Six rank and file killed.
21 August	Brigadier Macfarlane's brigade lands.
22 August	Lieutenant Treeve discovers source of Copenhagen's water supply.
26 August	One private killed in an outpost action and one killed by enemy bombardment.
27 August	Sir Arthur Wellesley storms enemy position at Kioge.
30 August	A captain, a lieutenant and seventy rank and file reinforcements come from the 2nd Battalion.
31 August	A piquet led by Lieutenant Harrison fights a brisk action, sustaining five rank and file wounded. One, Private Charles Bent, dies soon after.
1 September	Draft of seventy-six men received from the 2nd Battalion.

2 September	Bombardment of Copenhagen commences at 8.00 in the evening.
4 September	Lieutenant Jennings and two rank and file killed. Severe fires reported in Copenhagen in the vicinity of the University.
5 September	Steeple of the Church of our Lady destroyed by bombardment.
6 September	Negotiations commence.
7 September	Articles of capitulation signed. Battalion billeted in Copenhagen suburbs.
18 October	Battalion embarks from Copenhagen in the *Brunswick, Surveillante* and *Heir Apparent Frederick,* a Danish prize, for return to England.
20 October	Triumphant expedition leaves Copenhagen.
7 November	Battalion complete at Deal and commences return to Colchester.
13 November	Arrives back at Colchester barracks.

1808   **Battalion moves to Nova Scotia.**
A British force under Sir John Moore arrives in Portugal.
Battalion embarks for Martinique expedition.

18 January	Battalion marches to Portsmouth.
13 February	Battalion sails from Portsmouth for Nova Scotia on the *Lord Collingwood, Robert, Sea Horse, Traveller, Albion* and *Harriot.*
16 April	Arrives in Halifax, Nova Scotia. Battalion stationed at Annapolis Royal, Halifax and Digby. The battalion includes 49 sergeants, 22 drummers and 682 rank and file. Lieutenant Colonel Ellis in command.
10 August	Inspection at Annapolis by Lieutenant General Sir George Prevost. Present for inspection, 16 officers, 271 non-commissioned officers and men; on duty, 23 officers, 744 non-commissioned officers and men.
6 December	Battalion embarks at Halifax for Barbados.
29 December	Battalion arrives at Carlisle Bay, Barbados, rendezvous for Martinique invasion force.

1809   **Battalion participates in expedition to French island of Martinique.**
British force is evacuated from Portugal.
New British force under Sir Arthur Wellesley deploys to Portugal.

1st January	Parade state shows 35 officers, 43 sergeants, 37 corporals, 18 drummers and 853 rank and file embarked.
29 January	Battalion sails from Barbados for Martinique.
30 January	Battalion lands at Cul-de-sac Robert on the north-east of Martinique.
1 February	Battalion participates in the seizing of the heights of Mount Bruneau and severe action with the French. Battalion casualties of 1 sergeant, 14 rank and file killed, 2 sergeants, 79 rank and file wounded.
2 February	Action at heights of Sourier. Battalion casualties of 1 sergeant and 3 rank and file killed, Lieutenant Roskelly and Surgeon Power wounded, along with 19 rank and file; 1 sergeant reported missing.
19 February	Bombardment of Fort Desaix commences. Major Pearson wounded.

24 February	French garrison of Martinique capitulates.
1 March	Parade state gives battalion muster of 975 all ranks, including 104 sick, 1 wounded and 23 dead.
9 March	Battalion embarks at Martinique for Nova Scotia.
14 June	Inspection at Halifax by Lieutenant General Sir George Prevost.

1810   **Battalion sails for Portugal and the campaign against the French.**

2 August	Inspection at Halifax by Lieutenant General Sir George Prevost.
11 October	Battalion embarks at Halifax on the transports *Regulus* and *Diadem* for the Atlantic crossing. Parade state shows 814 embarked and 20 left sick in Halifax.
11 November	Arrives in Tagus Estuary, Portugal.
13 November	Disembarks at Lisbon.
16 November	Commences planned march to Santarém.
18 November	Battalion arrives at Sobral and joins the 4th Division, commanded by Major General Cole, becomes part of the Fusilier Brigade, commanded by Major General Pakenham.
19 November	Battalion directed into cantonments at Azambuja.

1811   **Battle of Albuera.**
             Wellington's army retreats to Portugal for winter.

19 January	Skirmish at village of Rio Maior. Captain Mercer and three rank and file killed.
24 January	Battalion departs Azambuja for Aveiras de Cima. Muster of the battalion: 50 officers, 54 sergeants, 22 drummers and 1,000 rank and file. However, these were split between Portugal, England and Canada, though with the vast majority present on active service in Portugal. On active service: 1 lieutenant colonel, 1 major, 9 captains, 15 lieutenants, 3 second lieutenants, paymaster, adjutant, quartermaster, surgeon, assistant surgeon, 35 sergeants, 18 drummers and 600 rank and file.
26 February	French force commanded by Soult commences investment of Badajoz.
5 March	French force commanded by Marshal Masséna completes withdrawal from cantonments at Santarém and begins retreat to Portuguese frontier. Colonel Myers takes command of the Fusilier Brigade. Battalion marches from Aveiras de Cima to Cartaxo as part of the general pursuit of the French.
6 March	Enters Santarém.
7 March	Marches to Golegao.
8 March	Reaches Thomar. French have left in the morning.
9 March	Harsh night out in the open, with only greatcoats and blankets as the battalion marches in pursuit of the enemy.
10 March	Reaches Pombal after a thirty-mile march. French set fire to Pombal and retreat.

11 March	Skirmish at Condeixa. French withdraw afterwards to Cazal Nova after setting fire to Condeixa. Badajoz occupied by the French.
12 March	Fierce rearguard action by French at Redinha.
13 March	Battalion enters Panella and then marches on to Espinhel.
14 March	French fight a further rearguard action at Cazal Nova. Battalion remains at Espinhel.
15 March	4th Division, commanded by Beresford, receives order to begin march for the recapture of Badajoz.
16 March	Battalion covers thirty-five miles marching.
18 March	Battalion crosses River Tagus at Tancos.
22 March	Enters Portalegre.
23 March	Rests at Portalegre.
24 March	Reaches Aronches.
25 March	Arrives at Campo Mayor. Muster of battalion: 32 officers, 25 sergeants, 13 drummers and 503 rank and file present fit; 4 sergeants, 3 drummers and 128 rank and file on march from Aveiras de Cima; at Belém, 3 officers, 8 sergeants, 4 drummers and 40 rank and file.
9 April	4th Division commences siege of Olivenza.
15 April	French garrison of Olivenza surrenders to 4th Division.
16 April	Moves to Zafra.
18 April	French retire to Guadal Canal.
25 April	Battalion at Valverde. Between this date and 25 March, the battalion received Captain Patten, Lieutenants G. Browne, Thorpe and Whalley, Second Lieutenants Enoch, Hall, Joiner, Palmer and Philipps, along with 5 sergeants and 198 rank and file as reinforcements from the 2nd Battalion in England.
8 May	Investment of Badajoz completed.
14 May	Siege is lifted due to approach of French force under Marshal Soult. 4th Division tasked to escort the movement of stores to Elvas.
15 May	4th Division marches to Albuera.
16 May	**Battle of Albuera.** Battalion casualties: Captain Montagu and Lieutenant Hall, 1 sergeant and 73 rank and file killed; Lieutenant Colonel Ellis, Captains Hurford, McDonald and Stainforth, Lieutenants Booker, Castle, Harris, Harrison, Ledwith, McLellan, J. McDonald, Thorpe and Treeve, 12 sergeants, 1 drummer, 232 rank and file wounded; 1 sergeant and 5 rank and file missing. Captain McDonald and Lieutenant Castle subsequently die of their wounds.
17 May	Both armies remain in positions occupied in morning.
18 May	Soult retires towards Seville with numerous wounded.
19 May	Siege of Badajoz actively resumed.
25 May	Wellington completes investment of Badajoz.

31 May	Battalion stationed at Almandralejo, screening further Badajoz siege. Captain Potter and Lieutenant Jocelyn posted to the 2nd Battalion.
3 June	Badajoz bombarded.
6 June	Unsuccessful assault on breach.
9 June	Unsuccessful assault on breach.
10 June	Siege of Badajoz lifted.
21 June	Battalion posted at Torre de Mouro. Effective strength of 463 all ranks. Since 25 May, 2 sergeants and 33 rank and file have died from various causes.
18 July	Battalion cantoned at Estremoz in support of the blockade of Ciudad Rodrigo. Sergeant Scott promoted to ensigncy in 11th Foot, in recognition of distinguished behaviour at the Battle of Albuera.
1 August	Lieutenant Wynn dies of fever.
2 August	Battalion located at Pedrogao. Major Dalmer, Lieutenant Walker, Second Lieutenants Butler, Curties, Fielding and Llewelyn, 6 sergeants, 2 corporals and 246 rank and file received as reinforcements from the 2nd Battalion in England.
28 August	Battalion effective strength given as 597.
23 September	Allied army withdrawn from blockade of Ciudad Rodrigo and takes up positions to meet the advance of a French corps under General Dorsène. As part of the 4th Division, battalion defends heights of Fuente Guinaldo.
25 September	Encounter with enemy on right flank of Fuente Guinaldo. Monthly return states Captain Keith dead, Captain Hill posted to Portuguese Army, 6 sergeants, 1 drummer and 51 rank and file invalided home to England.
26 September	Further encounter with enemy at Fuente Guinaldo. British position maintained.
27 September	Battalion covers retreat of 4th Division to River Coa by rearguard action at Aldea da Ponte. Captain Van Courtland killed, Major Pearson, Captain Cane and 13 rank and file wounded, 1 missing. French force retires to Ciudad Rodrigo.
1 October	Battalion moves into winter quarters at Gallegos, on the banks of the River Coa.
25 October	Battalion muster: 13 officers, 30 sergeants, 16 drummers and 445 rank and file.
1812	**Battalion supports siege of Ciudad Rodrigo.** **Battalion storms breaches of Badajoz with the 4th Division.** **Battle of Salamanca.**
1 January	Battalion leaves cantonment at Gallegos.
8 January	Investment commences of Ciudad Rodrigo, held by 2,000 French troops.
11 January	Four rank and file wounded.
14 January	San Francisco convent taken. One man killed, seven wounded.

19 January	Ciudad Rodrigo stormed by 3rd and Light Divisions.
20 January	Battalion moves to San Felices de Chico.
28 January	Battalion returns to Gallegos.
9 March	Battalion begins march to Badajoz.
16 March	Battalion and the 4th Division bivouacked south of Badajoz.
17 March	Start of investment of Badajoz.
18–22 March	Two rank and file killed, Brevet Major Potter (subsequently dies of wounds) and 17 rank and file wounded.
22–26 March	Four rank and file killed and seven wounded.
25 March	Picarina fort, one mile south of Badajoz Castle, captured.
31 Mar–2 Apr	One man wounded.
7 April	**Badajoz stormed.** Battalion casualties: Captain Maw and Lieutenant Collins killed, along with 1 ensign, 4 sergeants and 29 rank and file; Lieutenant Colonel Ellis, Brevet Major Leaky, Captains Hawtyn and Stainforth, Lieutenants G. Browne, T. Farmer, Fielding, Harrison, Tucker, Whalley and Wingate, Second Lieutenants Holmes and Llewelyn (subsequently dies of wounds), 7 sergeants, 1 drummer and 84 rank and file wounded; 1 sergeant and 19 rank and file missing.
13 April	Battalion in cantonments at Sabugal.
17 May	4th Division in defensive screen to north of Salamanca.
22 May	Muster parade at Traves. Present fit: 10 officers, 19 sergeants, 13 drummers and 289 rank and file; 1 sergeant and 23 rank and file have died during the month.
25 May	Battalion inspected by Major General Anson (temporary commander of the 4th Division) at Traves.
13 June	Battalion crosses River Agueda, part of Wellington's move to threaten the French line of communication through Valladolid and Bayonne.
16 June	Battalion poised six miles from Salamanca.
17 June	Battalion crosses River Tormes and occupies a position along with the main body of the army on the heights of San Christobal.
20 June	Skirmish on plain in front of San Christobal between opposing cavalry. Lieutenant Leonard killed.
27 June	Forts commanding the River Tormes captured.
28 June	Forts destroyed on order of Wellington.
30 June	Battalion reaches the River Guarena.
3–16 July	Allied and French armies remain drawn up in sight of each other.
19 July	French attempt to force a crossing over the River Douro. Battalion casualties: 2 rank and file killed, 2 missing and 9 wounded.
22 July	**Battle of Salamanca.** Battalion casualties: Major Offley and 10 rank and file killed; Lieutenant Colonel Ellis, Major T. Dalmer, Captain G. Browne, Lieutenants Clyde, Enoch, Fryer and J. MacDonald, 6 sergeants and 84 rank and file

wounded. Muster parade shows 13 officers, 27 sergeants, 15 drummers and 337 rank and file fit for duty.

31 July	Battalion enters Valladolid.
12 August	Wellington's army enters Madrid. Battalion posted at the Escurial.
21 October	Wellington lifts siege of Burgos.
31 October	Battalion leaves Madrid.
5 December	Wellington's army retreats to Portugal. Battalion resting at Soitella.
25 December	Muster parade shows 26 officers, 30 sergeants, 14 drummers, 294 rank and file present fit. Captains F. Dalmer and Strangeways, Lieutenants Cowell, Harris and Wingate, Second Lieutenants Gledstanes and Griffiths, Assistant Surgeon Smith, 2 sergeants and 72 rank and file arrive from the 2nd Battalion at Haverford West, Wales, as reinforcements.

1813   **Battle of Vitoria.**
               Engagements in the Pyrenees.
               Battle of Sorauren.
               Battle of the River Nivelle.

25 January	Sergeant Major Gordon promoted to ensigncy in the 13th Veteran Battalion.
2 March	Battalion leaves Soitella for Algodras. Nine rank and file die during month.
12 April	Battalion inspected by Colonel Skerritt at Algodras. Three sergeants and twenty-two rank and file transferred to the 13th Veteran Battalion.
16 May	The Anglo-Portuguese army advances on the French on the Douro. Battalion strength shown as 34 officers, 38 sergeants, 15 drummers and 394 rank and file. Twenty-five men have died during the stay at Algodras.
3 June	Wellington's army meets at Toro.
19 June	Engagement at Subijana-Morillas. Battalion casualties reported as one sergeant and three men wounded.
20 June	Wellington crosses River Ebro and encamps along River Bayas.
21 June	**Battle of Vitoria.**
	Battalion casualties: 1 man killed, 1 sergeant and 2 men wounded; Lieutenant G. Farmer (who has been a prisoner of war at Valladolid) is freed.
25 June	Battalion muster shows 27 officers, 33 sergeants, 14 drummers and 223 privates present fit; 1 sergeant and 43 privates prisoners of war; 5 sergeants and 72 rank and file have been invalided back to England.
26 June	Engagement at Tolosa.
25 July	Action at the pass of Roncesvalles. Battalion casualties: 1 sergeant and 5 rank and file killed; Captain Booker, Lieutenants Browne, Ledwith and O'Flaherty, and 15 rank and file wounded.
27 July	Battalion withdraws in a night march to take up position on heights near Sorauren.

28 July	**Battle of Sorauren**. Captains Stainforth and Walker, Volunteer Basset, 1 sergeant, 1 corporal, 1 drummer and 13 rank and file killed; Lieutenant Colonel Ellis, Lieutenants Neville, Harris and McLellan wounded.
30 July	Attack by army to dislodge French from final Pyrenees passes.
2 August	Allied army successfully drives the French through the Pyrenees passes, back into France.
7 August	Battalion encamped at Lesaca, north-east of San Sebastian. Battalion receives 5 sergeants, 1 drummer and 175 privates as reinforcements from the 2nd Battalion.
26 August	Siege artillery opens fire on fortress walls of San Sebastian.
31 August	Detachment from battalion participates as part of the storming party at San Sebastian. Battalion casualties: four men killed, Lieutenant Griffiths and four rank and file wounded.
3 September	Lieutenant Ledwith dies of wounds. Volunteer Fitzgibbon appointed second lieutenant.
8 September	San Sebastian garrison surrenders.
11 September	Battalion encamped at Yansi.
25 September	Battalion muster: 25 officers, 31 sergeants, 10 drummers and 333 rank and file present fit; 42 rank and file accounted for as prisoners of war.
7 October	Wellington's army crosses River Bidassoa and enters French territory. Battalion marches to Vera.
21 October	Volunteer Satchwell appointed second lieutenant.
10 November	**Battle of the River Nivelle.** 4th Division captures village of Sarre. No casualties in this engagement.
11 November	4th Division established across the River Nivelle. Battalion is encamped on Ascain heights and receives 2 sergeants and 46 privates as reinforcements from the 2nd Battalion.
8 December	4th Division and battalion move out of encampments to Saint-Barbe.
9 December	Allied army attacks French position on the River Nive.
10 December	Lieutenant Colonel Ellis is given command of the Fusilier Brigade.
11 December	Three battalions of Nassau troops desert to the British.
13 December	Concentrated French attack on British on right bank of River Nive. Battalion called upon to march as reinforcements, supporting the flank.
25 December	Battalion muster: 26 officers, 33 sergeants, 9 drummers, 409 privates; sick absent 1 officer, 10 sergeants, 3 drummers, 216 privates; sick present 6 privates; 40 privates accounted for as prisoners of war.

1814	**Battle of Orthez.** **Battle of Toulouse.**
1 January	Battalion cantoned at Ustaritz.
6 January	4th Division mounts attack against enemy positions between Joyeuse and Bidouse rivers.

18 January	One sergeant and four men captured whilst on a foraging party.
25 January	Three sergeants and thirty-three men discharged as unfit for service.
14 February	4th Division takes possession of La Bastide heights.
23 February	4th and 7th Divisions attack Hartingues and Oeyregave.
25 February	Battalion encamped at Sordes. Battalion muster: 26 officers, 35 sergeants, 11 drummers, 465 rank and file; sick absent 1 officer, 10 sergeants, 1 drummer, 168 rank and file.
26 February	4th and 7th Divisions cross the Gave de Pau.
27 February	**Battle of Orthez.**
	Battalion casualties: 1 sergeant, 15 rank and file killed, Captains Wynne, and Joliffe, Lieutenant Harris, 6 sergeants and 69 rank and file wounded.
1 March	Battalion crosses the Adour.
8 March	4th Division begins march on Bordeaux.
12 March	4th Division arrives at Bordeaux.
16 March	4th Division marches from Bordeaux to link up with Wellington.
18 March	Division links up with Wellington's force and makes contact with French at Tarbes.
20 March	Enemy pushed out of Tarbes.
25 March	4th Division reaches St-Foix.
26 March	4th Division moves into St-Lys, taking post on the Auch Road.
31 March	Allies enter Paris.
4 April	4th Division crosses River Garonne.
10 April	**Battle of Toulouse.**
	4th and 6th Divisions attack St-Sypière. Battalion casualties, one private killed, Lieutenant Thorpe and seven rank and file wounded.
11 April	French army evacuates Toulouse and town surrenders.
12 April	Wellington enters town.
14 April	Sortie by French garrison of Bayonne.
19 April	Convention signed by Soult for the suspension of hostilities.
25 April	Battalion encamped at Castera. During the month, the battalion has received Captain Farmer, Lieutenants Clyde and Fryer, Second Lieutenants Allan, Dunn and Stainforth, 2 sergeants, 3 drummers and 87 privates as reinforcements from the 2nd Battalion.
25 May	Battalion at Condom.
4 June	Lieutenant Colonel Ellis promoted to colonel by brevet.
6 June	Battalion moves to Blancfort, in the area of Bordeaux.
14 June	Battalion embarks in HMS *Egmont* at Pauillac for Plymouth.
25 June	Reaches Plymouth Sound. Battalion muster at landing: 4 captains, 15 lieutenants, 7 second lieutenants, 3 staff, 36 sergeants, 39 corporals, 13 drummers and 437 privates; 9 sergeants, 5 corporals, 167 privates and 40 prisoners of war have been left in the Peninsula. Lieutenant Colonel Ellis, 2 captains, 1 lieutenant and 10 privates remain at Pauillac for a court-martial.

5 July	Battalion moves to Ivybridge.
12 July	Battalion at Dorchester.
16 July	Battalion reaches Gosport and moves into 'New Military Barracks'.
18 October	Inspection by Major General Howard at Gosport.
24 October	The 1st Battalion receives 26 sergeants, 21 corporals, 23 drummers and 377 privates as reinforcements from the 2nd Battalion, which disbands. All officers of the 2nd Battalion are placed on half-pay in consequence. The 1st Battalion is made up to a strength of 1,197 non-commissioned officers and men, 20 above the establishment.
29 December	County and City of Worcester gift a vase by subscription to Colonel Ellis, in tribute of his meritorious services. On one side of the vase is the inscription: *'To Col. Henry Walton Ellis of the 23rd Royal Fusiliers this tribute to his meritorious and distinguished conduct, during fifteen years of active service in Holland, Egypt, America, The West Indies, Spain, Portugal and France is respectfully offered by the County and his native city of Worcester and presented at their desire by the Earl of Coventry Lord Lieutenant and Recorder. 1814.'*

1815	**Return of Napoleon.**
	Battle of Waterloo.
	With the Army of Occupation in France.
26 February	**Napoleon escapes from Elba.**
23 March	Battalion embarks on the transports *Ariel*, *Percival* and *Poniana*. Muster state shows 42 officers, 31 sergeants, 24 drummers, 36 corporals and 611 privates; 1 captain, 2 lieutenants, 1 second lieutenant, 14 sergeants, 11 drummers, 15 corporals and 190 privates are left at Gosport.
25 March	Transports sail for the continent.
28 March	Duke of Wellington appointed to command His Majesty's forces in Europe.
29 March	Battalion transhipped.
30 March	Battalion is landed at Ostend.
31 March	Battalion moves by canal boats to Bruges.
2 April	Arrives in Ghent.
7 April	Arrives at Oudenarde.
20 April	Colonel Mitchell's Brigade, including the battalion, is reviewed by the Duke of Wellington.
24 April	Moves into cantonment at Grammont, re-organization of the Army occurs. Colonel Mitchell's Brigade, known as the 4th British Brigade, is designated part of the 4th Division (British and Hanoverians) under the command of Lieutenant General Sir Charles Colville.
2 May	Brigade marches to Renaix.
9 May	Returns to Grammont.

16 June	Marches to Braine-le-Comte, via Enghien.
17 June	To Nivelles and then Braine-l'Alleud.
18 June	**Battle of Waterloo.**
	The strength of the battalion on the morning of the battle is: 3 field officers, 10 captains, 25 subalterns, 6 staff, 35 sergeants, 23 drummers and 639 rank and file. Battalion casualties are: Brevet Major Hawtyn, Captains Joliffe and T. Farmer, Lieutenant Fensham, 2 sergeants and 9 rank and file killed; Brevet Colonel Ellis (dies on 20 June), Brevet Lieutenant Colonel Hill, Captain Johnson, Lieutenants Clyde (dies on 3 July), Fielding, Griffiths and A. Sidley, 7 sergeants and 71 rank and file wounded. Brevet Lieutenant Colonel Dalmer stands in as commanding officer.
19 June	Battalion bivouacs at La Belle Alliance.
20 June	Moves to Mons.
21 June	Battalion reaches Valenciennes.
22 June	Enters Cateau-Cambrésis.
24 June	Assault and capture of Cambrai. Battalion casualties: Second Lieutenant Leebody and one private killed; two men wounded.
25 June	Battalion muster: 1 major, 2 captains, 14 lieutenants, 4 second lieutenants, 6 staff, 26 sergeants, 22 drummers, 37 corporals and 504 rank and file; 2 sergeants and 54 privates are sent over from the depot, now at Albany Barracks, Isle of Wight.
26 June	Leaves Cambrai.
4 July	Battalion reaches Bois de Boulogne.
5 July	Battalion marches to Neuilly. Receives reinforcements from the depot of Lieutenants Drury and Pemberton, 2 sergeants, 1 drummer and 52 rank and file.
20 July	Lieutenant Colonel Thomas Dalmer officially appointed as commanding officer.
24 July	Allied Army of Occupation reviewed by the Emperor of Russia.
16 August	Volunteer Ellis appointed second lieutenant.
20 October	Inspection of battalion by Major General Power at Neuilly.
30 October	Battalion moves from Neuilly into cantonments at Priel.
9 November	Strength of battalion given as 671 personnel.
24 November	New set of Colours arrives, delivered by Captain Harrison. Lieutenants Baillie, Boucher and Tower arrive from the depot. Lieutenant Cowell dies.
1816	**With the Army of Occupation in France.**
January	Battalion quartered at Montmarte.
February	Battalion moves to Hamelincourt and areas surrounding.
February	Strength of the battalion: 53 officers, 53 sergeants, 22 drummers, 48 corporals and 760 privates.

1817   **With the Army of Occupation in France.**

30 March   New recruits to the battalion are inspected by Colonel Sir Edward Blakeney.

14 April   Battalion ordered to move to Valenciennes to form part of the garrison of that town. Battalion strength recorded as 887 all ranks.

April   Recruiting parties are withdrawn due to the large numbers of men from other regiments being drafted in.

15 May   Battalion inspected by Colonel Sir Edward Blakeney.

24 July   Twenty-four privates join the battalion from the depot.

1818   **Battalion leaves France for Ireland.**

29 April   Major General Sir James Kempt inspects the battalion.

17 August   Battalion leaves Valenciennes and proceeds to a camp near Cambrai.

27 September   Roll call: 3 field officers, 8 captains, 17 subalterns, 4 staff, 36 sergeants, 20 drummers and 688 rank and file.

26 October   Battalion leaves Cambrai and marches for Calais.

31 October   Arrives Calais.

1 November   Sails for Dover.

19 November   Marches for Deal and embarks upon transports *Defence* and *Alfred* for Cork. On embarking the strength is 26 officers, 43 sergeants, 22 drummers and 612 rank and file.

20 November   Sails for Cork.

24 November   Reaches Cork.

1819   **On garrison duty in Ireland.**

        The regiment is stationed at Limerick. Establishment is 650 rank and file, 96 officers and non-commissioned officers, total 746 all ranks.

1 May   Inspection by Major General O'Loghlin at the New Barracks, Limerick.

1820   **In Ireland.**

        The regiment remains at the New Barracks, Limerick, with detachments at Shanagolden, Tarbet Island, Carrick Island, Scabbery Island, Newport and Kildimo.

12 May   Inspection by Major General Sir Thomas Brisbane.

25 November   Eight companies reported as being at Ennis and Numbers 5 and 6 on the march to Dublin.

25 December   Majority of the regiment stationed in Dublin.

1821   **In Ireland.**

10 May   Inspection by Major General Sir John Elley. He remarks, 'This Corps is in a high state of discipline, perfectly equipped, and in every respect fit for

any service.' Regimental establishment is 74 officers and non-commissioned officers, 576 rank and file, 650 all ranks.

12 September	Regiment moves to Londonderry.
5 November	Inspection by Major General Egerton.

1822   **In Ireland.**

April	Moves to Boyle, County Roscommon.
10 May	Inspection by Major General Sir John Elley.

1823   **Bentinck leaves Army.**

22 April	General Sir Richard Grenville, Colonel of the Regiment, dies. He is replaced by Major General Sir Colquhoun Grant.
1 May	Battalion garrisoned in Dublin.
3 June	Inspection by Major General Sir Colquhoun Grant.
28 October	Bentinck discharged from the Army.
7 November	Orders received for the battalion to embark for Gibraltar.
2 December	Embarks at Dublin. Remaining at Fermoy and acting as the depot are: Captain Sir W. Crosbie, Lieutenant E. Ellis, 1 sergeant, 2 corporals, 1 drummer and 3 privates.

Bibliography

Primary Sources

Heywood Advertiser, articles on Richard Bentinck, 9, 16, 23, 30 May, 13, 20, 27 June, 4, 11, 18, 25 July, 1, 22 August 1873.

National Archives of the United Kingdom, Kew, Surrey
  War Office 4, Secretary-at-War, Out-Letters; War Office 27, Inspection Reports; War Office 100, Waterloo Roll

Royal Welch Fusiliers Museum and Archives, Caernarfon
  Accession 1335, J. Harrison papers; Accession 2686, G. Booker papers; Accession 3777, J. Hill papers; Accession 5257, T. Farmer papers; Accession 5935, J. MacDonald papers

Suffolk Libraries, 'Life and Career of Richard Bentinck, the Waterloo Veteran'.

Discharge certificate and baptismal certificate of Richard Bentinck, copies held by the author.

Period Military Regulations

James, Charles, *The Regimental Companion, Containing the Pay, Allowances and Relative Duties of Every Officer in the British Service*. London: T. Egerton, 1798

Rottenburg, Francis de, *Regulations for the Exercise of Riflemen and Light Infantry, and Instructions for their Conduct in the Field*. London: T. Egerton, 1798

Published Sources

Journal Articles

'The Medals of Colonel Sir Henry Walton Ellis, KCB', *Y Ddraig Goch* [Journal of the Royal Welch Fusiliers], March 1934

'Memorial of Colonel Sir Henry Walton Ellis, KCB', *Y Ddraig Goch*, March 1938

'The Royal Welch Martinique Eagle', *Y Ddraig Goch*, Winter 1958

'The Puzzle of a Bundle of Love Letters and an MGSM', *Y Ddraig Goch*, April 1978

'The Youth who was to save our Flash', *Y Ddraig Goch*, March 1979

Richard Roberts, 'Incidents in the Life of an Old Fusilier', *The Workman's Friend*, Nos 1 & 2, 1862.

Books

Bell, Major General Sir George (ed. Brian Stuart), *Rough Notes of an Old Soldier*. London: G. Bell and Son, 1956

Bluth, B. J., *Marching with Sharpe*. London: Collins, 2001

Boutflower, Charles, *The Journal of an Army Surgeon during the Peninsular War*. Reprinted Staplehurst: Spellmount, 1997

Brett-James, Anthony, *Life in Wellington's Army*. London: Allen and Unwin, 1972

Broughton-Mainwaring, Ronald, *Historical Record of the Royal Welsh Fusiliers, late 23rd Foot*. London: Hatchards, 1889

Browne, Thomas Henry (ed. Roger Buckley), *The Napoleonic War Journal of Captain Thomas Henry Browne 1807–1816*. London: Bodley Head, 1987

Burroughs, George Frederick, *A Narrative of the Retreat of the Army from Burgos in a Series of Letters with an Introductory Sketch of the Campaign of 1812 and Military Character of the Duke of Wellington*. Cambridge: Ken Trotman Military Monographs, 2004

Cannon, Richard, *Historical Record of the Twenty-Third Regiment,* London: Parker, Furnival and Parker, 1847

Cary, A. D. L. & McCance, S., *Regimental Records of the Royal Welch Fusiliers (late 23rd Foot)* Volume I: *1689–1815,* Volume II: *1816–1914,* London: Forster Groom, 1921. Reprinted 1995

Cassidy, Martin, *Marching with Wellington: With the Inniskillings in the Napoleonic Wars*. Barnsley: Pen & Sword, 2003

Chandler, David, G., *Dictionary of the Napoleonic Wars*. London: Arms and Armour, 1979

——, *The Campaigns of Napoleon*. London: Weidenfeld & Nicolson, 1995

Chappell, Mike, *The King's German Legion (1) 1803–1812*. Oxford: Osprey, 2000

——, *The King's German Legion (2) 1812–1816*. Oxford, Osprey, 2000

Cole, Maud L. (ed.), *Memoirs of Sir Lowry Cole*, Cambridge: Ken Trotman Military Monographs, 2003

Cooper, John Spencer, *Rough Notes of Seven Campaigns 1809–1815*. 1969, reprinted Staplehurst: Spellmount, 2002

Costello, Edward, *Adventures of a Soldier: The Peninsular and Waterloo Campaigns*. London: Longman, 1967

Dempsey, Guy, *Albuera 1811: The Bloodiest Battle of the Peninsular War*. London: Frontline Books, 2008

Dobbs, John, *Recollections of an old 52nd Man*. Staplehurst: Spellmount, 2000

Donaldson, Joseph, *Recollections of the Eventful Life of a Soldier*. Staplehurst: Spellmount, 2000

D'Urban, Benjamin, *The Peninsular War Journal: 1808–1817.* London: Greenhill, 1988

Esdaile, Charles, *The Peninsular War: A New History*. London: Penguin, 2002

Fletcher, Ian, *In Hell Before Daylight*. Tunbridge Wells: Baton, 1984

—— (ed.), *A Guards Officer in the Peninsula: The Peninsular War Letters of John Edward Cornwallis Rous, Coldstream Guards, 1812–1814*. Tunbridge Wells: Spellmount, 1992

—— (ed.), *Voices from the Peninsula: Eyewitness Accounts by Soldiers of Wellington's Army 1808–1814*. London: Greenhill, 2001

——, *Badajoz 1812: Wellington's Bloodiest Siege*. 1999. Reprinted Oxford: Osprey, 2002

Fremont-Barnes, Gregory, *The Peninsular War 1807–1814*. Oxford: Osprey, 2002

Fortescue, J. A., *History of the British Army*. 13 vols, 1899–1930; reprinted Naval & Military Press, *c.* 2004

Gates, David, *The Spanish Ulcer: A History of the Peninsular War*. London: Pimlico, 1986

Glover, Gareth (ed.), *A Short Account of the Life and Adventures of Private Thomas Jeremiah 23rd or Royal Welch Fusiliers 1812–37*. Huntingdon: Ken Trotman, 2008

Glover, Michael, *Wellington's Army in the Peninsula, 1808–1814*, Newton Abbott: David and Charles, 1977

——, *Wellington as Military Commander*. London: Penguin, 2001

——, *The Peninsular War, 1807–1814: A Concise Military History*. London: Penguin, 2001

—— & Riley, Jonathon, *That Astonishing Infantry: Three Hundred Years of the History of the Royal Welch Fusiliers (23rd Regiment of Foot), 1689–1989*. Barnsley: Pen & Sword, 2008

Graves, Donald, *Fix Bayonets! Being the Life and Times of Lieutenant General Sir Thomas Pearson, 1781–1847*. Stroud: Spellmount, 2006

——, *Dragon Rampant, The Royal Welch Fusiliers at War, 1793–1815*. London: Frontline, 2010

Green, John, *A Soldier's Life 1806–1815*. Reprinted East Ardsley, E. P. Publishing, 1973

Griffith, Paddy, *Forward into Battle*. London: Penguin, 1992

Hamilton-Williams, D., *Waterloo New Perspectives: The Great Battle Reappraised*. London: Arms and Armour, 1993

Harris, Benjamin (ed. H. Curling), *Recollections of Rifleman Harris*. London: Cassell, 1970

Hay, William, *Reminiscences 1808–1815 Under Wellington*. Cambridge: Ken Trotman Military Monographs, 1992

Hayman, Peter, *Soult: Napoleon's Maligned Marshal*. London: Arms and Armour, 1990

Haythornthwaite, Philip J., *The Napoleonic Source Book*. London: Arms and Armour, 1990

——, *The Armies of Wellington*, London: Arms and Armour, 1996

——, *Die Hard! Dramatic Actions from the Napoleonic Wars*. London: Arms and Armour, 1996

Holme, Norman, & Kirkby, E. L., *Medal Rolls: 23rd Foot (Royal Welch Fusiliers) in the Napoleonic Period, 1801–1815*. London: Spink and Son, 1978

Holmes, Richard, *Redcoat: The British Soldier in the Age of Horse and Musket*. London: HarperCollins, 2001

Howarth, David, *Waterloo: A Near Run Thing*. London: Fontana, 1972

Isemonger, Paul, *Wellington's War: A Living History*. Stroud: Sutton, 1998

James, Lawrence, *The Iron Duke: A Military Biography of Wellington*. London: Weidenfeld & Nicolson, 1992

Kincaid, Sir John, *Random Shots from a Rifleman*. 1835. Reprinted Staplehurst: Spellmount, 1998

Kirby, E. L., *The Royal Welch Fusiliers, 23rd Foot*. 1969. Reprinted Andover: Pitkin Pictorials, 1974

——, *Officers of The Royal Welch Fusiliers (23rd Regiment of Foot) 16 March 1689 to 4 August 1914*. Caernarfon: Museum of the Royal Welch Fusiliers, 1997

Knowles, Robert, *The War in the Peninsula: Some Letters of a Lancashire Officer*. Staplehurst: Spellmount, 2004

Lawrence, William (ed. Eileen Hathaway), *A Dorset Soldier: The Autobiography of Sgt William Lawrence*. Tunbridge Wells: Spellmount, 1993

Leach, Jonathan, *Rough Sketches of the Life of an Old Soldier*. Cambridge: Ken Trotman Military Monographs, 1986

Mills, John (ed. Ian Fletcher), *For King and Country: The Letters and Diaries of John Mills, Coldstream Guards, 1811–1814*. Staplehurst: Spellmount, 1995

Murray, J., *The dispatches of Field Marshal the Duke of Wellington during his various campaigns in India, Denmark, Portugal, Spain, the Low Countries and France from 1799 to 1818*. London: John Murray, 1852

Myatt, Frederick, *British Sieges in the Peninsular War*. Staplehurst: Spellmount, 1987

Napier, W. F. P., *History of the War in the Peninsula and in the South of France* (6 vols), London: Thomas and William Boone, 1833

Nofi, Albert, *The Waterloo Campaign June 1815*. New York: Da Capo Press, 1998

Nosworthy, Brent, *With Musket, Cannon and Sword: Battle Tactics of Napoleon and his Enemies*. London: Constable and Company, 1995

Oman, Sir Charles, *History of the Peninsular War*. 7 Vols, 1902–30; reprinted London: Greenhill, 1995–8

——, *Wellington's Army 1809–1814*. Reprinted London: Greenhill, 2006

Palmer, Roy (ed.), *The Rambling Soldier: Life in the Lower Ranks, 1750–1900, through Soldier's Songs and Writings*. London: Penguin, 1985

Parkinson, Roger, *The Peninsular War*. 1973, reprinted London: HarperCollins, 2000

Rathbone, Julian, *Wellington's War*. London: Michael Joseph, 1984

Reid, Stuart, *British Redcoat 1793–1815*. 1997, reprinted Oxford: Osprey, 2002

Richards, D. S., *The Peninsula Years: Britain's Red Coats in Spain and Portugal*. Barnsley: Pen & Sword, 2002

Robertson, Ian, *Wellington at War in the Peninsula 1808–1814*. Barnsley: Pen & Sword, 2000

Robertson, William, *Old and New Rochdale*. Manchester: William Robertson, 1881

Schaumann, August (ed. Anthony Ludovici), *On the Road with Wellington: The Diary of a War Commissary*. London: Greenhill, 1999

Shaw-Kennedy, James, *Notes on the Battle of Waterloo*. Staplehurst: Spellmount, 2003

Sherer, Moyle, *Recollections of the Peninsula*. 1823. Reprinted Staplehurst: Spellmount, 1996

Siborne, H. T. (ed.), *The Waterloo Letters*, London: Cassell, 1891

Thomas, Howel, *A History of the Royal Welch Fusiliers, late the Twenty-Third Regiment*. London: T. Fisher Unwin, 1916

Thompson, W. F. K. (ed.), *An Ensign in the Peninsular War: The Letters of John Aitchison*. London: Michael Joseph, 1981

Weller, J., *Wellington at Waterloo*. London: Greenhill, 1998

Wheeler, W. (ed. B. H. Liddell Hart), *The Letters of Private Wheeler, 1809–1828*. London: Michael Joseph, 1951

Index

The author and the publishers
gratefully acknowledge the assistance
given by The Royal Welch Fusiliers
in the production of *The Very Thing*.

The Royal Welch Fusiliers Museum is situated in historic
Caernarfon Castle in Gwynedd, North Wales. On display
are artefacts, period uniforms, armaments and equipment
relating to the period in which Drummer Richard
Bentinck served.

For further information about the Royal Welch Fusiliers
Museum and about the history of one of the most
distinguished regiments in the British Army, visit the
Fusiliers' website at
www.rwfmuseum.org.uk